# BIBLICAL
# ELDERSHIP

By the same author:

Biblical Eldership: A Study Guide

Biblical Eldership: Restoring The Eldership To
Its Rightful Place In The Church

Using Your Home For Christ: What The New
Testament Teaches About Hospitality

# BIBLICAL ELDERSHIP

## AN URGENT CALL TO RESTORE BIBLICAL CHURCH LEADERSHIP

### ALEXANDER STRAUCH

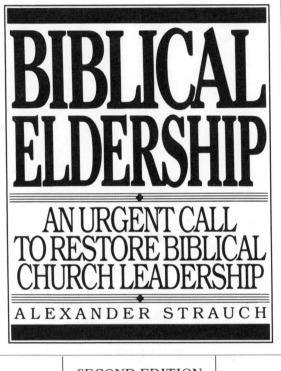

SECOND EDITION

LEWIS AND ROTH PUBLISHERS
Littleton, Colorado 80160 U.S.A.

Lewis and Roth Publishers, P.O. Box 569
Littleton, Colorado 80160-0569 U.S.A.

94  93  92                          7  6  5

All Scripture quotations, except those noted otherwise, are
from the New American Standard Bible, The Lockman
Foundation 1960, 1962, 1963, 1968, 1971, 1972, 1973, 1975, 1977,
and are used by permission.

Cover design: Stephen T. Eames

Library of Congress Cataloging-in-Publication Data


Strauch, Alexander, 1944–
  Biblical Eldership: 2nd ed.

  Includes bibliographies and indexes.
  1. Elders (Church officers)—Biblical teaching.
  2. Christian leadership—Biblical teaching. 3. Bible—
  Criticism, interpretation, etc. I. Title.
BS680.L4S77  1988  262'.15—dc19

ISBN 0-936083-03-4

# Table of Contents

[v]

# *Preface*

This book is primarily an exposition of the biblical passages on church eldership. I fully believe that if fair, reverent, and accurate exposition of God's Word will not convince men of the necessity and importance of biblical eldership, then nothing will. My prayer is that the Spirit of God will use this exposition of the Word to awaken more men to their God-given responsibility to care for the family of God.

Chapter 1 summarizes and briefly defends biblical eldership. I know that many readers will not study all the exposition chapters. That is unfortunate, for only the Word of the living God can properly transform our worldly thinking and attitudes so that they conform to Jesus Christ's. However, for the benefit of these readers, I have outlined in chapter 1 what biblical eldership is and why it best harmonizes with and promotes the true nature of the Christian assembly. In other words, I have explained why I believe biblical eldership is the right leadership structure for the Christian church.

Chapter 2, "Humble Servants," elaborates further on one of the major points in Chapter 1: the humble servant community. Humble servanthood is key to understanding the Christian community and its leadership structure and style. Jesus' teaching on humility and servanthood governs the practices and thinking of the New Testament writers. We want His teaching to govern our thinking and behavior also. Thus, I have placed this chapter at the beginning of the book. In the midst of life's daily pressures these glorious truths of God's kingdom are quickly forgotten, and the world's prideful ways and ideas of success are easily adopted—even in the work of God.

Chapter 3 surveys the Old Testament texts on elders, which is foundational to our New Testament study in chapters 4 through 19. Chapters 4 through 19 are the expositional chapters, the heart of the book.

The final chapter outlines general ideas and practical advice for churches that seek to implement biblical church eldership.

I have not had space in this volume to deal in depth with the practical issues and questions regarding church eldership. Therefore, I have prepared a study guide for this volume, which provides additional practical insight for implementing biblical church eldership. I urge you to read this supplementary guide in order to complete your study on eldership.

I gratefully acknowledge the support and encouragement of many dear Christian friends in writing this book. Special thanks is due to my diligent editors, Steve and Amanda Sorenson, my research helper, Chuck Harrison, and proofreader, Barbara Peek. Three special friends and associates who have consistently encouraged me in the project over the years are Doyle Roth, Barney Visser, and Paul Sapp. Finally, I thank God for the extraordinary privilege and joy of working with a body of fully dedicated elders in the spiritual care of God's church. I praise God for each of these men. Above all, I am thankful to my devoted wife, Marilyn, whose personal sacrifice and support cannot be measured or duly praised.

# Introduction: The Six Major Aims of this Book

In his magisterial epistle to the Hebrews, the inspired author writes, "Obey your leaders, and submit to them; for they keep watch over your souls . . ." (Hebrews 13:17). This book is about those who keep watch over the souls of the Lord's people—those who both Paul and Peter directly exhorted to shepherd the flock of God (Acts 20:28, 1 Peter 5:2). This book is about the church elders.

Regrettably a great deal of misunderstanding and indifference has surrounded this important subject. From an expository viewpoint, very little has been written on church elders. Although some writers have attempted to explain the doctrine of church eldership through small booklets, journal articles, or chapters within books, there is critical need for a full-length book that expounds all Scripture on the subject. To my knowledge, no book written in English fully expounds all New Testament passages regarding church elders, which is hardly believable when one considers the amount of explicit biblical teaching on this topic. Hopefully, this book will not only fulfill a need for exposition, but will inspire others to search the vast treasure of God's Word. Precious truths, no doubt, still await discovery.

I have written this book with six specific aims in mind:

### First, to accurately explain what biblical eldership is

Considering the elders' significant role as a leadership body in the first churches, and the number of Scriptures devoted to it, eldership should be a top priority in all discussion of church polity and pastoral care. However, most Christians today know little about biblical church eldership, its original purpose, or its noble character. As well-known Bible teacher John MacArthur, Jr. observes, even many church leaders think that biblical eldership is a frightening new doctrine:

[1]

Some have been vocal in characterizing it as a new and subversive concept that threatens the very life of the church. Yet, I find when I speak with pastors and other church leaders from all over the world, the most frequently asked questions I get are about elders. At our semi-annual Shepherds' Conferences, the most popular seminars invariably are those that deal with the issue of elders. Pastors want to know what elder rule is, and if government by elders genuinely strengthens the church, how they can implement it in their churches.[1]

I have found that most critics of biblical eldership do not really understand what it is. But that is not totally their fault. The exponents of eldership have been unclear and inarticulate about the doctrine. For example, pivotal texts like 1 Timothy 5:17,18 have been inadequately understood and explained. As a result, uncertainty, disagreement, and confusion still surround the doctrine. If we who believe in the plurality of elders send out an uncertain signal, we cannot expect others to hear and follow our teaching. Also, indecisiveness and disagreement hinders men from getting on with the all-important job of shepherding the flock of God. Therefore, one of the primary aims of this book is to explain, as simply and clearly as possible from Scripture, what biblical eldership is.

### *Second, to restore biblical eldership to its rightful place in the church*

The New Testament explicitly and repeatedly teaches that the elders are to shepherd (pastor) the local church. However, in the centuries that followed the New Testament period, radical changes took place in the leadership structure of the churches. An immense gulf developed between the New Testament apostolic churches and the emerging churches of the bishops. Soon a vast hierarchy of officials—with its exclusive, priestly caste—replaced the simple, brotherly oversight by elders found in the New Testament. In time, biblical church eldership vanished. John Calvin observes the demise of church eldership and supports his claim with this fascinating quotation from Ambrosiaster (circa A.D. 375):

> Gradually this institution degenerated from its original condition, so that already in the time of Ambrose the clergy alone sat in ecclesiastical judgments. He complained about this in the following words: "The old synagogue, and afterward the church, had elders, without whose counsel nothing was done. It has

fallen out of use, by what negligence I do not know, unless perhaps through the sloth, or rather, pride of the learned, wishing to appear to be important by themselves alone."[2] As centuries passed, church reformers made noble attempts to recover the church eldership. Particularly significant were the efforts of some sixteenth century reformers, such as John Calvin, who openly expounded oversight by elders in his *Institutes of the Christian Religion*.[3] But some of these mighty efforts suffered because they could not fully break free from the hardened soil of ancient clerical traditions. In the nineteenth century, George Muller and others in the Brethren movement tried to give the eldership its rightful place in the church.[4] But because of insufficient articulation, systematic exposition, and teaching, their efforts were short-lived and greatly confined.[5]

The effort to restore church eldership must go on, however. In faith, we cannot ignore Scripture's ample teaching on this vital topic. Moreover, local church leadership structure and style must harmonize with the true nature and teaching of the local church and the gospel. If not, as history sadly demonstrates, unscriptural forms of church organization will continue to distort the nature and purpose of the church of God.

Since the truth about the rightful place and function of elders is only found in God's Word, we will by God's grace, make a fresh and thorough exposition that is unfettered by human tradition of all Scripture pertaining to the New Testament doctrine of church elders. If there is any hope of restoring the eldership to its rightful place in the church, it must begin with the careful exposition of God's Word.

### Third, to challenge false traditions

A major premise of this book is that church eldership is plainly and adequately revealed in Scripture, but that false traditions and misconceptions have demeaned, obscured, and in some cases obliterated, the elders' true position and function. In addition, the accepted ecclesiastical terminology that supports these traditions and misconceptions seriously distorts the New Testament teaching on church leadership. Much of our church vocabulary today is unscriptural and misleading. In their modern sense, words such as clergyman, layman, reverend, priest, bishop, ordained, and ministerial convey ideas that are contrary to what Jesus Christ

[3]

and His apostles taught. Thus, our churches are in dire need of language reform.

Certainly it is no pleasant matter to learn that some of our most cherished and trusted traditions have no basis whatsoever in God's Word! But Jesus Christ, the greatest champion to stand against the giant of tradition, provides the inspiration and example we need to overthrow that which is contrary to God's Word, no matter how ancient it may be. We must listen afresh to the words Christ spoke to the hardened religious traditionalists of His day:

"'. . . Teaching as doctrines the precepts of men.'

"Neglecting the commandment of God, you hold to the tradition of men.

". . . You nicely set aside the commandment of God in order to keep your tradition.

". . . thus invalidating the word of God by your tradition which you have handed down; and you do many things such as that" (Mark 7:7-13).

If biblical eldership is to be restored to its rightful place in the church, false traditions and misconceptions that have obscured church eldership must be challenged and exposed in the pure light of God's truth.

### Fourth, to revitalize present elders

The deepest longing of my heart is that the Spirit of God will use this book's exposition of Scripture to awaken, revitalize, and challenge present elders to undertake their God-given task. There is almost no greater detriment to the protection and care of God's flock than uncommitted, half-hearted elders. Lacking vision, creativity, and whole-heartedness, such elders exist only to guard their own security and traditions. As shepherds of the church, elders have the greatest affect on the flock's direction and well-being. When elders are alive and excited about their task, unimaginable blessing, growth, and change await the church, resulting in better care for the Lord's people.

### Fifth, to raise up new elders

As a result of false ideas of ministry and polity, a tremendous source of manpower necessary to protect God's flock, to feed God's Word to His flock, and to guide God's flock in His perfect ways has been lost. I believe one of the most critical needs in churches today is for more men to take seriously their God-ordained responsibility to lead and serve in the church. For the future care and protection of local churches, it is absolutely essential to challenge the minds and hearts of able, spiritually-minded, young men. I pray that this book will help raise up a host of capable elders who will fill the tremendous need for leadership among the Lord's people. Hopefully this will be achieved by showing that the church elders' role is an exceedingly honorable and privileged work and is worthy of the congregation's most talented, spiritually mature men.

### Sixth, to teach believers their obligations to their elders

It is vitally important that the congregation understand its responsibilities to its spiritual leaders. When the assembly correctly honors and submits to its elders, the elders are able to do their work with greater joy and effectiveness. As a result, everyone is blessed and spiritually united. In Hebrews 13:17 we read, "Obey your leaders, and submit to them; for they keep watch over your souls, as those who will give an account. Let them do this with joy and not with grief, for this would be unprofitable for you."

Furthermore, people need to understand that God places shepherds in the church for everyone's spiritual protection and development. Those who think they know better than the elders, or who rebel against their admonitions, are heading for spiritual disaster or self-delusion. The children of Israel destroyed themselves because they continually rebelled against Moses and the elders. So it is for our own good that we honor and submit to our spiritual leaders. Biblical eldership, then, is not a topic to be studied only by scholars or church leaders. Rather, it should be studied by every believer because it directly affects each one's spiritual welfare.

### Holy Scripture: The Basis for Restoration and Reform

The basic assumption underlying this book is that Holy Scripture is the sole foundation and blueprint upon which to construct church reform, renewal, revitalization, and restoration. Reconstruction of church leadership can only begin when the distorted structure of human tradition is dismantled and replaced by a genuine return to biblical origins—including the apostolic teaching, the apostolic church model, and the primitive Christian brotherhood. Some will wonder if such a restoration is possible.

[5]

My emphatic reply is yes! Restoration is not only possible, but absolutely essential.

The apostolic record is the only means a Christian has to identify true or false Christianity, and as Alfred Kuen has said, "the Churches established by the apostles remain the valid models for churches of all times and places."[6] Quoting Merle d'Aubigne, Kuen goes on to state, "As we advance through the centuries, light and life begin to decrease in the Church. Why? Because the torch of the Scripture begins to grow dim and because the deceitful light of human authorities begins to replace it."[7]

As Christians, we are compelled to test everything by God's written Word—the sovereign, infallible, all-sufficient source of authority. Therefore, we must engage in continual reading, fresh study, deeper meditation, and bold, prayerful reexamination of God's unchanging Word, while at the same time humbly submitting our preconceived thoughts, denominational loyalty, and precious traditions to the authority of God's Word. In the words of Otto Riecher, "the life of the church depends on one thing: her return to biblical principles."[8]

## NOTES

1. John MacArthur, Jr., *Answering the Key Questions about Elders* (Panorama City, California: Word of Grace Communications, 1984), page 1.
2. John Calvin, *Institutes of the Christian Religion,* ed. J.T. McNeill, trans. F.L. Battles (Philadelphia: The Westminster Press, 1960), Book IV, ch. XI, page 6.
3. *Ibid.* Book IV.
4. George Muller, *A Narrative of Some of the Lord's Dealings with George Muller* (London: James Nisbet & Co., 1881), Vol. 1, pages 206, 207, 276-281. Henry Craik, *New Testament Church Order* (Bristol: W. Mack, 1863), pages 57, 58. H. Groves, *Memoir of the Late Anthony Norris Groves*, 2nd ed. (London: James Nisbet & Co., 1857), page 385.
5. F. Roy Coad, *A History of the Brethren Movement,* 2nd ed. (Exeter: Paternoster Press, 1976), pages 214, 215.
6. Alfred Kuen, *I Will Build My Church*, trans. Ruby Lindblad (Chicago: Moody Press, 1971), page 253.
7. *Ibid.*, page 27.
8. *Ibid.*, page 325.

# Chapter 1

# An Explanation and Defense of Biblical Eldership

> *For this reason I left you in Crete, that you might set in order what remains, and appoint elders in every city as I directed you.*
>
> Titus 1:5

\* \* \*

### The Importance and Relevance of the Doctrine

I am aware that many people find the issue of church government (or polity[1]) to be as irrelevant, boring, and unimportant as the color of the church pews. For many Christians, church government is a nonissue. But the fact is, church government is highly relevant and theologically significant. So I ask those of you who have not thought much about this subject, or have assumed that it is irrelevant, to consider the following points.

First, a society's beliefs should be expressed in its structure of government. No society can afford to be careless about the structure of its government. This is especially true of the Christian community. Not just any form of organizational structure will do, for great and precious principles are at stake. For example, to introduce a separate, priestly class would destroy the priesthood of every believer; to establish a lordly or sacred, hierarchical structure of rule would divide the family, ruin the living inter-play of spiritual gifts among members, distort the humble-servant character of the brotherhood, and obscure Christ's unique Head-ship over each local church.

Some of the worst havoc wrought to the Christian faith has been a direct result of totally unscriptural forms of church struc-ture. Only a few centuries after the apostles' death, Christian churches began to adopt both Roman and Jewish concepts of rule. As a result, a power-hungry, elaborately structured Church emerged in Christ's name that was in total contradiction to His teaching on humility, love, and, servanthood. But far worse, unscriptural ideas about church organization have demeaned Christ's superior place in the Church and falsely elevated men and the church institution. Our church governmental structures reveal how accurately we grasp our Lord's teachings, the gospel, and the nature of the Church of Jesus Christ.

Furthermore, there are critical, biblical issues in church polity that thinking, concerned Christians cannot avoid or term irrelevant. For instance, can women be pastors (elders)? Does the New Testament authorize the clergy-laity division? Does the New Testa-ment teach shared pastoral oversight? Is the local church to be subject to higher courts or ecclesiastical bodies?

I find it ironic that some evangelical leaders today are more concerned about the structure of the United States government than the structure of God's church. I doubt that evangelical leaders would say, "It doesn't matter how the U.S. government is structured so long as there is some form of leadership." Yet, that is precisely what I have heard some of our evangelical leaders say about the local church. The truth is, structure matters; it must enhance and suit society's beliefs, or serious philosophical dis-crepancies will ensue.

Second, God has provided explicit examples and instruction in His Word about the church elders. God has not been silent about the leadership structure of His household (1 Timothy 3:14,15). He knows what is best and wants the best for His people. Yet most Christian churches have totally ignored the Scriptures on eldership or misapplied them to the clergy. Such deliberate or inadvertent disobedience to God's Word always results in con-fusion and harm to the Lord's people. To the body of elders the Spirit of God gave the mandate to oversee and shepherd the local flock of God. Thus, if we are to be faithful to God's revelation, we must restore the church elders to their God-given place and role in the body.

I must add that if we truly grasp the meaning of our Lord's repeated teaching to His disciples about servanthood and humility of mind, we will understand how vitally significant the issue of leadership structure and style is to the Christian faith.

Third, the spiritual development of the leading men of the church is at stake. In Acts 20, Luke writes that the Spirit of God placed ordinary working men in the local church as overseers to pastor the flock of God. If this God-given work is taken away from the qualified men of the church because of false ideas about ministry, then they will never take their rightful place in God's program. They will not mature as they ought. They will not bear the yoke of responsibility given by God. They will not enter the spiritual battle as they ought. They will, at most, be advisors to the pastor—not the pastors God intended them to be.

Our churches today are filled with spiritually immature, weak men who are not fulfilling their proper role in the body. They have handed over their scriptural responsibilities to a professional minister (and criticize him if he can't do everything himself). So the very process of sanctification in the lives of our leading men is hindered.

What I am saying, then, is that false ideas about ministry and church organization severely hamper the spiritual growth of the very people who should be leading and caring for the Lord's people. This is a serious matter. Those who say that church structure is not essential do not know what they are saying, nor do they realize the long-term, debilitating effect their teaching will have on the work of God.

How the church is run is important. In his book *Liberating the Laity,* R. Paul Stevens confesses how he tried to equip the people in his church for doing the church's ministry, but failed because— as he discovered—the governmental structure of the church required *him* to do "the ministry." He writes, "Structure, I discovered, is important; there is no point in saying that every member is a minister if the structures of the fellowship 'says' the exact opposite—by making it hard for people to discover their gifts or to exercise loving service."[2]

I heard Chuck Swindoll say, in his usual, enthusiastic manner, that church government is an exciting and vitally important topic to everyone in the congregation. He challenged those who thought differently to look again at the last church split they had heard of or experienced to see if church government isn't a relevant and profoundly important issue. So, the topic of church polity is highly relevant, extremely practical, and vital to the proper functioning of the family of God.

### A Biblical Base for Government by Elders

Those who profess Scripture to be God's inspired Word to man are duty bound to construct their concepts and practices of church structure on the only true and reliable teacher—God's written Word. Only by returning to our source of life and light can we discern authentic Christianity. Only then are we able to check our continual waywardness, test our ideas, and reform the endless abuses of human authority and tradition. So, despite distinct differences that exist in church structure, there is still a God-given record of original, apostolic Christianity to which we must all refer for correction and guidance concerning church life and order (1 Timothy 3:14,15).

Although many others would agree that church organization is relevant, they would say that the New Testament gives us little or no specific guidance on the topic. Many scholars teach that the New Testament is ambiguous or silent on the topic of church polity, so no one can insist upon a biblical model of oversight for all churches because the Bible does not. George Eldon Ladd in his book *A Theology of the New Testament,* writes, "It appears likely that there was no normative pattern of church government in the apostolic age, and that the organizational structure of the church is no essential element in the theology of the church."[3] Ladd's statements, I believe, are completely unwarranted for the following reasons: (1) A consistent example of elder rule exists among most of the churches established by the apostles. (2) Instruction about elders is given to the churches. (3) Important instruction and exhortation are given directly to elders. (4) It can be demonstrated that oversight by a plurality of elders best suits and promotes the true brotherly, saintly, and servant nature of the congregation. Also, eldership suits the character of the church as a body—a spiritually gifted body of Spirit-indwelt saints.

[10]

Theology inevitably affects church organizational structure. We see in the New Testament that Paul's practice and counsel were rooted in doctrine; doctrine determines behavior and structure. The gospel is to be practically embodied in the life and structure of our churches, but most church structures (e.g., the clergy-laity structure) are contrary to the gospel message. Indeed, they demonstrate that we have inadequate and incomplete views about the Church and God's program for His people. So, Ladd is quite wrong when he says, "the organizational structure of the church is no essential element in the theology of the church."

The fact is, Christ's apostles established a specific type of oversight in nearly every church, and the New Testament provides detailed instructions concerning it (Titus 1:5-9). So those who dismiss its necessity or relevance for the same type of oversight today are obligated to demonstrate why the apostles' specific practice and instruction should be abandoned. I have yet to see good reasons for abandoning oversight by the plurality of elders, and have seen nothing better suited to take its place.

There are sufficient New Testament examples and instructions to fully justify insistence on spiritual oversight by a plurality of elders, yet there is no command from the Lord, "Thou shalt have a plurality of elders." (Although Titus 1:5 ff. and possibly a few other passages come close to that.) There are several reasons for not expressly commanding leadership by a plurality of elders. First, the New Testament is not written that way. It is not written on the order of Moses' five books of the Law. The New Testament simply does not contain lists of minute regulations and laws. Second, many churches could not keep such a command; it would be an unreasonable requirement because many local congregations lack a qualified body of men to serve as elders. (This may have been the situation at Corinth during Paul's labors among them.) Many churches exist in less-than-ideal conditions. There may only be one qualified man in a congregation who can lead or teach. So the freedom allowed in the New Testament permits a local congregation to function without disobedience if no body of elders is available.

Let us now define biblical eldership and review the evidence from the New Testament for leadership by a plurality of elders in a nonclerical church structure. Indeed, any honest, biblical discussion or study of church leadership or pastoral care must first deal with the doctrine of eldership as taught and practiced by our Lord's own apostles.

### An Explanation of Biblical Eldership

Despite all the New Testament says about church elders, the subject has been deeply misunderstood or ignored. Many evangelical churches that sincerely claim to base their church structure on holy Scripture do not even have a body of elders. These churches have ignored the pastoral oversight of the church by a plurality of elders—a concept plainly set forth in Scripture—and replaced it with a one-man pastor, which is inadequately defensible by Scripture. Even most Presbyterian churches (and others that claim to be governed by a scriptural plurality of elders) have redefined church eldership so that its original purpose and noble standing have, in practice, been eclipsed by the ordained minister and his staff.

I define biblical eldership as the official oversight body of the local church, which is open to all males of the congregation who meet Scripture's qualifications and have a Spirit-imparted desire to jointly oversee the spiritual welfare of God's household. To better clarify biblical eldership in light of contemporary church practices, I present the following six distinguishing features of biblical eldership.

*Humble, servant character.* A biblical eldership is to be a humble, servant body of men who sacrificially and lovingly care for the family of God. The organizational structure of a church is important and the structure of shared leadership by elders suits a humble, servant community, yet the spirit of those who make up the organizational structure is equally important. The elders must be humble, servant-like, caring, and brotherly (Matthew 23:1-12; Mark 9:34,35; 10:32-45).

*Shared oversight.* This means that the elders jointly govern the local church under Christ. Other terms for this form of structure are plurality or collegiality. However, there is diversity of gift and diligence among those who unitedly shepherd the church. Some elders, indeed, are to be honored for their diligent labor in leading or teaching by receiving material assistance from the congregation (1 Timothy 5:17,18).

*Nonclerical structure.* There is no division between lay elders and an ordained minister. The New Testament does not give the slightest hint that the eldership is to be presided over by a pastor. There is no office of pastor, only the offices of elder and deacon. Elders pastor the flock. Biblical eldership cannot coexist with a clergy-laity division.

*Scriptural qualifications.* Those who comprise the church eldership must meet Scripture's objective, moral, and spiritual requirements (1 Timothy 3:2-7; Titus 1:5-9). Included in the qualifications are a heartfelt desire for the work and the leading of the Holy Spirit (1 Peter 5:2; Acts 20:28). Elders serve for as long as they desire the work and meet the qualifications outlined in Scripture.

*Male leadership.* The Christian church eldership is to be restricted to male members of the congregation (1 Timothy 2:8-3:13).

*Congregational submission.* The eldership oversees, leads, and shepherds the local congregation of God. It has no jurisdiction outside the local assembly. Further, the New Testament does not suggest that the elders are under the authority of the congregation. The elders are *Christ's undershepherds and stewards,* thus the congregation is to obey and submit to their guidance, protection, and care (Hebrews 13:17). Yet there is to be close, mutual cooperation between elders and congregation, for all are under the authority of the Lord Jesus Christ and His holy Word. The chief, guiding principle for church government is that Jesus Christ is supreme Lord, Head, and Pastor. (1 Peter 5:1-4).

A word of warning is urgently needed at this point. Let no one think that all a church needs is correct organization. Nothing could be further from the truth. Certainly a congregation can have a plurality of elders and be cold, lifeless, and spiritually underdeveloped. Ultimately, the character and life example of the men who lead are most important. Proper structure, however, greatly facilitates the development of good men in their oversight-leadership task.

## A Defense of Biblical Eldership

*Apostolic practice and teaching as revealed in the New Testament.* The New Testament record clearly reveals that the pastoral oversight of many of the first churches was committed to a council of elders. This was true of the earliest Jewish Christian churches in Jerusalem, Judea, and neighboring countries, as well as many of the first Gentile churches:

- Barnabas and Saul gave their offering for Judea's poor to the elders (Acts 11:30).
- The elders at Jerusalem united with the twelve apostles to deliberate over doctrinal controversy (Acts 15).
- The biblical record reveals oversight by the plurality of elders in the churches of Derbe, Lystra, Iconium, and Antioch (Acts 14:23); in the church at Ephesus (Acts 20:17; 1 Timothy 3:17; 5:17-25); the church at Philippi (Philippians 1:1); the churches on the island of Crete (Titus 1:5); and, according to Peter, the churches in Pontus, Galatia, Cappadocia, Asia, and Bithynia (1 Peter 1:1; 5:1).
- Both the apostles Paul and Peter directly charged the elders of the church to pastor (shepherd) and oversee the local congregation (Acts 20:28; 1 Peter 5:1,2).
- At both the beginning and end of Paul's ministry, he appointed a plurality of elders to care for the churches he planted (Acts 14:23; Titus 1:5). According to the Titus 1:5 passage, Paul did not consider a church to be fully developed until it had functioning, qualified elders.
- Paul calls on the congregation to render double honor to the elders who "rule" the church well, especially the elders who work hard at "preaching and teaching." This honor includes financial help (1 Timothy 5:17,18). *Here is a confounding, uncomfortable passage of Scripture that does not fit into most theories of pastoral oversight.*
- Paul states that the elders are the stewards, or household managers, of the local assembly (Titus 1:7).
- Paul states that the elders are the church's overseers (Acts 20:28; Philippians 1:1).
- The elders are solemnly charged to protect the church from false teachers (Acts 20:28-31; Titus 1:9-11).
- Elders are men placed in the church as overseers by the Holy Spirit of God (Acts 20:28).
- Peter warns the elders against being too authoritative. (1 Peter 5:3).
- James instructs the saints to call for the elders of the church if they are sick (James 5:14).
- Men must be qualified before they can serve as elders. Particularly relevant here is the fact that they must all be able to teach the Word, exhort, and stop false teachers with sound teaching

(1 Timothy 3:2; Titus 1:9).

• Paul states that the elders "take care of the church of God" (1 Timothy 3:5).

So according to the New Testament, elders aren't just board members of a religious corporation with whom the pastor cautiously consults. On the contrary, they protect the church from false teachers, exhort the saints in sound doctrine, visit the sick and pray, and judge doctrinal issues. In general terms, they lead, oversee, shepherd, and care for the local church.

It's odd that the great apostles—Peter, Paul, and James—do not once address or give instruction about the "pastor" of the church. (Ephesians 4:11 refers to the *gift* of shepherd, which is a spiritual gift like teaching or leading that one or several of the elders will possess.)

In its major features, then, church oversight by the plurality of elders is plainly and amply set forth in the New Testament. Not only does the New Testament record the existence of elders in numerous churches, it also gives considerable instruction about the elders. In fact, the New Testament offers more instruction regarding elders than on other important church subjects such as the Lord's Supper and baptism. When one considers the New Testament's characteristic avoidance of detailed regulations and church procedures, the attention given to elders is amazing. In addition, biblical church eldership is presented more directly and simply than many other doctrines. As Jon Zens observes, "This is why we need to seriously consider the doctrine of eldership: it jumps out at us from the pages of the New Testament, and yet it has fallen into disrepute and is not being practiced as a whole in local churches."[4]

*The proper structure for governing the church of God.* I am convinced that biblical eldership, as defined above, best harmonizes with the true nature of the church. Let us look at the church as a body, a brotherhood, and servant community in order to better understand this statement.

First, the church is a spiritually gifted body. We must never forget that the church of Jesus Christ is a supernatural, Spirit-indwelt, Spirit-empowered, living community of Christ-like servants who minister Christ's love and care to one another (1 Corinthians 12:7, 25; 1 Peter 4:10). The same Spirit Who links Christians together in one body also empowers and enables every

Christian to serve and build up the body (Ephesians 4:1-6).

The indwelling Holy Spirit is the truly distinctive feature of the community of God's people that was formed on the day of Pentecost. In contrast to the people of Israel who lived under the old covenant, the Holy Spirit came to indwell each and every believer and thereby formed the body of Christ. Through the indwelling Holy Spirit, a glorious, new bond—a dynamic interdependence—was created within the community of believers. That bond is unlike any other relationship in the world. To illustrate this new mutuality and wondrous interdependence among believers, Paul used the imagery of the body and its many parts. Romans 12:4-6 (a) says, "For just as we have many members in one body and all the members do not have the same function, so we, who are many, are one body in Christ, and individually members one of another. And since we have gifts that differ according to the grace given to us, let each exercise them accordingly. . . ." So, each member of the body has a spiritual gift and function to perform for the good of all (1 Corinthians 12:7).

Therefore, within the body of Christ, ministry is the sacred privilege and duty of every believer. There is to be no passive, inactive majority. All members are to perform a vital function—caring for one another, building up one another, and ministering to one another. When each and every member of the body functions as God intended, the community of believers will grow, and an amazing, living interplay of gifts and services will result.

Since ministry is the duty of every believer, no one person or group is responsible to provide the total ministry for the rest of the congregation. The concept that only a professional, lawfully ordained man is qualified to perform "the ministry" totally contradicts the fact that the church is a ministerial body. Also, nothing in the New Testament suggests the concept of "the laity" with its passive, negative connotations. Therefore, the one-man-professional-ministry concept is totally unsuited for the body of Christ. Outwardly it may be successful, but in reality it is harmful to the sanctification of the members of Christ's body. Shared, brotherly leadership by ordinary men, who are empowered by the Holy Spirit (Acts 20:28), is the structure established by the apostles because it best enables the church to function as the body of Christ.

Second, the church is a brotherhood. Of the different New Testament terms used to describe the nature of the church—the

[16]

body, the bride, the temple, the flock—the most frequent is the family, particularly the fraternal aspect of the family, *brethren.* Robert Banks makes this observation in his book, *Paul's Idea of Community*: "Although in recent years Paul's metaphors for community have been subjected to quite intense study, especially his description of it as a 'body,' his application to it of 'household' or 'family' terminology has all too often been overlooked or only mentioned in passing."[5] Banks further comments on the frequency and significance of these family expressions: "So numerous are these, and so frequently do they appear, that the comparison of the Christian community with a 'family' must be regarded as the most significant metaphorical usage of all. . . . More than any of the other images utilized by Paul, it reveals the essence of his thinking about community."[6]

The reason behind this preference for the family aspect of the church is obvious. Only the most intimate of human relationships could express the love, closeness, privileges, and new relationships that exist between God and man, and man and man, because of Christ's incarnation and death. The local Christian community is to be a close-knit family of brothers and sisters. The reality of this relationship saturates the New Testament. The New Testament writers most commonly refer to the believers as *brethren.* For instance, Peter directly refers to Christians as "the brotherhood" (1 Peter 2:17; 5:9). The terms *brethren, brother,* or *sister* occur 250 times throughout the New Testament, particularly in Paul's letters.

In the early churches, the family-like life of the Christian brotherhood displayed itself in many practical ways:

• The early Christians met in homes (Romans 16:5; 1 Corinthians 16:19; Colossians 4:15; Philemon 2).

• They shared material possessions (Acts 2:44,45; 4:32; 11:29; Romans 12:13,20; 15:26; 1 Corinthians 16:1; 2 Corinthians 8; Galatians 2:10; 6:10; Hebrews 13:16; James 2:15,16; 1 John 3:17,17).

• They ate together (Acts 2:46; 20:11; 1 Corinthians 11:20 ff; Jude 12).

• They greeted one another with a holy kiss (Romans 16:16; 1 Corinthians 16:20; 2 Corinthians 13:12; 1 Thessalonians 5:26; 1 Peter 5:14).

• They showed hospitality (Acts 16:15; 21:8,16; Romans 12:13; 1 Timothy 3:2; 5:10; Hebrews 13:2; 1 Peter 4:9: 3 John 5-8).

[17]

- They cared for widows (Acts 6:1-6; 9:39; 1 Timothy 5:1-16).
- When appropriate, they disciplined their members (1 Corinthians 5-6; 2 Corinthians 2:1-11; 2 Thessalonians 3:6-15; 1 Timothy 5:19,20).

But most important to us, brotherliness provides the guiding principle of conduct between Christians (Romans 14:15,21; 1 Corinthians 6:8; 8:11-13; 2 Thessalonians 3:14,15; Philemon 16; James 4:11). Our Lord, Himself, insisted that—because His followers were brethren—they must never imitate the ways of the world's religious leaders who pridefully separate and elevate themselves above the people for their own interest and glory:

"But they do all their deeds to be noticed by men; for they broaden their phylacteries, and lengthen the tassels of their garments.

"And they love the place of honor at banquets, and the chief seats in the synagogues, and respectful greetings in the market places, and being called by men, Rabbi.

"But do not be called Rabbi; for One is your Teacher, and you are all brothers" (Matthew 23:5-8).

In complete obedience to Jesus Christ, the first Christians and their leaders resisted self-elevating, lordly forms of rule—including special titles, sacred clothes, and chief seats. In choosing an appropriate form of oversight for their local congregations, they knew that the profoundest spiritual principles were at stake. No form of government that might disturb the order and function of the household of God could be permitted (1 Timothy 3:15). The early Christians found within their biblical heritage a structure of government that was compatible with the new family—leadership by the plurality of elders. Israel was a great family and found rule by the plurality of elders to be a natural and fair form of self-government. Who but the elders could best represent the people? Who but the elders would be closest to the people—the actual families of Israel—to provide for counsel and help?

Government by elders worked well for the family of Israel. The early Christians also found corporate leadership by a council of elders to be exceptionally well suited for governing the Christian household of brothers and sisters. (Remember the local church is an extended family, not a single family. So it is inappropriate for one individual to be head of the extended family of God's people.) Such government gives all brothers who desire, and

[18]

qualify, the full right and opportunity to share leadership responsibilities in the community they love. The problem with many churches today is that they are structured and run on a corporate or bureaucratic model, as if the church were a large, corporate institution. But the church is a brotherhood, and it should have a leadership structure that suits brotherhood.

Even the term *elder* is appropriate to describe the leaders of the church. Since the Christian community does not need—and cannot tolerate—any mediator, priest, cleric, or lord in its midst, the leaders of the early Christian community were appropriately called *elders*. The term itself most approximates the idea of leadership and supervision that is necessary in the Christian household. In contrast to all hierarchical or sacred titles, nothing in the name *elder* or *overseer* violates the church's family character, humble-servant nature, or holy status in Christ. Indeed, the terms well suit the leaders of God's family, who are its respected and mature members.

Third, the church is a humble, servant body. Not only does the New Testament stress the guiding principle of brotherly love in the Christian community, it also teaches the necessity of humble servanthood. Actually, Jesus gave more explicit instruction about servanthood than about brotherhood. Repeatedly, He taught His disciples that true greatness in His Kingdom is achieved by humility. So the church is not only to be a close-knit family of brothers and sisters, it is to be a humble, servant body that manifests the lowly, servant character of its Lord.

Tragically, Christians have shown a polite indifference to these supreme Christian virtues. Of course we give lip service to the importance of these great qualities, but in reality humility and servanthood do not guide our thinking, relationships, church leadership style, and structure the way they should. Indeed, in many practical ways it can be demonstrated that we do not really grasp the meaning of servanthood, or the humble, servant nature of the church. Pride and selfishness plague much of the Lord's work. The world's concepts of power, honor, and authority in leadership permeate our churches. Because this point is so important, we will consider this topic in much greater detail in the next chapter. Here, it is sufficient to say that the plurality of elders suits not only the church's family nature, but also fits and promotes its humble, loving, servant nature.

[19]

## AN EXPLANATION AND DEFENSE

*An effective form of oversight for God's church.* Biblical eldership is a very effective form of pastoral leadership—much better than one-man church leadership. Critics say eldership doesn't work because a church board cannot properly care for a church. To these critics I answer with a hearty "Amen!" Most organizational boards I have seen or been part of are quite passive, uninformed, and uninvolved. But biblical eldership is something quite different. From the Greek word *kopiao* (work hard) in 1 Thessalonians 5:12 and 1 Timothy 5:17, we learn that the elders are strenuously working to the point of weariness for the sake of the assembly. They are laboring men, workmen, watchmen who care for the souls of the Lord's people. So, true biblical eldership means that a group of Spirit-moved men are working hard to care for the flock of God.

Elders are men placed as overseers in the flock by the Holy Spirit of God (Acts 20:28). Their desire to shepherd the flock comes from God, and each has been given a spiritual gift (or gifts) to contribute to the shepherding task. The resulting interplay of gifts helps lighten the heavy workload and balances out the deficiencies of any one man. The plurality of overseers adds greater perspective and wisdom to decisions that need to be made. In addition, the different ages and personalities of each elder give the people a choice of whom to consult about their needs and problems.

Many devout, Christian men are not multi-gifted leaders, nor are they well suited to singularly lead a congregation effectively. But when placed in a leadership body, these same men excel and make important contributions. (I believe the vast majority of traditional pastors fit into this category. That is why they are so severely criticized by the congregation and thus move on to another pastorate after five or six years.)

*The perennial question.* The big question that always arises when discussing eldership is, "Who leads the elders? The buck has to stop with one person, not a board. Didn't Israel have only one deliverer at a time, like Moses or David? Everyone knows that one-man rule is most effective." I respond to this question with the following truths and observations.

First, we have one Head, one Shepherd, one Master, one King, one High Priest, one Leader—the Lord Jesus Christ Who is always present with His people through the Holy Spirit (Matthew 18:20; 28:20). This is not a theory or a theological platitude; it is a

[20]

glorious, blessed reality. I believe the professional, ordained clergy-man obscures this central truth of the Christian assembly.

Second, the real error to be contended with is not simply that one man provides leadership for the congregation, but *that one man in the holy brotherhood has been elevated to a sacred, unscriptural status.* In practice, the ordained clergyman—*the* minister, *the* reverend, *the* lone professional—is the Protestant priest.[7] He alone is qualified to lead in worship and administer the Lord's Supper, preach, and baptize. All other believers are merely laymen who have been declared unqualified to carry out these functions.

The awful result of this doctrine is clerically-dependent congregations that are hindered from growing into spiritual maturity. To Paul, maturing in the faith was one of the supreme goals of the Christian life. The very concept of a sacred minister is unbiblical, and the persistence of belief in the concept is the chief reason why most churches will never accept biblical eldership. The New Testament Scriptures, however, neither authorize nor speak of such a sacred person who rules over the saints of God. This concept is foreign to the gospel and the assemblies established by the apostles of the Lord Jesus Christ.

Third, do we think we are wiser and more intelligent than the apostles of our Lord Jesus Christ? Do we think they would have established a form of oversight that would be inferior or ineffective? There were good reasons why the apostles avoided one-man oversight—which was very common in their day—and instituted collective pastoral oversight.

Fourth, many people falsely pit local church eldership against the special deliverer or the charismatic, multi-gifted leader, favoring the single leader. But both are needed and have a place in God's plan. For example, some people think Moses is the model for every local congregation. Moses, however, was a unique, one-time, special deliverer for the nation of Israel. He was not a permanent institution. It is hard even to describe his position and role (Deuteronomy 34:10-12; Numbers 12:6-8; Exodus 33:11), yet he is an example to all godly leaders. After the people settled in their cities they were to be led primarily by their local elders and the priestly family, with God as their King and Master. Unfortunately, Israel never appreciated or practiced this blessed truth (1 Samuel 8).

Today, God raises up extraordinarily gifted men to teach and lead His people. Such men may or may not be local elders. There are great teachers of the Word, evangelists, and church planters who God has used to build up and redirect the Lord's people, but who are not (and should not be) local elders. The fact is, there are very few such gifted men. Local elders need to call upon these gifted men for help.

Let us never forget that God uses ordinary people to accomplish His plans. There is too much emphasis today on the charismatic super-leader. This kind of emphasis is not in the New Testament. I am convinced that the majority of people who are converted to Christ are reached and built up in the faith by ordinary, common people who allow themselves to be used by the Holy Spirit of God. So let us take our eyes off the superstars and focus on the whole body of Christ—a body in which each member functions and serves one another in love (Ephesians 4:15,16). We need both the superstar and the ordinary, obedient saint.

Fifth, most people don't realize that biblical eldership actually combines the best of both leadership structures; an exceptionally gifted leader can lead and teach with all his zeal and might, yet he is subject to his fellow leaders and brothers who jointly lead and guide the congregation. Biblical eldership provides necessary protection from the all-too-common pitfalls of egoism and personality imbalance. So the gifted leader or teacher is the person who can greatly profit from the checks and balances biblical eldership provides.

There is a dark side to the super-pastor concept that is seldom talked about: many churches are lead by highly independent, domineering, egotistical men *who desperately need accountability and balance.* The superstar approach is the wrong model for a body that preaches and practices humble servanthood and close interdependence on one another's gifts and services. Furthermore, when ruled by a superstar pastor, qualified men remain in spiritual infancy rather than growing into maturity as they share in the oversight of the church.

I have found that most critics of biblical eldership don't really understand it. They don't understand how much more flexible and adaptable it is to every culture and local situation than the rigid, one-man-professional-minister-structure of most churches today. An eldership may have one or more elders who serve full time, or it may have no full-time elders and operate very effectively.

## AN EXPLANATION AND DEFENSE

One elder may be a gifted public teacher, or no elders may have that gift. Another brother may be an effective teacher, but not a qualified elder. Under biblical eldership, all of these situations are possible and equally effective. There are many variations of how an eldership may operate. The only fixed responsibility is that the elders share the overall pastoral oversight of the assembly.

*Conclusion.* We have every right to believe that the Spirit of God had good reasons for establishing rule by elders in the first churches—both Jew and Gentile, from Jerusalem to Rome, and in many varied cultural situations. To say that we are free to discard eldership and deaconship and establish other forms of church oversight is dangerous. In the end, such reasoning does not do justice to Scripture, particularly the mandate given to the first elders who were appointed by the apostles. Yet this apostolic mandate has, for the most part, been taken from church elders and placed into the hands of a single, professional minister.

By departing from biblical eldership, man has produced nothing better. On the contrary, man has produced a great deal of error: the clergy with its mass of passive laity, a priesthood separate from the rest of God's people, women pastors, and an obsession with honorific titles and hierarchical forms of rule that demean the glorious status of the Lord's people and greatly limit their participation in the life of the Christian community. Be assured that if we do not cling to scriptural instruction, we will continue to establish forms of church rule that are more like the secular and religious forms of rule Jesus so vigorously and repeatedly denounced (Matthew 20:25-28; 23:1-12). As Alfred Kuen suggests, we do best when we follow what the Spirit of God led the apostles and first Christians to practice and teach:

Has not the history of twenty centuries of Christianity proved that the plan of the primitive church is the only one which is suitable for all times and places, is most flexible in its adaptation to the most diverse conditions, is the best able to resist and stand against persecutions, and offers the maximum of possibilities for the full development of the spiritual life?

Each time that man has believed himself to be more intelligent than God, that he has painstakingly developed a better religious system "better adapted to the psychology of man," more conformable to the spirit of our times, instead of simply following the neotestamentary model, his attempt

[23]

has been short-lived because of failure due to some unforeseen difficulty.[8]

If, as I have contended, the New Testament gives sufficient example and instruction regarding the oversight of the household of God, then we can see that most churches have strayed—in some cases very far—from God's design for His people. Most churches have followed the paths of institutionalism, denominationalism, professionalism, clericalism, and sacramentalism. Under present church structures, many qualified men will never take their rightful place in the church or grow into spiritual maturity.

The concept of the church as a brotherhood of free men; as a ministerial body; as one people; and as a humble, servant community is unrealized in most churches. The issue, then, as always, is simple faith and obedience to God's Word, which means honoring Him above our thoughts and traditions and being loyal to our great God. To be sure, the incorporation of biblical eldership into the local church is not the cure-all for every problem. In fact, a church may experience even greater difficulties if it tries to establish a biblically functioning council of elders. Nevertheless, faithful obedience to our Lord is the true measure of success and the only thing that counts for eternity.

---

### NOTES

1. The term government is used here in the sense of a system or structure by which a society is governed. It is used interchangeably with polity, organization, structure, form, order.
2. R. Paul Stevens, *Liberating the Laity* (Downers Grove: InterVarsity Press, 1985), page 17.
3. George Eldon Ladd, *A Theology of the New Testament* (Grand Rapids: William B. Eerdmans Pub. Co., 1974), page 534. Other evangelicals say the same. Well-known missiologist George W. Peters writes, "No permanent pattern can be established conclusively and defended exegetically" (*A Theology of Church Growth*, Grand Rapids: Zondervan Publishing House, 1981, page 145). A Bible study series by The Navigators on 1 Peter, states, "The New Testament gives no clear picture of how churches were organized" (*1 Peter,* Life Change Series, Colorado Springs: Navpress, 1986, page 115).
4. Jon Zens, "The Major Concepts of Eldership in the New Testament," *Baptist Reformation Review* 7 (Summer, 1978): 28.
5. Robert Banks, *Paul's Idea of Community* (Grand Rapids: Wm. B. Eerdmans Publishing Co., 1980), pages 53, 54.
6. *Ibid.*

## AN EXPLANATION AND DEFENSE

7. In their book, *What's Happening to Clergy Marriages?*, observe how David and Vera Mace refer to the protestant pastor:
   Something else, too, must be considered. The pastor is not simply a leader, an authority. He also exercises priestly functions that are forbidden to all other members of the church. He administers the sacraments, receiving the power to do so from his ordination. In this capacity he acts directly as the representative of Christ, and this gives him a special aura of holiness (Nashville: Abingdon Press, 1980, pages 57, 58).

8. Alfred Kuen, *I Will Build My Church* (Chicago: Moody Press, 1971), page 7.

# Chapter 2

# *Humble Servants*

*If I then, the Lord and Teacher, washed your feet, you*
*also ought to wash one another's feet. For I gave you*
*an example that you also should do as I did to you.*

John 13:14,15

\*   \*   \*

Just as Christianity influenced the Roman empire, the Greco-
Roman world affected the course of Christianity. Renowned
historian Kenneth Scott Latourette, when citing pagan influences
on early Christianity, states that the Roman concepts of power
and rule, in particular, corrupted the organization and life of
the early churches: ". . . the Church was being interpenetrated
by ideals which were quite contrary to the Gospel, especially
the conception and use of power which were in stark contrast
to the kind exhibited in the life and teaching of Jesus and in
the cross and the resurrection."[1] This, Latourette says, proved to
be "the menace which was most nearly disastrous" to Christianity.[2]

I believe it is more accurate to say that the organizational
changes that occurred during the early centuries of Christianity
were indeed disastrous. Christianity, the humblest of all faiths,
degenerated into the most power-hungry and elaborate hierarchical religion on the face of the earth. After the emperor
Constantine elevated Christianity to the status of a state religion
in A.D. 312, the once-persecuted faith became the fiercest
persecutor of all its opposition. An unscriptural clerical and
priestly caste arose that was consumed by questions of power

[26]

and authority. Even Roman emperors had a guiding hand in the care of God's churches. Nearly everything Jesus Christ had taught and lived was distorted; the pristine character of Christianity was lost. Particularly relevant to our study was the loss of the humble, servant character of Christianity that was so evident in the New Testament churches.

As we read the Gospels, however, we see that the principles of humility and servanthood are at the very heart of Christ's teaching. Unfortunately, like many of the early Christians, we have been slow to understand these great virtues, especially their application to church structure and leadership. Worldly concepts of power, success, and prominence are easily perpetuated and hard to break—even among Bible-believing Christians. Because these principles of humility and servanthood are essential to Christian leadership and community life, let us briefly survey our Lord's teaching on the subject.

*Matthew 5:3.* This verse is the key to understanding the Beatitudes. Jesus declares that only those who are "poor in spirit" will enter the kingdom of heaven. To be poor in spirit means that we see our utter spiritual poverty apart from God and recognize our total dependence on Him for help. Being poor in spirit is acknowledging, like the tax collector in Luke 18:13, our spiritual destitution, helplessness, and unworthiness before an infinite and holy God. It is the opposite of pride, self-reliance, and self-satisfaction. The psalmist confesses an attitude of being poor in spirit in Psalm 51:17: "The sacrifices of God are a broken spirit; A broken and contrite heart, O God, Thou wilt not despise."

*Matthew 11:29.* In contrast to the instruction of the oppressive religious leaders of His day, Jesus tells the people to "take my yoke upon you, and learn from Me, for I am gentle and humble in heart." In this verse, Jesus explicitly tells us what He is like as a person: meek and lowly in heart. Too many religious leaders, however, do not have gentle, humble hearts. They use people to advance themselves. They exploit others to gain money, success, prominence, and satisfy their own egos. But Jesus is radically different, and His followers—especially those who would lead His people—are to be humble and gentle like He is.

*Mark 9:33-35.* On the first recorded occasion of the disciples' struggle for position among themselves, Jesus teaches, "If anyone wants to be first, he shall be last of all, and servant of all." By means of this paradoxical statement, our Lord begins to transform His disciples' thinking about greatness. He declares that true greatness is not achieved by striving for prominence over others or grasping for power, but by a humble, self-effacing attitude of service to *all*—even the most lowly people. An enormous amount of literature today tells people how to become "number one," how to be self-fulfilled, and how to achieve personal happiness and success. "Me-ism" is the idol of modern man. But we find that the teaching of Jesus Christ is in stark contrast to this attitude. He tells us to be "servant of all." Being a servant of all is an attitude that inflicts a deathblow to selfishness and "me-ism." It is a disposition that leads one to genuinely and generously care for the welfare and interests of others. It is a lowly attitude that reflects our position as people under our Master's authority. Thus we must submit to our Master Who calls us to lovingly sacrifice ourselves for the advancement and care of others.

In Matthew's parallel account of the Mark 9:33-35 incident, Jesus states the supreme importance of humility even more explicitly: "Whoever then humbles himself as this child, he is the greatest in the kingdom of heaven" (Matthew 18:4). We must seek to be humble. Humility does not come like lightning out of the sky; it is something we must actively pursue. We must submit our thoughts and lives to His will. We must agree and submit to God's assessment of ourselves as revealed in His Word. We must see that, like a child, we are small and helpless. We must see our complete dependence on God for everything and realize that all gifts we possess come from His hand. We must not be jealous of others who are more gifted or prominent than we are. Rather, we must use our God-given talents and gifts to glorify Him and to serve others.

*Matthew 20:20-28.* In bold display of selfish ambition, the mother of James and John asks Jesus to give her sons the two more prominent seats in His kingdom. She says, "Command that in Your kingdom these two sons of mine may sit, one on Your right and one on Your left." We could almost laugh at her crass selfishness, but at heart we know that we are like her. We, too, want the best places for ourselves. We want to climb the ladder of success. We want to be known. We want to be a part of something big and successful. We want to secure a good, comfortable place for ourselves. Jesus knows how much we desire importance and how contrary it is to His ways. So as He answers the mother of James and John, He teaches about true greatness in God's kingdom. He says, "You know that the rulers of the Gentiles lord it over them, and their great men exercise authority over them. It is not so among you, but whoever wishes to become great among you shall be your servant." Our Lord reminds His disciples that His principles of success and greatness are different from those of this godless world's. So He summons His disciples to be truly distinct. How distressing that so many Christian leaders strive to be more like the world's leaders than their lowly, obedient Savior. In the age to come, such leaders will lose out on rich rewards and true praise from God.

*Matthew 23:1-12.* In this emotionally charged passage, Jesus castigates the awful pride, selfishness, and hypocrisy of the religious leaders of His day. As totally self-centered men, they separated and exalted themselves above the people. They lusted after titles, special clothes, special treatment, and the chief seats among their fellow men. They loved to have a high-profile public ministry; they loved the limelight. They demanded special greetings from ordinary people.

In marked contrast, Jesus prohibits His disciples from using honorific titles; from calling one another Rabbi, Father, or Master; from elevating themselves in any way that would diminish their brotherly relationship; or from usurping the unique place that Christ and the Father have over each believer. These words are as needed and applicable to today's religious scene as when they were first spoken.

*Luke 22:24-27.* During the last Passover meal, the disciples strive for the most prominent place at the table. Again, we witness how our Lord patiently teaches them not to act like worldly leaders: "But not so with you, but let him who is the greatest among you become as the youngest, and the leader as the servant" (Luke 22:26). In his book, *Jesus and Power,* David Prior shows how churches today still strive over the same issues of prominence.

This rivalry among his disciples was a constant thorn in the side of Jesus. It was endemic in the church at Corinth (cf. 1 Cor. 3:1-15). It is frequently found today among and within large evangelical congregations which strive to be larger, better and more famous than each other. The very size of these congregations often produces an envious attitude among not-so-large churches, an attitude which reveals precisely the same competitive spirit in those churches also. During the last twenty years I have been a member of four congregations with attendances which happen to have been much higher than most in the neighborhood. Being an Anglican, these four have all been Anglican churches. One of the most difficult obstacles to overcome has been the unholy combination of pride-in-numbers in the local church on the one hand, and envy-at-success in the diocese on the other. Competitiveness is a cancer. Jesus recognized it as completely hostile to the reality of power which he was teaching and demonstrating."[3]

*John 13:3-17.* Jesus further illustrates His humble, servant role during the last Passover meal by washing His disciples' feet. Here we see that the symbol of our Lord is the towel, not elaborate clerical garments. Only when we learn what it means to wash one another's feet and clothe ourselves in humility will we be able to live together in peace and unity.

I believe it is impossible to correctly understand church elder-ship or true Christian community without first grasping Jesus' teaching on humility and servanthood. Yet, as Andrew Murray observes, it is in understanding humility that we are most likely to fail:

> When I look back on my own religious experience, or on the Church of Christ in the world, I stand amazed at the thought of how little humility is sought after as the distinguishing feature of the discipleship of Jesus. In preaching and living, in the daily activities of the home and social life, in the more special fellowship with Christians, in the direction and per-formance of work for Christ—how much proof there is that humility is not esteemed the cardinal virtue.[4]

Our Lord's repeated insistence on humility and servanthood teaches us at least three important truths.

First, God hates pride. Proverbs says, "Everyone who is proud in heart is an abomination to the Lord" (Proverbs 16:5a). Those are strong words. In the list of seven sins that God especially hates, pride is at the top (Proverbs 6:16-19). James says, "'God is opposed to the proud, but gives grace to the humble'" (James 4:6). God hates pride so much that He gave Paul a thorn in the flesh to keep him from exalting himself and to force him to be dependent on his Creator (2 Corinthians 12). One of the awful things about pride is that it deceives us; we may think we are serving God, when in reality we are serving ourselves.

Second, Christ's repeated teaching on humble servanthood proves how difficult it is for the human heart to understand humility. Our Lord often repeated His teaching on humble servanthood because the disciples failed to understand what He was saying. Pride and selfishness continually strive to dominate and deceive the human heart. Many of the ugly divisions, power struggles, wounded feelings, and petty jealousies in our churches and personal relationships exist because we are not truly humble, loving servants. We may talk about humble servanthood, but pride and selfishness guide much of our thinking and behavior. The history of Christianity clearly reveals that those who lose sight of Christ's spirit of humility, love, and servanthood quickly revert to the world's proud, selfish, and authoritarian ways. So we need to constantly pray that we will be humble minded. We need to gladly accept the situations and problems that God allows in our lives so that He can break us of our pride and selfishness.

Third, our Lord's repeated teaching shows us the ideal characteristics of the Christian community and its leadership. Humility and servanthood are vital leadership qualities because they express the mind and disposition of God's beloved Son. God calls upon us to emulate His Son's character: "Do nothing from selfish or empty conceit, but with humility of mind let each of you regard one another as more important than himself; do not merely look out for your own personal interests, but also for the interests of others. Have this attitude in yourselves which was also in Christ Jesus, who, . . . taking the form of a bond-servant, . . . humbled Himself . . ." (Philippians 2:3-8). Despite these wonderful words, we have to admit that too much of the Lord's work is marked by pride and strife. Many Christian leaders are characterized by an independent spirit. That is why they have so little ability to work with others unless they are the boss. Leaders of parachurch organizations and local churches often set up organizational structures that give them greater control and power over the organization.[5] But New Testament teaching and examples emphasize shared leadership, interdependence within the body, mutuality, and brotherly community. These must be our goals and ideals!

### The Proper Structure of Leadership

In light of our Lord's extraordinary teaching on servanthood and His humble manner of life, there are several crucial questions we must ask ourselves: How does leadership operate in a community that is to preach and practice humility and servanthood? How does leadership organize itself in such a community? How is this leadership different from that of this prideful, selfish world? The answers to these questions are important. I am convinced that one of the major reasons the apostles chose the elder system of oversight for the first churches was because it enhanced the humble, servant nature of the Christian brotherhood. Although many Christians today have a new awareness of Christ's teaching on servanthood, we still have a long way to go toward fully implementing these principles in our church leadership practices.

The New Testament provides a consistent example of shared, brotherly leadership as the ideal means of leadership in the congregation where humility and servanthood are paramount. To function properly, shared leadership, that is, plurality, requires a greater exercise of humble servanthood than does unitary leadership. In order for an eldership to effectively operate, the elders must show mutual regard for one another, must submit themselves one to another, must patiently wait upon one another, must genuinely consider one another's interests and perspectives, and must prefer and defer to one another. Eldership, then, enhances brotherly love, humility, mutuality, and loving interdependence—qualities that mark the Christian assembly.

Furthermore, shared leadership is often more trying than unitary leadership. It exposes our impatience with one another, our awful pride, bull-headedness, selfish immaturity, domineering disposition, lack of love and understanding of one another, and prayerlessness. It also shows us how underdeveloped and immature we really are in humility, brotherly love, and the true servant spirit. Like the saints at Corinth, we are quick to develop our knowledge and public gifts, but slow to mature in love and humility. Our churches are in desperate need of a revival in love, humility, and the servant spirit, and it must begin with our leaders. Biblical eldership provides the structure for leaders to work together in mutual love and humility. It is the model for the entire congregation to follow. Thus, the plurality of elders suits the assembly of God.

### The Proper Style of Leadership
Proper leadership structure is meaningless without the right spirit of humility, love, and servanthood. Elders must be humble,

loving, and servant minded in spirit. A group of elders can easily become authoritarian or self-serving. God requires, therefore, that church elders be humble, servant leaders like the Lord Jesus. In 1 Peter 5:3, Peter uses the same terminology as Jesus when instructing the elders of Asia: "nor yet as lording it over those allotted to your charge, but proving to be examples to the flock." Just as Jesus clothed Himself in humility, taking the towel of a servant, Peter charges the elders, as well as everyone else, to be clothed in humility, ". . . all of you, clothe yourselves with humility toward one another, for God is opposed to the proud, but gives grace to the humble" (1 Peter 5:5). Paul reminds the Ephesian elders of his example of humility in Acts 20:19, "serving the Lord with all humility. . . ." He implies that they, too, must serve the Lord in a spirit of humility. Paul also makes it clear that new Christians cannot qualify for eldership because of the temptation for pride. "And not a new convert, lest he become conceited and fall into the condemnation incurred by the devil" (1 Timothy 3:6). Further, when describing the qualifications for elders, Paul insists that an elder must be gentle, not self-willed, uncontentious, and not pugnacious.

What is of supreme importance to God, then, is the way in which elders shepherd God's people. God measures success by the spirit in which elders handle people, solve problems, and perform their duties—not so much by the outward results. Thus, humility and servanthood are at the very heart of Christian eldership. We must understand that it is possible for a church to be governed by a body of elders, yet be totally unscriptural because of the manner in which the elders operate. Like Pharisees or worldly rulers, the elders may wrongly separate and elevate themselves above the people. The elders may serve chiefly to satisfy their egos. They may serve because they need to dominate people. But only elders who operate in humble servanthood are true, biblical elders. Only they can genuinely manifest the life of Jesus Christ to the congregation and a watching, seeking world.

Furthermore, if the elders do not live as humble servants, they will never experience unity and peace among themselves. If the church elders fight among themselves, how can the congregation live in peace? The elders are examples—a microcosm of the Christian community. Humble, loving mutuality and true, servant regard for one another must characterize them. Yet conflict among elders remains a common and serious problem. The solution, however, is not to revert to one-man rule. That is the easy way out. God desires that the elders humble themselves, wash one another's feet, repent, pray, turn from pride, shun impatience, and love as Christ loved. That is the kind of leadership God wants the elders to exemplify for His flock. Thus, true success in pastoral oversight is not measured by wealth, numbers, or programs. Instead, success is measured by the quality of spiritual life, the church's unity, peace, humility, love, fidelity to truth, and loving service to one another.

At this point we need to clarify a concept that is easily misunderstood: the humble servant character of church elders does not imply that they have no authority. The New Testament terms that describe the elders' position and work—God's stewards, overseers, shepherds, leaders—all imply a measure of authority. Peter could not have warned the Asian elders against "lording it over those allotted to your charge" if they had no authority that could be abused. The writer of Hebrews also confirms the elders' authority by saying the saints must submit to and obey their leaders because the leaders have the solemn duty of watching over the souls of the saints (Hebrews 13:17).

The issue, then, is the way in which elders exercise their authority. Elders must never wield authority in a heavy-handed way, use manipulative tactics, or be arrogant and aloof. They must not enslave others or create a repressive atmosphere. They must never think they are unanswerable to their fellow brethren. They must never act like the false teachers of Corinth who took advantage of the people (2 Corinthians 11:20). Nor must they act like Diotrephes, the church tyrant, who sought first place for himself (3 John 9). In other words, elders must never be authoritarian. Such an attitude is incompatible with humble servanthood. J. I. Packer's powerful contrast between proper authority and authoritarianism will help us understand the difference:

> Exercise of authority in its various spheres is not necessarily authoritarian. There is a crucial distinction here. Authoritarianism is authority corrupted, gone to seed. Authoritarianism appears when the submission that is demanded cannot be justified in terms of truth or morality. . . . Any form of human authority can degenerate in this way. You have authoritarianism in the state when the regime uses power in an unprincipled

way to maintain itself. You have it in churches when leaders claim control of their followers' consciences. You have it in academic work at high school, university or seminary when you are required to agree with your professor rather than follow the evidence of truth for yourself. You have it in the family when parents direct or restrict their children unreasonably. Unhappy experiences of authority are usually experiences of degenerate authority, that is, of authoritarianism. That such experiences leave a bad taste and prompt skepticism about authority in all its forms is sad but not surprising.

Authoritarianism is evil, anti-social, anti-human and ultimately anti-God (for self-deifying pride is at its heart), and I have nothing to say in its favor.[6]

Humble servant elders, therefore, must use their God-given authority as shepherds to build up and protect the congregation—never for the purpose of gaining prominence or material advantage. True elders must never use their authority to demean the glorious status and privileges of their brothers and sisters in Christ. Because the local church is made up of a body of priests, Spirit-indwelt saints, and gifted servants of God, elders must never treat the people like their subjects.

### A Good Example to Follow

If you cannot imagine how humble leaders operate, study the life of Paul; he is a concrete illustration of how a humble servant exercises God-given authority. Paul received authority as an apostle from the Lord Jesus Christ. Yet he viewed this authority as a means of building others up, not as a means of dominating people or gaining prominence and material advantage for himself. In 2 Corinthians 10:8, Paul writes, "For even if I should boast somewhat further about our authority, which the Lord gave for building you up and not for destroying you . . ." In another portion of Scripture similar to 1 Peter 5:3, Paul, by his own example, displays his attitude toward lordly oversight: "Not that we lord it over your faith, but are workers with you for your joy; for in your faith you are standing firm" (2 Corinthians 1:24). Paul always promoted Christ, never himself. He knew he was to be a servant, an instrument in God's plan. Thus he gave all the glory to God.

Paul's restraint in his use of authority is striking: He would rather suffer than risk wounding his children in the faith.[7] He would rather appeal than command, dealing with people in love and gentleness rather than "with a rod."[8] Although he used his authority and power when needed to stop false teachers, his patience was extraordinary. He so identifies with his converts that their discipline, weakness, and humiliation become his.[9] He would lower and sacrifice himself so that he might raise others in faith and maturity.[10] He sacrificed all personal gain and advantage for others. He did not get rich off of his converts. Indeed, he avoided celebrity status.

For example, although he was at Corinth for a year and a half, he never once mentioned his extraordinary experience of being taken up to the third heaven. He mentioned his heavenly experience only after he was compelled to do so because the Corinthians had fallen prey to boasting false teachers.[11] He did not speak of his experience earlier because he knew the Corinthians would have exalted him, and he wanted them to trust only in Christ.

Humility was the key to Paul's use of authority in his relationships with erring and contentious converts. His great intellectual powers and fiery zeal were used to build up God's people. In everything, his converts' spiritual welfare was foremost in his mind.

However, because of his extraordinary humility and lowly display of apostolic authority, Paul was terribly misunderstood. Many even considered him to be weak and cowardly.[12] Because our minds are so accustomed to the world's images of leadership, it is easy to think of a humble person as passive, weak, timid, or cowardly. But look at Jesus Christ. He was totally humble, yet He taught vast crowds, faced grueling intellectual debate, taught with great authority, and boldly confronted the hypocritical, religious clerics of His day with scorching criticism. In righteous anger, He took a whip and drove the moneychangers out of the temple. Humility is not a symptom of weakness or incompetence!

The humble servant, Paul, was a strong, brave warrior and leader for Christ. He served God and cared for His people with all his might and zeal. During his life he faced many conflicts, debates, and struggles; he even rebuked Peter and Barnabas for their hypocrisy. The man who could say that he "served the Lord with all lowliness of mind," handed over an impenitent believer to Satan for the destruction of his flesh, struck the false teacher Elymus with blindness, and stood bravely before Roman courts and judges.

Nevertheless, despite the many problems he confronted, Paul consistently responded to his brethren in humility and love. He knew that acting in pride would make things worse and divide God's people. When we consider Paul's example and that of our Lord's, we must say that true elders do not dictate, but direct. They do not command the consciences of their brethren, but appeal to their brethren to faithfully follow God's Word. Out of love they suffer and bear the brunt of difficult people and problems so the lambs are not bruised. They bear the misunderstanding and sins of others so the assembly may live in peace. They lose sleep so others may rest. They make great personal sacrifices of time and energy for the welfare of others. They see themselves as men under authority. They depend on God for wisdom and help, not on their own power and cleverness. They face the false teachers' fierce attacks. They guard the community's liberty and freedom in Christ so the saints are encouraged to develop their gifts, mature, and serve one another.

**NOTES**
1. Kenneth Scott Latourette, *History of Christianity,* 2 vols. (2d ed., New York: Harper & Row, Publishers, 1975), 1:269.
2. *Ibid,* page 261.
3. David Prior, *Jesus and Power* (Downers Grove, InterVarity Press, 1987), page 82.
4. Andrew Murray, *Humility* (Springdale, Pennsylvania: Whitaker House, 1982), page 7.
5. Listen to this honest confession by Anthony Campolo, Jr.:
   Few people know the rhetoric of servanthood better than the clergy. And yet so many of them, even unconsciously, are on power trips. It may be that some were attracted to the ministry because they saw in the role of minister the opportunity to exercise power. Clergymen of this type have learned to play their power games with a cleverness that keeps most people from ever suspecting what they are really about.
   One way for the minister to gain and maintain power is to do all the work of the church himself. As a young pastor I was very guilty of this tactic. I called on all the church members, ran the youth groups and the Daily Vacation Bible School, supervised the Sunday School, mimeographed the church bulletin, organized the church choir, unofficially chaired every committee, and did half of the janitorial work. For the most part, the church people stood back in amazement at my boundless energy and seeming dedication. Yet what I was really doing was keeping church members out of positions

of power by occupying them all myself. I was in charge of everything. I controlled the church and my power was everywhere evident. When church members wanted to take over some of the roles I monopolized, I treated them as threatening people. When I met with fellow clergy of my community, our discussions often revolved around ways to handle such uppity members.

"Don't they realize what I am trying to accomplish?" "Why do they want to hold me back?" "Why are they interfering with my plans?" "If they would just move out of my way, I could really get the church rolling! . . ."

Pastors who try to do everything themselves often complain about the lack of adequate lay leadership in the church. In reality, they are keeping lay workers out of leadership roles because of their own need for power. Sometimes a power-oriented pastor will con his congregation into hiring an assistant pastor whom he can control; then the two of them are able to do all the church work, and it becomes unnecessary for the church members to do anything. The pastor is more powerful than ever, the church program grinds on, and the laity remain unchallenged and dormant (*The Power Delusion*, Wheaton: Victor Books, 1984, pages 42-43.).

6. J. I. Packer, *Freedom and Authority* (Oakland: International Council on Biblical Inerrancy, 1981), page 8.
7. 2 Corinthians 1:23-2:4; 13:7.
8. 1 Corinthians 4:21; 2 Corinthians 10:1,2; 13:8-10; Galatians 4:20.
9. 2 Corinthians 11:29; 12:21; Galatians 4:12.
10. 2 Corinthians 11:7,21; 13:9.
11. 2 Corinthians 12:1-13.
12. 1 Corinthians 4:18-21; 2 Corinthians 10:1-11.

# Chapter 3

# *The Elders of Israel*

*And they shall bear the burden of the people*
*Numbers 11:17*

\*   \*   \*

Before looking at the role of elders in the New Testament, we must explore the eldership of the Old Testament. The Old Testament is full of rich background material essential to our study of New Testament elders. Also it provides many practical insights for elders today.

In the ancient Near East, including the nation of Israel, society rule by a body of elders was widespread.[1] Simply defined, government by elders is corporate rule by the qualified, leading men of society. To our dislike, the Old Testament does not explain who the qualified, leading men of Israel were. Although Israel's elders are mentioned some 100 times throughout the Old Testament, no detailed description of their organization, appointment, or qualifications is given. Obviously the Old Testament writers were not led by God's Spirit to give detailed explanations of all ancient institutions. Since it is unnecessary to expound every Old Testament passage regarding elders, we will briefly survey selected Old Testament passages and summarize facts that shed helpful light on the New Testament elders.

### *Age and Office*

It is generally agreed that the institution of elder rule, as the word itself indicates, originally was based on age: the older, more influential men of society naturally formed a ruling council. The origin of the office is easily traced. Under the primitive conditions of society that prevail in the early history of all nations age is an indispensable condition of investment with authority. . . . The title, which at first is inseparably associated with the idea of age, came afterwards to designate merely the dignity to which age was formerly the necessary passport.[2]

In Hebrew, the word for elder (*zaqen*) is the same word used to describe old or older men. Throughout the Old Testament, *zaqen* bears the twofold meaning of an age designation and a title of office. Because of the dual meaning of the word *zaqen*, it is in some passages difficult to know if the writer meant older men or the more technical meaning of community leader.[3] Most of the time, however, the context makes the intended meaning of the word obvious. The majority of Old Testament occurrences of the term *zaqen* refer to a collective body of leading men with official, recognized status to act for the people, not just to all the society's old men. Often the term *elder* is found alongside terms for other official positions such as judges, heads, officers, and priests.

The ancient Greek translation of the Old Testament (the Septuagint) generally renders *zaqen* as *presbyteros*, which, like the Hebrew word, also bears the twofold meaning of age and official title depending on the context. The Septuagint also uses the word *gerousia* (senate or council of elders) in a number of places, indicating that the elders were an official senate or council of leaders. The English translations of the Old Testament acknowledge the twofold meaning of *zaqen* by translating it as *old* or *elder*, depending on the context.

The twofold meaning of *zaqen* must not be overlooked. You must not think of Israel's elders as simply the old men of Israel. That would be inaccurate and misleading, a point John L. McKenzie illustrates well: "In all but a few instances, the elders in the Old Testament appear as a distinct social grade or collegiate body with certain political and religious functions, and not merely as 'old men.' . . . but we must bear in mind that the word in actual usage need not by its etymology signify an old man any more than 'Senator' or 'alderman' does in the United States."[4]

Although the strict sense of age has been dropped from the meaning of *elder*, certain connotations such as maturity, experience, dignity, authority, and honor are retained. The term *elder* also

ISRAEL'S ELDERS

conveys the positive concepts of honor and dignity for a wise, stable, and experienced man. Of course, maturity, experience, and recognition by the community as a wise and respected leader takes time, so no youngster will sit with the elders, the community leaders. Even so, the Old and New Testaments give no specific age requirement for elders.

The Old Testament reveals specific age limits for service for the Levites (25/30 to 50 years of age, Numbers 4:3; 8:23-26). But there is no basis for imposing these age limits on other institutions, since not all institutions require the same amount of physical labor as the Levites' work. The absence of any age requirement for eldership is part of God's perfect wisdom as revealed in His Word. Great flexibility and recognition of individual diversity in experience and maturity is displayed by Scripture's silence concerning the age of elders. Although an elder is a community leader who is respected for his wisdom, maturity, and stability—all of which take some time to accomplish—it is unsound to set age requirements for elders because Scripture does not set such requirements.

*Israel's elders*

From the time they were slaves in Egypt, Israel was governed by a council of elders. God acknowledged the elders' place of leadership by sending Moses to them first to announce the people's deliverance: "Go and gather the elders of Israel together . . ." (Exodus 3:16). The elders appear as the people's chief representative leaders (Exodus 4:29, 31) and as Moses' chief assistants—standing by his side when he confronts Pharaoh (Exodus 3:18) and assisting him as he prepares the people for the first Passover (Exodus 12:21).

At God's command, the elders were Moses' constant attendants and witnesses to his leadership and actions during the wilderness wanderings.[5] They played a key role in all important events during Israel's wanderings. Of particular significance is the role of the 70 elders Moses selected to closely assist him in leading and caring for the people (Numbers 11:16,17): The Lord therefore said to Moses, "Gather for Me seventy men from the elders of Israel, whom you know to be the elders of the people and their officers and bring them to the tent of meeting. . . . and I will take the Spirit who is upon you, and will put Him upon them; and they shall bear the burden of the people with you, so that you shall not bear it all alone." Thus,

[41]

the 70 elders helped Moses bear the burden of the people, shepherding the congregation during their wilderness wanderings.

Upon entering the Promised Land, the elders continued the same relationship with Joshua as they had had with Moses.[6] At the close of the book of Joshua, a glorious tribute is paid to the elders' faithfulness—a tribute every elder should earnestly desire: "And Israel served the Lord all the days of Joshua and all the days of the elders who survived Joshua, and had known all the deeds of the Lord which he had done for Israel" (Joshua 24:31). This verse demonstrates the elders' important influence over the people. After Israel conquered many of the heathen nations and settled in her new cities, the elders exercised considerable military, spiritual, judicial, and political authority in the cities and the entire nation. The elders were intimately involved in every aspect of society, from making national decisions to judging family matters. Unfortunately, the accounts of their leadership unfold a sad history of moral and spiritual failure. But their failures reveal valuable lessons for elders today.[7]

First Samuel records one of the worst disasters in Israel's history—a direct result of Israel's elders' counsel. Their counsel in this situation demonstrates their utter ignorance of spiritual matters. After the enemies of God had beaten Israel in war, ". . . the elders of Israel said, 'Why has the Lord defeated us today before the Philistines? Let us take to ourselves from Shiloh the ark of the covenant of the Lord, that it may come among us and deliver us from the power of our enemies'" (1 Samuel 4:3). Failing to recognize the chastening hand of God, of which they had ample warning (Deuteronomy 28:25), the elders acted no better than their heathen Philistine neighbors. Superstitiously, ignorantly, and unlawfully, they moved the ark of the covenant—the most sacred object of God's presence—and exposed it to the enemies of God, by whom it was captured (1 Samuel 4:22). What a price to pay!

Another example of the elders' failure to understand and appreciate God's ways is also found in 1 Samuel. As the supreme council of the nation, the elders of Israel rejected the Lord's rule over them (1 Samuel 8:4). They wanted a king like the kings of the heathen nations around them: "Nevertheless, the people refused to listen to the voice of Samuel, and they said, 'No, but there shall be a king over us, that we also may be like all nations . . .'" (1 Samuel 8:19,20).

## ISRAEL'S ELDERS

The spiritual failure of the elders of Jabesh-Gilead to rely upon the Lord for help against the fearsome Ammonite army further illustrates the underlying unbelief that lies at the root of their failures (1 Samuel 11). Unbelief was the worst of their sins and caused most of their troubles. A further cause of these many failures was due to the elders' (and people's) inadequate understanding and appreciation of their glorious privilege and blessing as God's chosen people. They were a nation with no heartfelt praise for the Lord, which the Psalmist says they should have had, "Let them extol Him also in the congregation of the people, And praise Him at the seat of the elders" (Psalm 107:32).

I am sad to say, but the fact is, the same failures exist today among many of God's elders—ignorance of God's precious Word, earthly mindedness, little understanding of the exalted privilege of being in Christ, and unbelief. As a result, the same multitude of spiritual problems abound among God's people.

### The Monarchy

During the early monarchy, the kings depended much on the elders' cooperation for successful rule. When the kingdom was taken away from Saul, for example, he pleaded with Samuel to uphold his royal reputation before the elders (1 Samuel 15:30). Of all Israel's kings, David had the closest and most frequently recorded association with the elders (2 Samuel 12:17; 1 Chronicles 15:25; 21:16). He diligently sought the elders' support (1 Samuel 30:26). The covenant he made with them reveals his desire to secure their loyalty (2 Samuel 5:3). He knew their weakness and fickleness, especially in their unstable political condition. He also knew that he could shepherd the nation effectively only with their cooperation. In a real way, the elders in each city functioned as David's undershepherds. Indeed, of King David's skillful leadership, the Psalmist wrote: "So he shepherded them according to the integrity of his heart, and guided them with his skillful hands (Psalms 78:72).

Throughout the Old Testament, the elders closely followed the direction of their king, and no king better led the elders than David. Years later, however, after Absalom skillfully won their loyalty, the elders broke their covenant with David (2 Samuel 17:4,15). How easily people—even elders—are fooled and misled by clever men!

During King Solomon's reign, because of an increasingly

[43]

elaborate royal organization, the elders' influence must have been curtailed. However, this probably did not disrupt the inner organization of the cities to any great extent. Despite further governmental changes during the later monarchy, the elders still counseled the king on military matters (1 Kings 20:7,8), consulted with the prophet Elisha (2 Kings 6:32), and made top political decisions (2 Kings 10:1,5). But during this period of deep spiritual decline, two incidents especially illustrate the elders' failure to obey God's Word and reveal the terrible consequences their disobedience had on the people.

The first account records the worst of Israel's elders' social and religious corruption (1 Kings 21:8,11). The story discloses how godless Israel's elders and king had become, and why God punished them. At the urging of Queen Jezebel, the elders of Jezreel staged a mock trial in which an innocent Israelite, Naboth, was condemned to death. This enabled wicked King Ahab to seize the property Naboth had rightfully refused to sell him. The elders' action was a vile outrage to God's Law and His people—an abomination of everything they were instructed to do in Deuteronomy. The very men commanded to protect the family and uphold God's Law became its most heinous offenders.

The second account took place under the rule of King Josiah. As unbelievable as it sounds, God's Law, which God commanded the priests and elders to read to the people every seven years (Deuteronomy 31:9,10), had been lost. What an example of how little value God's Word has to man! When the Law was found, Josiah gathered all the elders, priests, prophets, and people together and ". . . read in their hearing all the words of the book of the covenant, which was found in the house of the Lord" (2 Kings 23:1,2).

### The Prophets

The prophets are especially critical of Israel's wayward elders. Isaiah, for example, prophesied against the kind of elders who lied and murdered Naboth. In Isaiah 3:14,15, he vividly portrays the Lord entering His courtroom in judgment against the elders and princes, saying, ". . . It is you who have devoured the vineyard; The plunder of the poor is in your houses. What do you mean by crushing My people, And grinding the face of the poor? . . ." What an awful scene! The vineyard is a beautiful figure of speech for God's people. The elders should have tenderly loved and cared for the vineyard as their own. They should have been conscientious, self-sacrificing farmers. Instead, they plundered the vineyard and ate it up. They exploited God's people for their own pleasure and profit, even using the poor to gain riches. They violently oppressed the people and treated them with utter contempt. Such elders have no love for God's people, no heart for humble service, and no understanding of God's sure judgment. What a contrast they are to the leaders God intended them to be!

The prophet Ezekiel also denounced the elders of Israel. In Babylon, the exiled elders of Judah visited Ezekiel for a word regarding the homeland. To their dismay, Ezekiel received a vision of Jerusalem's abominable idolatry and further judgment—and the elders of Israel were most heavily involved (Ezekiel 8:11,12)! In his vision, Ezekiel saw Israel's 70 elders secretly worshipping the most detestable idols. Lacking the basic knowledge of God's omniscience, omnipresence, and loving kindness, the elders even blamed God saying, ". . . 'The Lord does not see us; the Lord has forsaken the land'" (Ezekiel 8:12). What a contrast they are to the 70 elders who helped Moses ratify the covenant on Mount Sinai! How far from God they had strayed! Hence, judgment soon came upon them (Ezekiel 9:6).

The elders in exile, however, were no better. Externally they honored God, but they still loved idols in their hearts. On several occasions they visited Ezekiel and acted as if they wanted to hear what God had to say, but through His prophet God exposed and rebuked their hypocrisy (Ezekiel 14:3; 20:1,3). These elders are the ancestors of the lifeless, legalistic, and hypocritical elders of Jesus' day.

In Lamentations we read of the judgment Israel's elders and other leaders brought upon themselves. The priests and elders—the chief men of the city—were starved to death in their own city (Lamentations 1:19). They were silent, with no wise words to counsel their destroyed city. Sorrow and despair overwhelmed them (Lamentations 2:10). They were no longer respected (Lamentations 4:16; 5:12) and no longer fulfilled their role as city administrators (Lamentations 5:14). Only judgment awaited them.

### Back to the Land
After returning to the Promised Land in 538 B.C., the people of Israel resettled their cities (Ezra 2:70). They had a great desire

to reestablish what they had lost in exile. Their homeland, cities, and temple were all vitally related to their identity as God's people. It is not surprising, then, that the elders once again functioned as local leaders and administrators.

Evidence of the elders' role is seen by their involvement in the problem of mixed marriages (Ezra 10:8,14). Ezra heeded the elders' and other leaders' counsel to exclude those who refused to assemble with the rest of the people concerning the matter. Furthermore, the elders helped arbitrate and implement the separation procedure for those within their city who had foreign wives. The expression "elders of the Jews" is applied to the leaders responsible for building the temple in Jerusalem (Ezra 5:5,9; 6:7,8,14. In each of these verses, the Aramaic word *sib* is used, which in the plural means elders). Exactly who these elders were is not clear. But, for the next 400 years the elders unquestionably continued to be a well-recognized institution both in the local cities and the nation as a whole.

### Divine Legislation

Laws regarding the elders' responsibilities appear in the legislative portions of the Old Testament. Six specific situations demand the elders' counsel:

• Seeing a murderer brought to justice. In the case of an intentional murder, the local elders ". . . shall send and take him from there and deliver him into the hand of the avenger of blood, that he may die" (Deuteronomy 19:12).

• Protecting the manslayer in a city of refuge (Joshua 20:4). In case of an accidental killing, there were cities of protection where a manslayer could live until a trial could vindicate him. The elders of those cities admitted and protected the slayer until the death of the high priest.

• Protecting the land from unsolved murders (Deuteronomy 21:2-4,6). If a person was found murdered and the murderer was unknown, the elders, representing the city, along with the judges and priests, performed the proper expiation rite.

• Judging the case of a rebellious son (Deuteronomy 21:19,20). Especially noteworthy is the elders' involvement in the family's protection. They heard and judged even the most intimate family matters.

• Judging a husband's accusation against his wife's virginity (Deuteronomy 22:13 ff.). The elders were to judge the evidence and enforce proper punishment.

• Hearing a widow's charge against her brother-in-law in levirate marriages (Deuteronomy 25:7-9). The elders sought to persuade the brother-in-law of his duty, and if they could not, they witnessed the humiliating legal transaction between the widow and her brother-in-law.

The elders' duties extended also to the entire nation:

• Representing the congregation in the sin offering, the elders were clearly the people's leading representatives: "'Now if the whole congregation of Israel commits error. . . . Then the elders of the congregation shall lay their hands on the head of the bull before the Lord . . .'" (Leviticus 4:13-15).

• Reading the Law to the people (Deuteronomy 31:9-13). The elders and the priests were jointly responsible to read the Law to the people every seven years. After all, how could the elders administer the Law if they and the people did not know it?

## Summary

We could make many interesting observations about Israel's elders, but for the sake of space, I will list only the most important points that directly affect our study of New Testament elders.

*Their Importance.* The eldership was Israel's oldest and one of its most fundamental institutions. It is nearly as basic as the family. Throughout Israel's history, the elders appear to exercise an important and pervasive influence (both positive and negative) over daily community life. Their vital leadership role is displayed by the many references to them and their participation in all crucial events of the nation's history.

*Official Designation.* The term *elder* is used predominantly in the Old Testament as a designation for an official community leader like a judge, officer, prince, or priest. Elders clearly represent a distinct governing body of men with certain political and religious functions—not merely older men. Conrad correctly observes, "The elder is thus a member of a special committee representing a specific, clearly defined social community; he must be thought of primarily as the holder of an office, not the representative of a particular age group."[8]

*Corporate Rule.* The elders always appear as a corporate body of community leaders, a council of leading men. The nature of this governmental structure requires the elders' work and authority to be exercised jointly, as a collective body, not individually.

# ISRAEL'S ELDERS

Nowhere in the Old Testament do we find a head elder or senior elder who rules over the eldership.

*Family Rule.* Eldership is a form of rule particularly suitable to a tribal, family-oriented society like Israel. It is a form of self-government that fairly and fully represents the people: a government in which the community is governed by its most qualified men, however that may be defined at different times or in different circumstances.

*A Tenacious Form of Self-government.* One of great strengths of this ancient, simple, self-government structure is that eldership can exist and perpetuate itself under all conditions—even the most oppressive and primitive, as shown through Israel's captivity in Egypt and Babylon.

*Honored Men.* The term elder is used in the Old Testament in a positive way. Since it conveys the ideas of wisdom, authority, experience, and leadership, the term implies honor, respect, dignity, and veneration. Elders, then, are men to be highly honored by the community. Jeremiah portrays the nation's doom when the people did not respect or favor the elders (Lamentations 4:16; 5:12). At the second advent of Christ, Isaiah sees the elders honored as those who especially witness His glory (Isaiah 24:23).

*A Male Leadership Structure.* From all appearances, the elders—whether of tribes, cities, or nations—were males.

*The Elders' Role.* The Old Testament elders were community leaders. They were the men who protected, governed, and administered justice. As community leaders, they were not without authority. By Mosaic Law, as well as by society's law, the elders had considerable authority in specific civil, domestic, and religious matters. They were not mere figureheads or advisors.

In the Old Testament, elders are characterized as men of counsel and wisdom. The concept of wisdom and discernment is implied in the word elder itself: "'Wisdom is with aged men, With long life is understanding'" (Job 12:12, also 1 Kings 12:8,13). This idea of wisdom also carries over to the restricted, official meaning of elder. Many illustrations in the Old Testament reveal the elders' counseling role in the local community and entire nation. According to Ezekiel, visions belong to the prophet, law to the priest, and counsel to the elders (Ezekiel 7:26). Jeremiah appears to refer to the elders as the sages who give counsel (Jeremiah 18:18). Job refers to the sovereign God who takes away the discernment of the elders (Job 12:20). Joseph taught Egypt's elders wisdom (Psalms 105:22). The Psalmist states: "I understand more than the aged [elders], Because I have observed Thy precepts" (Psalm 119:100). Moses calls upon the new generation to question the elders concerning God's past work on behalf of the nation (Deuteronomy 32:7). The judgment and doom of Jerusalem is depicted by the deadening silence of the elders' counsel (Lamentations 2:10) and by their absence at the city gate (Lamentations 5:14).

As leaders of a highly religious community, the elders were responsible for the spiritual well-being of the people, particularly their response to the Law of God.[9] Moses had delivered the Law to the priests and elders of Israel and ordered them to read the Law to all the people every seven years (Deuteronomy 31:9-13). Therefore, the elders as well as the priests were responsible for the people's education in God's Law. Among the people, the elders were to be the chief examples of knowing, teaching, and administering the Law of God. As exemplary citizens of God's nation, they also helped lead the people in repentance and spiritual renewal (Leviticus 4:15; Joshua 7:6; 1 Chronicles 21:16; Joel 1:14).

*Failure.* The divine record reveals that Israel's elders, as a whole, failed to lead the people in the way of obedience to God's Law. As a result, the people strayed from the Law and followed false gods, bringing unimaginable misery upon themselves: ". . . O My people! Those who guide you lead you astray, And confuse the direction of your paths" (Isaiah 3:12).

---

## NOTES

1. Genesis 50:7; Numbers 22:4,7; Joshua 9:11; Psalm 105:22.
2. *A Dictionary of the Bible*, s.v. "Elder," by J. A. Selbie, 1 (1908): 676,677.
3. 1 Kings 12:6ff; Joel 1:2; 2:16.
4. John L McKenzie, "The Elders in the Old Testament," *Biblica* 40 (1959): 522.
5. Exodus 17:5,6; 18:12; 19:7; 24:14; Leviticus 9:1; Numbers 16:25; Deuteronomy 5:23; 27:1; 29:10; 31:28.
6. Joshua 7:6; 8:10,33; 23:2; 24:1.
7. Judges 8:14,16; 11:1-11; 21:16 ff.
8. *Theological Dictionary of the Old Testament*, s.v. " זקן ," by J. Conrad, 4 (1980): 123.
9. Leviticus 4:15; Deuteronomy 27:1; 31:9-13,28; Joshua 24:31; 2 Kings 23:1; 1 Chronicles 15:25.

# Chapter 4

# *The Jewish Christian Elders at Work*

> *And in the proportion that any of the disciples had means, each of them determined to send a contribution for the relief of the brethren living in Judea. And this they did, sending it in charge of Barnabas and Saul to the elders.*
>
> Acts 11:29,30

\* \* \*

### *Receiving Money for the Poor*

The first time Luke mentions the Jewish Christian elders is in Acts 11:27-30.[1] Luke offers no word of identification as to who the elders were, when they originated, how they were organized, or why the Jewish Christians chose the term *elder* to describe their leaders. It is commonly assumed that the Jewish Christians simply borrowed the elder-system of oversight from the synagogue. However, A. E. Harvey has challenged this view.[2] He has shown that little is known about the synagogue elders of Palestine in the first century. Thus, he claims, we cannot be so certain that the first Christians adopted the elder rule from the synagogue.

What is clear and relevant to our study is that the chief official of the synagogue (called "the ruler of the synagogue" in Luke 8:49; 13:14; and Acts 18:8,17) never appears in a local Christian congregation. The Christian congregations were led by elders with no mention of rulers of the synagogue, while the synagogues were led by rulers with scarce reference to elders. Although similarities existed between the synagogue and the Christian congregation, it is obvious that the early Christian congregations were not merely reorganized synagogues. Oversight by elders was familiar enough to any Jewish community (from the Old Testament and the example of contemporary society) to easily adopt. We can be sure that the establishment of congregational oversight by a plurality of elders was no arbitrary decision. Prayer and the Spirit's leading guided the first Jewish Christian communities to organize themselves in this manner.

At the beginning, the twelve apostles were the overseers of the Christian community in Jerusalem. But at some unrecorded date, a group called the elders emerged, who were fully recognized by the brethren and apostles as the community leaders. The saints at Antioch specifically sent their contribution to the elders, although the elders' role in the actual distribution of the funds is not indicated. But the fact that money was placed into the elders' care shows that they were the recognized community leaders.

The elders of the church, then, were involved in the practical care of the people. According to James, the elders were also responsible for praying for the sick (James 5:14). God expects elders to have compassionate hearts for the physical as well as spiritual needs of the people. Job could say, "'Have I not wept for the one whose life is hard? Was not my soul grieved for the needy'" (Job 30:25)? Moses writes, "'For the poor will never cease to be in the land; therefore I command you, saying, "You shall freely open your hand to your brother, to your needy and poor in your land"'" (Deuteronomy 15:11). Was not our Lord also concerned for the poor and needy? Loving, material care for people is one of the most beautiful marks of true Christianity (Acts 4:32-37). It is one truly significant way we have of expressing the love of Christ within our hearts. So let us not be like the loveless, selfish shepherds who Ezekiel denounced. They were shepherds with no heart for the needy. Their only concern was caring for themselves: "'Woe, shepherds of Israel who have been feeding themselves! Should not the shepherds feed the flock?'" (Ezekiel 34:2).

### Solving Doctrinal Controversy

*And some men came down from Judea and began teaching the brethren, "Unless you are circumcised according to*

[51]

*the custom of Moses, you cannot be saved." And when
Paul and Barnabas had great dissension and debate with
them, the brethren determined that Paul and Barnabas
and certain others of them, should go up to Jerusalem to
the apostles and elders concerning this issue (Acts 15:1,2).*

*And when they arrived at Jerusalem, they were
received by the church and the apostles and the elders,
and they reported all that God had done with them
(Acts 15:4).*

*And the apostles and the elders came together to
look into this matter (Acts 15:6).*

*Then it seemed good to the apostles and the elders,
with the whole church, to choose men from among them
to send to Antioch . . . and they sent this letter by them,
"The apostles and the brethren who are elders, to the
brethren in Antioch and Syria and Cilicia who are from
the Gentiles, greetings" (Acts 15:22,23).*

*Now while they were passing through the cities, they
were delivering the decrees, which had been decided
upon by the apostles and elders who were in Jerusalem . . .*
                                                    *(Acts 16:4).*

The name frequently used in reference to this Jerusalem council,
"The Apostolic Council," could imply that only the apostles
deliberated together. This, however, was not the case. Luke writes
that, "the apostles and the elders came together to look into this
matter" (Acts 15:6). Clearly, "the apostles and the elders," as they
are repeatedly referred to, jointly shared in the proceedings. This
close association with the apostles demonstrates the elders' significant place within the church at Jerusalem. As the apostles
gradually left Jerusalem, the daily, permanent supervision of the
church became the elders' responsibility. The apostles and elders
are thus joined because both shared, at one time or another, the
local leadership of the church at Jerusalem. The apostles' unique
universal ministry, commission, and gift, however, caused them to
travel throughout the world while the elders, who exercised only
a local community ministry, remained in Jerusalem.

When Paul and Barnabas arrived in Jerusalem, they were
welcomed "by the church and the apostles and the elders" (Acts
15:4). The apostles and elders, however, did not eclipse the church,

for the whole church shared in the proceedings (Acts 15:22). To communicate the decision reached at the council, the apostles and elders composed a letter, "'to the brethren in Antioch and Syria and Cilicia who are from the Gentiles'" (Acts 15:23).[3] At the start of their second missionary journey, Paul and Silas delivered this letter to the churches (Acts 16:4).

The decision of the apostles and elders at Jerusalem was vitally important to the Gentile mission. Containing the apostles' own greeting, the letter bore their authority. Despite the apostles' universal, foundational position in the church (Ephesians 2:20; 3:5), they did not command or appeal to their higher ecclesiastical position. In fact, the letter's very wording lacks any terms of command: "For it seemed good to the Holy Spirit and to us . . . that you abstain from things sacrificed to idols and from blood and from things strangled and from fornication; if you keep yourselves free from such things, you will do well. Farewell" (Acts 15:28,29).

In keeping with the spirit of the New Testament, the apostles and elders at Jerusalem wrote as brethren to brethren, respecting one another as free men in Christ. In his book, *The Christian Ecclesia,* F.J.A. Hort's well-known comments on the council's use of authority bear repeating:

> The letter itself at once implies an authority, and betrays an unwillingness to make a display of it. . . .
>      . . . The New Testament is not poor of words expressive of command . . . yet none of them is used. . . . But along with the cordial concurrence in the release of Gentile converts from legal requirements there gets a strong expression of opinion, more than advice and less than a command, respecting certain salutary restraints. A certain authority is thus implicitly claimed. There is no evidence that it was more than a moral authority; but that did not make it less real.[4]

Both Roman Catholics and Protestants have used the Acts 15 account to justify the authority of church councils and church courts. James Bannerman, a Presbyterian scholar of the last century, wrote, "Now, in this narrative we have all the elements necessary to make up the idea of a supreme ecclesiastical court, with authority over not only the members and office-bearers within the local bounds of the congregations represented, but also the Presbyteries or inferior Church courts included in the same limits."[5] However, attempts to prove later systems of church government by this account always project many of our own ideas into this momentous historical event. Such attempts then distort the meaning and significance of the original event.

We need to understand that Jerusalem held a unique and influential place among the first churches. It was the birthplace of the Church and home base for Christ's apostles. So, when a group of legalistic Jews, who claimed connection with the church at Jerusalem, taught at Antioch of Syria that circumcision was necessary for Gentile salvation (Acts 15:1), the church at Jerusalem was obligated to respond. Many strong forces were at work in Jerusalem (Galatians 2:1-12). Trouble was brewing in Jerusalem and Judea; it was a hot bed for legalistic, zealous Jews who worried over Gentile salvation that was free from the Law and circumcision (Acts 15:5; 21:20-26). It was the profoundest wisdom, then, to locate the circumcision debate on the highest Jewish soil—Jerusalem—and allow the Jewish Christians to judge the issue.

Of course the church at Antioch could have solved the issue of Gentile liberty on its own ground, through its own able leaders. But by going to Jerusalem, the church at Antioch demonstrated a humble, deferential Christian spirit. At the same time, chief Jewish leaders decisively defeated error on its home ground. William Kelly says, "It was true wisdom, therefore, to transfer the further discussion of the question to the source from which the mischief had come."[6] In the end, resolving the matter at Jerusalem resulted in a greater victory for the gospel and the Gentiles than if Antioch had settled it alone.

It was important for the Gentiles to hear from Peter, James, the elders at Jerusalem, and the rest of the apostles. The Gentiles had been disturbed by the legalists' unsettling words (Acts 15:24), and the council assured them of salvation by grace: "But we believe that we are saved through the grace of the Lord Jesus, in the same way as they also are" (Acts 15:11). "Therefore it is my judgment that we do not trouble those who are turning to God from among the Gentiles (Acts 15:19).

It is evident that the elders played a leading role at the council. Even though the elders could not claim the same distinction as the apostles, they represented at that time (even more than the apostles) the local leadership of the church at Jerusalem. So the elders' role was absolutely essential in answering false rumors and combating error and confusion that emanated from Jerusalem.

As the leading men of the community, the Jerusalem elders had to hear and answer doctrinal conflict involving their congregation. The actions of the council do not imply that the elders had official authority over the church at Antioch. Because of the elders' close association with the twelve apostles, their leadership of the first Christian assembly, and their conservative Jewish character, they possessed unique status and influence. Yet there is no indication that the Jerusalem elders had any formal jurisdiction over other churches. Again, Hort clarifies the issue: "The independence of the Ecclesia of Antioch had to be respected, and yet not in such a way as to encourage disregard either of the great mother Ecclesia, or of the Lord's own Apostles, or of the unity of the whole Christian body. . . . It is impossible that, as such, they (the elders) could claim any authority properly so called over the Ecclesia of Antioch."[7]

Note that the only elders recorded in this account are the elders of the church at Jerusalem. There is no indication that elders from other churches met, forming a higher council or court of authority over a federation of churches. Instead, the Jerusalem elders, together with the Twelve as the primary leaders, had to answer a burning issue in their own midst that was brought to attention by Antioch because of its large Gentile membership.

The apostles and elders at Jerusalem were forced to deal with a growing problem among their own congregation concerning the Gentiles' relationship to Israel and its Law. It was the elders', and particularly the apostles', disavowal of the false teaching that was of utmost importance to the Gentile and Jewish Christians at Antioch, and later to the other Gentile churches.

From this account, then, we learn that one of the major duties of the church elders is to hear and judge doctrinal issues. Elders must be men of the Word: men of sound judgment, discernment, and counsel. In a hostile world filled with satanic lies and false teachings, churches desperately need men of knowledge and sound judgment. Without men who know and love God's truth, the local congregation is doomed to corruption and failure. That is why one of the qualifications for an elder is to hold "fast the faithful word which is in accordance with the teaching, that he may be able both to exhort in sound doctrine and to refute those who contradict" (Titus 1:9).

## A Local Pastoral Ministry

Acts 15 does not teach or prove that higher ecclesiastical bodies have the right to rule over an association of churches or church unions. The New Testament gives absolutely no authorization for establishing a presbytery or ruling council over a group of churches. It solely authorizes the appointment of a body of elders within a local church.

• After leaving the island of Crete, Paul wrote to Titus instructing him to appoint qualified elders in every local church in each city. He did not instruct Titus to establish a body of elders over a fellowship of churches (Titus 1:5-9).

• In Acts 14:23, Paul appointed a council of elders for each of his newly planted churches in the region of Galatia. He did not establish a higher council over these churches.

• When Paul departed from Ephesus, he entrusted the elders to the hands of God and the "word of His grace." He did not entrust them to the care of a higher body of officials (Acts 20:32).

• Peter addressed the elders of the different churches of Asia, yet he never indicated that they had anything more than local church authority (1 Peter 5:1-5).

First Timothy is the primary New Testament book that offers instruction on church order. Yet it reveals no hint of any organizational structure above the local congregation. Robert Banks writes, "Nor does Paul speak of any organizational framework by which the local communities are bound together. He nowhere prescribes an ecclesiastical polity of this kind and nowhere suggests that the common life which communities share should be made visible in this way."[8]

Indeed, we would have to add that for nearly the next 200 years there was no formal interchurch federation, denominational union, association, or official church organization. This is historical fact. In his classic work, *The Organization of the Early Christian Churches*, church historian and classical scholar Edwin Hatch demonstrates that no superior individual or organizational body originally ruled over local Christian congregations. Each congregation was self-governing and independent, with the jurisdiction of its elders restricted to the local congregation:

> In the course of the second century the custom of meeting in representative assemblies began to prevail among the Christian communities. . . .

At first these assemblies were more or less informal. Some
prominent and influential bishop invited a few neighbouring
communities to confer with his own: the result of the delibera-
tions of such a conference was expressed sometimes in a
resolution, sometimes in a letter addressed to other Churches. . . .
But so far from such letters having any binding force on other
Churches, not even the resolutions of the conference were
binding on a dissentient minority of its members. . . .

But no sooner had Christianity been recognized by the
State than such conferences tended to multiply, to become
not occasional but ordinary, and to pass resolutions which
were regarded as binding upon the Churches within the
district from which representatives had come, and the accept-
ance of which was regarded as a condition of other provinces.
There were strong reasons of imperial policy for fostering
this tendency. . . .

It was by these gradual steps that the Christian Churches
moved from their original state of independence into a great
confederation. . . .

. . . Every such community seems to have had a complete
organization, and there is no trace of the dependence of any
one community upon any other. But, as time went on, there
were several groups of circumstances which modified in various
ways this original completeness and autonomy.[9]

In the face of such clear and overwhelming historical evidence
for the original autonomy of the local church, Acts 15 cannot
be made to justify interchurch organizations and courts above
the local church.

In the New Testament, each local church is complete in
itself. Each is a holy temple filled with God's presence (1 Corinthians 3:16,17). The New Testament does not view a local church
as part of a bigger church. Rather, each local church is the Church
of God manifested in a particular place. And each church is
dependent upon its Head for life and strength.

Although each local church was a separate and complete
entity, there were varied and important links between the first
Christian churches. Churches sacrificially shared their finances
with poorer churches. Churches sent greetings and letters to one
another. Teachers traveled freely among all the congregations.
Hospitality was considered a responsibility that all believers were

to offer to traveling Christians and preachers. Believers from all churches were to pray for one another and love one another. They were to see themselves as a worldwide brotherhood that transcended all cultural and racial boundaries. Therefore, the idea of some churches forming an association separate from other Christian churches would have been absolutely abhorrent to the apostles.

### Providing Guidance

> *And now the following day Paul went in with us to James, and all the elders were present. And after he had greeted them, he began to relate one by one the things which God had done among the Gentiles through his ministry. And when they heard it they began glorifying God; and they said to him, "You see, brother, how many thousands there are among the Jews of those who have believed, and they are all zealous for the Law; and they have been told about you, that you are teaching all the Jews who are among the Gentiles to forsake Moses, telling them not to circumcise their children nor to walk according to the customs.*
>
> *"What, then, is to be done? They will certainly hear that you have come.*
>
> *"Therefore do this that we tell you. We have four men who are under a vow; take them and purify yourself along with them, and pay their expenses in order that they may shave their heads; and all will know that there is nothing to the things which they have been told about you, but that you yourself also walk orderly, keeping the Law.*
>
> *"But concerning the Gentiles who have believed, we wrote, having decided that they should abstain from meat sacrificed to idols and from blood and from what is strangled and from fornication"*
>
> *(Acts 21:18-25).*

Paul's appearance in Jerusalem to deliver the Gentiles' offering for the poor furnishes the background for Acts' third mention of the Jewish Christian elders. Naturally, the first question that arises when studying this passage concerns James' position in the church.

Several Scripture portions strongly suggest that James was an apostle (1 Corinthians 15:7; Galatians 1:19; 2:9). But all of these passages are plagued with uncertainty. It is significant that James' apostleship is never clearly stated.

One might think that the biblical writer's first and immediate interest would be James' title or position in the church. Plainly it is not. But why? The answer is found in Jesus' teaching. Jesus taught His disciples to act differently from the worldly rulers and religious leaders of His day who loved titles and high rank. The practical reality of Christ's teaching, then, is found throughout the New Testament, and this passage is a good example of the biblical writers' disinterest with title and rank.

Whatever James' position or gift, he stands out as the distinguished brother of the church at Jerusalem. Some viewed James on equal status with Peter and John as pillars of the church (Galatians 2:9). James' letter "to the twelve tribes who are dispersed abroad" reveals his widespread influence and great stature among Jewish Christians. It also exhibits his outstanding personal character and remarkable prophet-like teaching. So highly was James esteemed by the believers that Jude could identify himself simply by stating that he was a brother of James (Jude 1). Peter's command to notify James of his deliverance from prison (Acts 12:17), James' leading role at the Jerusalem council, and Paul's contacts with him further demonstrate his unquestionable leadership position and prominence among Jewish Christians. If James was an apostle, as is most likely the case (Galatians 1:19), he was unique in that his ministry was primarily to the church at Jerusalem. But Jerusalem had special need for a conservative, conciliatory leader like James. The church was massive in size (Acts 21:20) and severely strained by groups of rigid Jewish believers (Acts 6:7; 11:3; 15:1,5,24; 21:20; Galatians 2:12). Without a man of great stature and respect, the church would have been torn to pieces. Thus, James must have given immense support to the Jerusalem elders.

The second question that arises concerning this passage is the official relationship between James and the elders. A number of answers have been suggested, including the placement of James as bishop and the elders as his clergy. But such a conclusion is based on human tradition and contradicts history and gospel truth. Judging the record itself (Acts 21:18-25), this unpretentious, simple account of James and the elders was exactly what it appeared to be. A relationship of mutual brotherly cooperation existed between James and the elders in which the elders deferred to James out of respect for his God-given gifts (especially as an apostle) and sterling character. James, in turn, provided much needed moral support and guidance for the elders. Although the account begins with James as the central person whom Paul visits, the dialogue is between Paul and the assembly of brothers (Acts 21:18-25). Note that Luke uses the plural form throughout this passage:

"And after he had greeted *them*"
"And when *they* heard it *they* began glorifying God"
"And *they* said unto him"
"Therefore do this that *we* tell you"
"*We* have"
"*We* wrote"

The meeting between Paul and the Jerusalem elders was of critical importance. Luke recalls that all the elders were present, although he doesn't give a specific number. This statement demonstrates, however, that there was a distinct, recognizable body of elders. The bond of Christian fellowship between Paul, James, and the elders was renewed at their meeting. They rejoiced at Paul's report of what God had done among the Gentiles, but their own pressing problems—created by their zealous fellow-Jews—quickly dominated the meeting: "'You see, brother, how many thousands there are among the Jews of those who have believed, and they are all zealous for the Law; and they have been told about you, that you are teaching all the Jews who are among the Gentiles to forsake Moses, telling them not to circumcise their children nor to walk according to the customs'" (Acts 21:20,21).

Many difficult and complex problems confronted the Jerusalem elders. Under great pressure from both believing and non-believing Jews concerning Gentile fraternization and the Law of Moses, the Jerusalem elders knew they would suffer no matter what solutions they chose. Rumors spread by anti-Pauline teachers had poisoned the Jewish believers' attitude towards Paul, and he was their key target. The elders were clearly caught in the middle—a place elders frequently find themselves. Together, they devised a solution whereby Paul could publicly disavow false criticism before the Jews while they maintained their previous council decision. The wisdom of their plan, however, is highly questionable. It appears they made too many concessions to Judaism for the sake of peace. History soon showed they could not please both Judaism and Christ.

---

**NOTES**

1. Only once does the New Testament mention what appears to be a local body of Jewish elders: "And a certain centurion's slave, who was highly regarded by him, was sick and about to die. And when he heard about Jesus, he sent some Jewish elders asking Him to come and save the life of his slave" (Luke 7:2,3).

   All other references to elders in the Gospels and Acts are associated with the Sanhedrin of Jerusalem. Their frequent appearance is due to their leading role in the rejection and death of Christ: "And He began to teach them that the Son of Man must suffer many things and be rejected by the elders and the chief priests and the scribes . . ." (Mark 8:31).

   The Sanhedrin was the supreme court of the Jewish people. The New Testament indicates a three-fold classification of its members: high priests, scribes, and elders. Judging from the meager historical information available, it appears these elders were part of the non-priestly nobility—heads of important, wealthy Judean families, Joseph of Arimathea, who Matthew identifies as a rich man of Arimathea (Matthew 27:57), was one such elder.

   Furthermore, the entire Sanhedrin is referred to three times in the New Testament as the council of elders (Greek, *presbyterion*, Luke 22:66; Acts 22:5; *gerousia*, Acts 5:21). Those referred to in the phrase, "the tradition of the elders" (Matthew 15:2; Mark 7:5), are the great Jewish scholars of past generations. The term elder is flexible enough that over the centuries it was applied to different groups of people deserving of honor and respect.

2. A. E. Harvey, "Elders," *The Journal of Theological Studies* 25 (October, 1974): 319.

3. The phrase, "the apostles and the brethren who are elders," is literally written in Greek as: "The apostles and the elders brethren." Knowing exactly how to translate this unusual phrase is a problem, assuming the text is correct.

   Of interest to this study is the translation found in the *Revised Version*: "the apostles and the elder brethren." According to this translation, elders is an adjective. This is significant. If "elder brethren" is the correct translation, this is a definite identification of who the Jerusalem elders were. They were, indeed, the older men.

   There is good reason for rejecting this rendering, however. Greek grammar does not absolutely require the translation *the elder brethren.* Greek usage of the article in such appositional constructions is too imprecise to be certain, as H. Hyman concludes in *The Classical Review* 3 (1889): 73. Following most modern English translations, then, it is better to understand brethren as a noun without an article—apposed to both the apostles and the elders, hence, the apostles and the elders who are your brethren.

Furthermore, this rendering best fits the context. Luke's designation on the other five occasions is, "the apostles and elders." Why would he change it just one time? By adding the apposition, brethren, a closer brotherly spirit is communicated, a letter from the apostles and the elders (their brothers in Christ, not over-lords) "to the brethren in Antioch and Syria and Cilicia who are from the Gentiles" (Acts 15:23).

Nowhere else does the New Testament suggest that elders are older men. The list of qualifications says nothing about age.

4. Fenton John Anthony Hort, *The Christian Ecclesia* (1897; reprint ed., London: Macmillan and Co., Limited, 1914, pages 81-83.
5. James Bannerman, *The Church of Christ,* 2 vols (1869; reprint ed., Cherry Hill, New Jersey: Mack Pub. Co., 1972), 2:326. See also, William Cunningham, *Historical Theology,* London: The Banner of Truth Trust, 1969, Vol. I, page 59 ff.
6. William Kelly, *An Exposition of the Acts of the Apostles,* 3rd ed., (1890; reprint ed., Denver: Wilson Foundation, 1952), page 209.
7. Hort, *Ecclesia,* pages 82, 83.
8. Robert Banks, *Paul's idea of Community,* (Grand Rapids: Wm. B. Eerdmans Publishing Co., 1980), page 47.
9. Edwin Hatch, *The Organization of the Early Christian Churches* (London: Longmans, Green, and Co., 1901), pages 170-172, 175, 195.

## Chapter 5

# *Praying for the Sick*

*Is anyone among you suffering? Let him pray. Is anyone
cheerful? Let him sing praises. Is anyone among you
sick? Let him call for the elders of the church, and
let them pray over him, anointing him with oil in the name
of the Lord; and the prayer offered in faith will restore
the one who is sick, and the Lord will raise him up, and
if he has committed sins, they will be forgiven him.*

*James 5:13-15*

\*　\*　\*

James' letter begins and ends with prayer. James offers believing
prayer as the ultimate solution to all the problems he addresses
in his letter. He says a righteous man's effective prayer can accomplish much (James 5:16). He also says that self-centered prayers
and a lack of prayer are the first steps to worldliness (James 4:1-5),
and the chief reasons believers fail (James 1:2-8). James concludes
his letter with three basic exhortations: first, keep on praying
when suffering; second, keep on singing spiritual songs of praise
when cheerful; and third, call for the elders of the church to
pray when sick. Within this third category, James includes instruction involving the church elders.

### *Praying for the Sick*
James envisions a bedridden Christian whose weakened condition calls for special attention. In this circumstance, he instructs
the sick person to call for the church elders to come and pray: "Is

anyone among you sick? Let him call for the elders of the church."
As an act of personal faith and obedience to God's Word, the sick
person is to initiate the call for prayer. Besides demonstrating
personal faith, the call for prayer would, as Tasker points out,
aid those who need assistance in prayer and encouragement for
their spirits due to serious illness:

In the case of serious illness . . . when the body may be
racked with pain and the mind considerably disturbed, it is not
easy for the sufferer unaided to turn his thoughts in any
articulate or concentrated manner to prayer, and he needs
the consolation of other Christians in what may be for him
a period of much spiritual distress. James, accordingly, bids
any of his readers who may find himself in such a condition
to call for the elders of the church.[1]

James specifically exhorts the sick to "call for the elders," not
deacons, friends, or miracle workers. He assumes that all congregations, as in Jerusalem, have an official, recognized body of
elders to call on for help. The term *elder* cannot be rendered
here as *older man*, for "the elders" James refers to are the official
community leaders, just as in the Old Testament. This is the earliest
New Testament record of Christian elders. From the beginning of
the first century church, there was a body of elders in each
Jewish Christian congregation. Knowing this, James instructs the
infirmed to summon elders of their assembly to pray.

Note carefully that the call James mentions in verse 14 is
directed to the official body of elders (plural), not an individual
elder. James is not referring to a traditional, pastoral hospital
call or a visit to a faith-healing rally. No less than two elders,
if not more, ought to be present at the sick person's bedside. This
important point, easily missed or ignored because it is inconvenient,
is an essential feature of the biblical counsel.

James' primary instruction to the elders is to pray. Prayer
is the chief subject of this entire section, in which the word
prayer is used seven times (James 5:13-18). The sick need prayer,
and the issue of anointing with oil must not overshadow prayer,
which is the main point. It is perfectly clear from these verses
that the sick should summon the church elders to come and
pray. The question is, do we believe there is power in prayer
when the church elders are called to the bedside of the sick?
Do we practice it? We must not allow other issues to obscure

God's command for prayer for the sick by the church elders. The phrase, "over him," in verse 14 does not suggest a special position of prayer or the laying on of hands. Rather, it depicts the actual situation, with the sick person lying upon the bed and those who are praying standing close by over him. In the presence of suffering, prayer comes alive and is endowed with a great deal more vitality and reality. In the elders' presence, the sick person is encouraged and comforted. Tasker develops these ideas even further:

> While it is true that they could intercede for the sick man without being present at his bedside, nevertheless, by coming to the actual scene of suffering and by praying within sight and hearing of the sufferer himself, not only is their prayer likely to be more heart-felt and fervid, but the stricken man may well become more conscious of the effective power of prayer uttered in faith, by which, even in moments of the most acute physical weakness, communion with God can be maintained.[2]

Indeed, James portrays an offical church prayer gathering at the sick person's bedside. What a deeply moving experience such a gathering would be for both the one who is ill and the elders!

### Anointing with Oil

Because of confusion and fear over the phrase, "anointing him with oil," James' teaching on the subject has been ignored or relegated to the world of scholarly debate.[3] This should not be. Along with prayer, James plainly tells the elders to anoint the sick, "with oil."[4] James does not explain the meaning of oil or its function. But we can assume that the Jews he was writing to understood its meaning. There is a very good possibility that anointing with oil had been practiced in Jerusalem. If this practice had an obscure or new meaning, James would have had to explain himself better. Thus, it is best to look for a simple, obvious meaning.

In the Bible, oil is a symbol of God's Holy Spirit. The prophet Zechariah, for example, had an extraordinary vision of Israel's immense, supernatural supply of oil pouring forth from two olive trees beside a golden lampstand (Zechariah 4:2,3). When Zechariah asked the meaning of this vision, an angel of the Lord answered him, ". . . 'This is the word of the Lord to Zerubbabel saying, "Not by might nor by power, but by My Spirit," says the Lord of hosts'" (Zechariah 4:6). Clearly the oil bears reference to the Holy Spirit, as Feinberg explains: "What was the meaning of the oil in the vision? Hengstenberg has the support of all, surely, when he maintains the 'Oil is one of the most clearly defined symbols in the Bible.' Everywhere in Scripture oil is seen as the type of the Holy Spirit. The oil of consecration for prophet, priest, and king was understood to symbolize the work and presence of the Holy Spirit."[5] As Feinberg mentioned, anointing kings with oil is closely associated with the Holy Spirit's presence and power.[6] When all facts are considered, the primary symbolic usage of oil throughout Scripture is to create an awareness of the Spirit's presence and power.

According to Scripture, the sick or mournful would not normally anoint themselves with oil.[7] The reason for this is that oil is also a sign of refreshment, gladness, and joy.[8] In light of these considerations, anointing the sick with oil as James suggests appears to express refreshment, joy, and gladness, which would stimulate faith and anticipation in what God's Spirit will do. Anointing with oil is a comforting and encouraging physical symbol that is applied to sick people to help awaken their faith to the Holy Spirit's presence, power, and protection.

The physical symbol of oil is applied "in the name of the Lord." There is no power in the oil, or in the elders. All power and authority is in Jesus Christ exalted in heaven. Within His sovereign will lies the power to heal through the Spirit; nothing is too great for Him to do. So the elders act and the sick are healed in Christ's name alone (Luke 10:17). All glory goes to Him.

James concludes this passage with words of encouragement and assurance: "and the prayer offered in faith will restore the one who is sick, and the Lord will raise him up." What makes the difference is not the oil, but the kind of prayer the elders offer to God—prayer that proceeds from faith (James 1:6,7). Prayerless, spiritually impotent elders cannot offer such a prayer. Here, as in a number of Gospel accounts, the prayers and faith of those trying to effect healing (not those being healed) actually bring about healing.[9] This places a solemn responsibility upon the elders to be men of living, vital faith and prayer.

James' unqualified promise of recovery is not surprising: "and the prayer offered in faith will restore the one who is sick, and the Lord will raise him up." It is similar to many unconditional statements about prayer found in the Gospels: "'And all things you ask in prayer, believing, you shall receive'" (Matthew 21:22; cf. Mark 9:23; 11:22-26; Luke 11:5-13). These absolute, unrestricted statements forcefully teach the power of faith and prayer. The prayer of faith is so powerful that James, like our Lord, states its effectiveness in limitless terms.

Such limitless expressions are part of a rich variety of images used to vividly and dramatically teach men, who by nature are dull to spiritual matters (Romans 6:19). The teacher rightly expects his listeners to understand that there are legitimate, unexpressed qualifications to such statements. Otherwise, one would be faced with contradictions and absurdities. For example, Paul, in 2 Corinthians 12:8,9, did not receive what he asked for in prayer. That did not mean he lacked faith. God, however, had His perfect reasons for answering in a different way (2 Corinthians 12:9). Fortunately for us, God does not grant everything we ask. James obviously expects his readers to understand that his statement about recovery has unexpressed limitations. Even Elisha, one of the great Old Testament miracle workers, could not cancel God's sovereign determination of his death (2 Kings 13:14).

James does not say when or how the Lord will restore one who is sick. God has many ways to cure man's ills, as demonstrated by the case of Epaphroditus in Philippians 2. Epaphroditus was extremely ill, almost to the point of death, and Paul seemed powerless to prevent it. Why didn't Paul pray and receive immediate, miraculous healing for Epaphroditus? How could a death-bed experience occur with two mighty men of faith? The answer is that even apostles could not indiscriminately heal (cf. Galatians 4:13,14; 1 Timothy 5:23; 2 Timothy 4:20). Consequently, Paul writes that God had mercy on Epaphroditus (Philippians 2:27). God certainly cares for His own. Epaphroditus recovered, but not by the spectacular means we might have expected. The means of healing is not revealed, only its ultimate source, God. James' teaching does not mean that a divine miracle must take place. He writes in a general manner that says nothing specific about how the Lord will heal. James' instruction, therefore, cannot be brushed aside as a unique, temporary, first century practice.

### Dealing with Sin

James leaves the possibility open that sin may have caused the sick person's illness: "and if he has committed sins, they will be forgiven him." Elders must be aware of this possibility in order to help the sick person deal with the sin that may have caused the sickness. God does, indeed, chasten His children with sickness because of sin. Paul's advice to the Corinthian Christians is a good example of God's chastening: "For this reason many among you are weak and sick, and a number sleep. But if we judged ourselves rightly, we should not be judged. But when we are judged, we are disciplined by the Lord in order that we may not be condemned along with the world" (1 Corinthians 11:30-32). King Asa is another example of God's chastening through sickness: "And in the thirty-ninth year of his reign Asa became diseased in his feet. His disease was severe, yet even in his disease he did not seek the Lord but the physicians" (2 Chronicles 16:12).

A person who is willing to call on the church elders is more inclined to confess sin and receive total physical and spiritual recovery. Assuming there has been a genuine confession, James says that the sick person's sins will be forgiven. So, the visiting elders may deal with far more than sickness. Their visit may turn out to be a time for spiritual counsel, confession, encouragement, or restoration.

Not all sickness is a result of personal sin. This passage clearly says, "if he has committed sin." Many fine men and women of faith and prayer have suffered illness for much of their lives. In fact, Paul himself suffered from physical infirmities. Sickness became a means of guidance for him (Galatians 4:13,14), and if his "thorn in the flesh" (2 Corinthians 12:7-10) refers to a physical illness, his sickness also became a means of spiritual development and protection. However, if someone's sickness is due to sin, elders must be prepared to deal with the situation accordingly.

What blessing, help, and comfort is denied to God's people when this portion of Scripture is not taught faithfully! Most Christians have never witnessed or been taught to practice James' instruction to the sick. Local congregations pray for the sick, the pastor visits and prays for the sick, but few elders are ever called upon to pray for the sick. Why is it so difficult to call for the shepherds of the church to come and pray when Scripture plainly teaches that this is the thing to do? Is not our lack of faith the problem? Those who have faith will respond in obedience to God's Word when it says, "Is anyone among you sick? Let him call for the elders of the church."

In conclusion, I must point out a fact crucially important to our study of eldership that is uniquely illustrated by this passage; the elders of the church are not church board members, executives, or advisers to the pastor, as is the case in most churches today. Rather, this passage demonstrates that elders are shepherds of the people. Board members don't go to the bedside of the sick. They don't deal with people's sins. Indeed, they may not deal directly with the people at all. But church elders do pray for the sick. In fact, they must be men of strong faith and prayer. They must have spiritual perception and knowledge in order to deal with people's personal problems and sins. They must be caring and compassionate. They must be ready and able to visit needy, hurting sheep. Thus, elders are shepherds of people. They care for the people's practical as well as spiritual needs.

Let us not be shepherds like those Ezekiel had to denounce, "Those who are sickly you have not strengthened, the diseased you have not healed, the broken you have not bound up . . ." (Ezekiel 34:4).

## NOTES

1. R.V.G. Tasker, *The General Epistle of James*, The Tyndale New Testament Commentaries (Grand Rapids: Wm. B. Eerdmans Publishing Co., 1957), page 129.
2. *Ibid.*
3. Some hold a "medicinal view" in which elders were to treat the sick medically with oil as well as pray for their recovery. Hence, the lesson is that medicine and prayer work together. This of course is true, but to conclude that James intends this to be taught through this passage is unlikely for the following reasons:

    (1) Mark 6:13 is the clue to interpreting James 5:14. The disciples anointed (Greek, *aleipho*) the sick with oil as they preached that men should repent (Mark 6:12). It is unlikely that the disciples applied oil as medicine only to those whom they worked upon as physicians. Such action would have weakened and confused their miracle-working ministry that confirmed their messianic message.

    In all probability, the oil was symbolic of God's Spirit being poured out in abundant measure (Zechariah 4:6). The refusal of Israel's leaders to recognize the Spirit's miraculous work through Jesus and His disciples brought Jesus' fierce condemnation that blasphemy against the Spirit will not be forgiven (Matthew 12:31,32). So oil was a symbolic aid to teach that God's Spirit was the source of power in healing.

    (2) One cannot use James' word for anointing (Greek, *aleipho*)

to make a strong case for the medicinal use of oil. The more sacred word for anointing is the Greek *chrio*. *Aleipho* could be used for sacred acts in the Old Testament, however (Genesis 31:13; Exodus 40:15; Numbers 3:3).

W.E. Vine challenges Trench's conclusion "that *aleipho* is the mundane and profane, *chrio*, the sacred and religious word" (*An Expository Dictionary of New Testament Words*, 1969 ed., page 59). Vine contends that Trench's conclusion is not borne out by evidence. For example, a papyrus document uses *chrisis* to describe "'a lotion for a sick horse' (Moulton and Milligan, *The Vocabulary of the Greek Text*)."

Both James and Mark intend the practice of anointing with oil to teach, help, and awaken men. James' choice of the Greek word, *aleipho*, fits his purpose and helps avoid any false sacred or ritualistic connotations.

(3) It's doubtful that James means to comment on medicine. If he believes oil should be used for all diseases, he is a very poor doctor. We can assume that if oil were needed, it would have been applied long before the elders arrived. The elders' primary task is prayer, and oil accompanies prayer in the Lord's name.

4. The aorist participle suggests that anointing precedes prayer, but the participle can be contemporaneous with the main verb, pray. The former order—anointing followed by prayer—seems most likely.

5. Charles L. Feinberg, *God Remembers*, 4th ed. (Portland: Multnomah Press, 1979), page 59.

6. 1 Samuel 16:13; 2 Samuel 1:14,16; 23:1,2; Isaiah 61:1. Oil is the perfect symbol for the Holy Spirit. Oil was used for healing (Isaiah 1:6; Luke 10:34). The Holy Spirit is the power of life (John 6:53; Romans 8:11; 2 Corinthians 3:6) and has the power to heal (Luke 4:18; Acts 10:38; 1 Corinthians 12:9). Oil was used for lighting darkness, and the Holy Spirit illuminates man's darkness (Genesis 41:38,39; 1 Corinthians 2:10,12). Oil was used to set things apart for God, and the Holy Spirit sanctifies believers (2 Thessalonians 2:13). Oil was used to express joy and feasting, and the Holy Spirit is the source of joy (Galatians 5:22; Ephesians 5:18-20). Oil was used to comfort and bless, and the Holy Spirit is the ultimate source of grace, rest, and comfort (Isaiah 44:3; 63:14; Haggai 2:5; Zechariah 12:10; Hebrews 10:29).

The Gospels also portray oil as a symbol of the Holy Spirit. This appears to be the case in the parable of the ten virgins (Matthew 25:1-13). In Mark 6:13, the sick are anointed with oil: "And they were casting out many demons and were anointing with oil many sick people and healing them." Here, the disciples' symbolic action taught the people that God's Spirit was among them and was the source of power for healing. Elsewhere, we read that God's Spirit had been poured out on Christ (Luke 3:22; 4:14,18; Acts 10:38), and worked through Him to heal (Matthew 12:28).

The extraordinary presence and working of the Holy Spirit was

## JAMES 5:13-15

not to be missed (Isaiah 61:1). The disciples' anointing with oil was a means of awakening and instructing the Jews to the truth of the Spirit's presence.

7. 2 Samuel 12:20; 14:2; Daniel 10:3; Matthew 6:17,18.
8. Psalms 23:5; 45:7; 92:10,11; 141:5; Proverbs 27:9; Ecclesiastes 9:8; Isaiah 61:3; Luke 7:46.
9. Matthew 8:5-13; 9:18-26; 15:21-28; 17:14-21; Mark 2:5.

# Chapter 6

# *Appointing Elders*

*And when they had appointed elders for them in every church, having prayed with fasting, they commended them to the Lord in whom they had believed.*

*Acts 14:23*

\*   \*   \*

As the great apostle and teacher of the Gentiles, Paul's appointment of elders is vitally significant. This passage becomes more significant because in his letters to the churches Paul never uses the term elder or indicates that he even appointed elders. Thus, Acts 14:23 provides the crucial historical background both for Paul's method of organizing the first churches and the doctrine of eldership.

The historical occasion of this passage—the beginning of Paul's church planting ministry among the Gentiles—was a momentous event in the history of Christianity, and adds to its significance. In a new and special way, Paul's first missionary journey opened the door to the Gentiles. The churches he planted had congregations of both Jews and Gentiles together. At this time, Paul began preaching directly to the Gentiles rather than just the Jews (Acts 13:46,48). This was indeed the beginning of the work the Lord had called Paul to in Acts 22:21: "'And He said to me, "Go! For I will send you far away to the Gentiles."'"

Both J. B. Lightfoot and William Ramsey claim the significance of this passage is in Luke's usage of it as a summary of Paul's customary method of organizing newly planted churches. Lightfoot writes: "On their very first missionary journey the Apostles Paul and Barnabas are described as appointing presbyters in every church. The same rule was doubtless carried out in all the brotherhoods founded later; but it is mentioned here and here only, because the mode of procedure on this occasion would suffice as a type of the apostles' dealings elsewhere under similar circumstances."[1] William Ramsey comments: "It is clear, therefore, that Paul everywhere instituted elders in his new churches; and on our hypothesis as to the accurate and methodical expression of the historian, we are bound to infer that this first case is intended to be typical of the way of appointment followed in all later cases."[2] Thus, we are dealing here with one of the most significant statements about elders recorded anywhere in the New Testament.

### Original Apostolic Appointment

A well-known and longstanding problem persists in the meaning of the word, "appointed," (Greek, *cheirotoneo*) in Acts 14:23. Ancient churchmen erroneously changed this word to mean ordination by laying on of hands, which threw later commentators and translators off the right track. In Luke's day, however, the word had nothing to do with ordination or the laying on of hands. In fact, Luke employs a distinct Greek verb (*epitithemi*) to designate the laying on of hands, which he doesn't use here. Nothing stated or implied in this passage suggests the laying on of hands or the rite of ordination. The word *cheirotoneo* simply means to appoint.

Furthermore, the word "appointed" carries no indication of how Paul and Barnabas actually appointed elders. F. F. Bruce makes the point very clear: "In Acts 14:23, therefore, we are simply told that Paul and Barnabas appointed elders in the recently founded churches of South Galatia, but the verb itself tells us nothing about the method of appointment."[3] To insist, as some scholars do, that Paul and Barnabas followed the procedure of Acts 6:1-6 when appointing elders is unjustified. The congregations' involvement is simply not revealed in this passage. Therefore, one must be satisfied with the simple statement that Paul and Barnabas appointed elders for the churches.

However, numerous commentators have attempted to explain the appointment procedure by arguing that the word's root meaning (to extend the hand) indicates election by the people. They claim the church founders merely presided over the churches' election. But this is plainly false. *Cheirotoneo* can mean to appoint without reference to election. Context determines the word's usage, and in this case Greek lexicons and dictionaries agree that appoint is the correct translation.[4] In short, Luke used a perfectly good Greek word to mean appointing. The problem is not with Luke, but with biblical interpreters who trifle with etymology. Thus, ordination, laying on of hands, or election of elders by the congregation cannot be proven from this single word.

Before elders had been appointed in every church, Luke writes, "And the disciples [new believers] were continually filled with joy and with the Holy Spirit" (Acts 13:52). Although the churches existed for a short time without elders, they were still called churches (Acts 14:23). Thus, the ministry of elders is not essential to the existence of a church; only the Holy Spirit's presence is essential. But God doesn't neglect the basic human need for leadership, so God's Spirit guided the apostles to leave a body of elders in each church to oversee the flock.

Some have suggested that Paul appointed a single elder in each church, but this view is incorrect. (The Greek word *presbyteroi*, meaning "elders" is plural, and the word "church" is singular, preceded by the distributive use of the preposition, *kata*.) Literally, Luke writes: And having appointed for them "church by church, elders," or, "according to church, elders." Thus, each individual church had a body of elders. Furthermore, "elders" is plural because that is the structure of corporate oversight as practiced in the Old Testament. Lange's commentary confirms this point: "Not *one* elder, but *several* elders, in each congregation; the customs of the Israelitic authorities alone, without referring to other considerations, show that no other view can be entertained."[5]

The second half of the verse is a solemn farewell in which Paul and Barnabas prayerfully, "commend them to the Lord." One naturally asks whether the "them" refers to the newly appointed elders or the disciples in general. Most likely, it refers to the disciples in general, including the elders, because this appears to fit the entire context (verses 21-23) best. As Paul and Barnabas prepared to depart, they keenly felt the trials the new believers would soon face without their missionary founders and teachers. Paul and Barnabas knew, more than anyone else, the dangers and problems ahead. Therefore, they earnestly prayed and fasted in every church as they placed their converts into the Lord's care and safekeeping.

Believing Christ for salvation, the new converts continued by faith and daily trust to depend on Him for everything. Paul and Barnabas did not leave the new congregations in the care of apostles, priests, clerics, or even the newly appointed elders—and this is vitally important to understand—but ultimately in Christ's care. The new believers had entered the life of faith, the life of prayer, and the life of obedience to and dependence on the indwelling Holy Spirit. To increase and preserve their newly planted congregations, they were totally dependent on God. They would grow only as they understood and relied upon Him more.

Paul's and Barnabas' departure was an occasion for prayer and fasting. The clause, "having prayed with fasting," is related to the verb "commended" not the verb "appointed." Prayer was the means whereby the apostles handed over the church to the Lord's protection and care. Prayer was accompanied by "fasting," which adds intensity and urgency (Ezra 8:21-23; Acts 13:1-3). The apostles put aside their natural needs in order to concentrate on God, giving themselves completely to the occasion. Their self-renunciation demonstrated their earnestness to God.

### Perpetuating the Eldership

Although there is no New Testament example of elders appointing elders, perpetuation of the eldership is implied in the elders' role as community leaders, shepherds, stewards, and overseers. Perpetuating the eldership is a major aspect of church leadership responsibility. It is absolutely vital to the life of the church and the eldership that the elders recognize the desire of others to shepherd the flock. It is all too easy to allow personal feelings or fear to prejudice one's judgment toward aspiring elders. *One must have biblical reasons to keep a man from church oversight.* Yet many qualified men are refused their rightful place as elders because they are a threat to the status quo. Indeed, good men are often a threat to the status quo. Far too often, church politics rule in these matters instead of God's Word, prayer, and the leading of God's Spirit.

If a brother desires to shepherd the Lord's people and truly exhibits that desire through appropriate action, and if he is morally qualified, then the leaders are obligated to see that he is not frustrated in his desire. Such a brother needs to be officially placed on the council of elders.

When elders consider a candidate for eldership, the congregation's recognition and counsel regarding the candidate's labor and character is absolutely essential. That which affects everyone in God's household ought to concern everyone. The entire assembly is responsible to see that *its leaders are scripturally qualified for the office.* Since the qualifications for eldership are recorded in Scripture, both elders and congregation are bound by them. Everyone is under Scripture's authority, and the elders—as the spiritual leaders—are obligated to see that Scripture is obeyed. In this way the elders are accountable to the congregation.

Early in the life of a church, Paul or one of his colaborers evaluated the moral and spiritual character of potential elders and appointed them to lead the various congregations (Acts 14:23; Titus 1:5). Even in these first appointments (meaning the actual placement or installment into office or responsibility), we assume that the missionary-founders sought the congregation's counsel regarding the moral fitness and work of those they appointed to the eldership. After all, who would know the potential elders better than the brothers and sisters who lived and worked with them in the community?

Congregational involvement and responsibility in appointing elders is plainly seen in 1 Thessalonians 5:12,13. Before Paul appointed elders at Thessalonica, he wrote to the church, exhorting the congregation to know and esteem those who labored among them. Presumably, Paul planned to return on a later occasion and officially appoint those who were known and esteemed by the assembly for their labor. This being the case, the men would have been doing the work and been recognized for it by the congregation before their official appointment as elders. Recognition of potential elders' qualifications and service comes before official, public appointment to eldership. Henry Craik comments on Timothy's and Titus' appointment of elders:

The qualifications for the overseership (1 Timothy 3:1, ff.), are clearly laid down, and there can be no reasonable doubt but that they honestly sought to ascertain, by inquiry from the brethren generally, the character of those who might express a desire for the position. If, as Clement tells us, the approval of the church went along with the Apostolic appointment, there can be no reason given why Timothy and Titus, who appear to have acted as the deputies of Paul, should not have respected the testimony of the brethren to the fitness of the candidate, or even the selection made by them out of their own number.[6] The existing elders and congregation should give much prayer to the matter of appointing elders. The appointment of elders must not be done hastily or flippantly, for the elder is the Lord's steward and undershepherd. "The issue is always," as Jon Zens says, "Who has Christ equipped for this office? Better have no elders than the wrong ones."[7]

The existing elders (or founding missionaries) are responsible to officially appoint elders who they and the congregation recognize for their labor, desire, and qualification for the position. Scripture allows freedom to have or not have a ceremony—such as the laying on of hands and prayer (Acts 6:6; 1 Timothy 5:22)—in connection with the elders' appointment. Even though elaborate ceremony is not seen in the New Testament church, and Scripture commands no ceremonial rite for appointment, the first Christians were not adverse to simple, public ceremony (Acts 6:6; 13:3; 1 Timothy 4:14; 5:22). Because there was an official, public appointment of elders and deacons, the first Christians knew who the elders and deacons were (Acts 6:6; 14:23; 1 Timothy 5:17, ff.). For example, the sick could call for the church elders, and there was no confusion about who would come (James 5:14; cf. Acts 20:17; 21:18; Philippians 1:1; I Peter 5:1). Official appointment by the acknowledged leadership was necessary because of the elders' and deacons' highly responsible and delicate work on behalf of the congregation. Official appointment greatly facilitated their effectiveness, helped avoid confusion and infighting, and added a greater sense of accountability.

It is absolutely essential to understand that the New Testament never shrouds the appointment of elders in mystery or sacred ritual. There is no holy rite to perform or special ceremony to observe. Appointment to eldership is not a holy sacrament. The appointment confers no special grace or empowerment, nor does one become a priest, cleric, or holy man at the moment of appointment. No one has special power to appoint elders. The truth is, Scripture gives little detail about the actual appointment of elders. Luke, for example, merely records that Paul and Barnabas appointed elders (Acts 14:23). The newly planted Christian assemblies needed leadership, so Paul and Barnabas appointed a council of men to oversee each new church—men who were spiritually qualified and had been moved by the Holy Spirit to shepherd the flock.

Even Paul's and Barnabas' right to appoint elders appears to lie in their Spirit-appointed task of preaching the gospel in new lands (Acts 13:2), not in their role as apostles. Scripture gives no indication that Paul and Barnabas appointed elders because they, as apostles, had exclusive rights to do so, or that appointing elders was a highly sacred act that only they could execute. It is unwise to make more out of this subject than Scripture does.

The fact that the New Testament does not elaborate on the official appointment of elders should not be surprising. Scripture gives almost no detailed instruction about administering the Lord's Supper or baptism either. The absence of elaborate regulations is a characteristic of new life in Christ. All such detail is left to the local Christian community's discretion. Even under the Mosaic Law, which prescribed detailed regulations for every area of life, certain matters such as the appointment and organization of elders were left to the people's discretion. God expects His saints to use the creativity and wisdom He has given to organize all such matters within the guidelines of His Word, and to do so in a way that exemplifies the gospel's truth and the true nature of the church. In his book, *A Noble Task,* Neil Summerton captures the biblical spirit of elder appointment when he writes,

> It is characteristic of Technological Man of the twentieth century to worry abnormally about the precise mechanism of selection. But biblically of much greater importance is its manner and spirit. Be we never so precise about the *modus operandi*, it will be of no avail if the mechanism still succeeds in choosing the wrong men. For this reason it may not matter much whether selection of elders is by church planters, the existing elders, or the congregation as a whole, so long as all are certain that the outcome is the choice of God.[8]

### How a Man Becomes an Elder

In order to better explain how a man becomes an elder, and what requirements precede the appointment to eldership, we must consider three key terms in more detail: desire, qualifications, and examination.

*Personal desire.* The Bible says, ". . . if any man aspires to the office of overseer, it is a fine work he desires to do" (1 Timothy 3:1), so the first step to eldership is the desire to be an elder. The desire to be an elder is not sinful or self-seeking, but is the result of God's Holy Spirit. Paul told the Ephesian elders that the Holy Spirit had placed them as church overseers (Acts 20:28). Ultimately, a man becomes an elder because God's Spirit has created within him a burden for the local flock and a compulsion and love to shepherd the Lord's people. In a similar vein, Peter speaks of the need for an elder to have a willing spirit to shepherd God's people voluntarily, not under compulsion (1 Peter 5:2). Without a deep desire and willing spirit for the work, a man cannot—and should not—be an elder. Considering how few men really desire to shepherd the Lord's people, it is wonderful when a man desires to be an elder. We should thank God for men who desire this honorable task.

A Spirit-given burden for oversight demonstrates itself in action and deed. It cannot be held in. The person lets others know his desire to be an elder, and there is nothing wrong with that. But more important, the person who desires to be an elder devotes much time and energy to caring for the saints. There is no such thing as a Spirit-given desire for oversight without corresponding evidence of sacrificial, loving service. The reason for this is that eldership is a strenuous, shepherding task—not just another position on a decision-making board. In fact, the stronger a man's desire for eldership, the stronger his leadership and love for people. So, the first step to be an elder is a Spirit-given desire that manifests itself in sacrificial service to the congregation (1 Timothy 3:1; Acts 20:28; 1 Thessalonians 5:12).

*Qualifications.* The New Testament is perfectly clear and positively emphatic that only scripturally qualified men can be appointed as elders. In addition to a subjective desire for eldership, Scripture demands that a candidate for eldership meet certain objective qualifications (1 Timothy 3:1-7; Titus 1:5-9).

The biblical requirements for elders protect the local congregation. Self-seeking, sinful, deluded men who pursue positions of influence to fulfill their own needs will hurt the Lord's people and bring shame on God's house and name. An unqualified man in the position of elder will inevitably be a detriment to the church and the gospel's testimony. God, in His grace, gives clear and ample instruction in His Word regarding the moral and spiritual requirements for those seeking church oversight.

*Examination.* God fully expects His people to take the requirements for elders seriously, so it follows that some sort of human
examination and consultation about the proposed elder is necessary.
First Timothy 3:10 states: "And let these [deacons] also [like the
elders] first be tested; then let them serve as deacons if they
are beyond reproach." In addition, 1 Timothy 5:22-25 teaches that
a human evaluation of character and deeds is necessary to avoid
placing the wrong people in responsible positions, and to approve
those worthy of leadership. Throughout history, hasty appointment
of people to influential positions has been a source of great harm
to churches (1 Timothy 5:22). If all prospective elders were
honestly examined, many unworthy and non-functioning elders
would not be appointed.

The elders, as official church leaders, naturally take the lead
in evaluating an aspiring elder's desire and qualifications. Opportunity must be freely provided, however, for all members of the
congregation to express their questions, doubts, or approval of a
candidate for eldership. Since God's Word provides an objective
standard, everyone is responsible to see that God's requirements
for eldership are followed.

A word of warning: no group (or individual) has the right to
add their own standards of education, social status, personality,
success, age, or even quality of spiritual life to the biblical requirements. Eldership is open to all Christian men who truly desire
to serve and meet God's requirements.

### The Problem of Frustrated Aspiration

Appointment to eldership can easily become a source of
jealousy and frustration, particularly when one's desire for eldership is blocked. Such frustrated aspiration can cause much ill feeling
and fighting in the church. The great Indian evangelist and church
planter, Bakht Singh, referring to the rebellion against Moses and
Aaron (Numbers 16), observes:

> In Christian churches also we find many men who are very
> ambitious to become elders over their congregations. If they
> are not given such places they are prepared to fight for them.
> Some will fight with their tongues, some with their money and
> some by other means. Some have a trick of looking very
> angrily at you whenever they meet you; but as soon as you

are willing to give them power they will speak very kindly to you. Such is human nature.[9]
Some men will believe they are elder material, but for various reasons the elders or congregation will not consider them for eldership. This can be very frustrating for a man who desires the work of oversight. But God uses these frustrating experiences to test and develop character. For example, will a man react in anger, with hurt feelings, or will he humbly and patiently pray, continuing to serve until God changes the circumstances? In one of his letters on preparation for leadership, D. E. Hoste writes:

> Are our loved ones taken from us, our health and strength reduced, or our pecuniary resources diminished? Is our outward sphere of service curtailed, is our good name attacked? In each and in all of these circumstances we may with confidence remember that God is providing "some better thing" for us; and that in no other way can we be led on into this higher and richer experience. Those who are appointed to exercise spiritual oversight must needs be prepared for their ministry in this way.[10]

To have one's desire for appointment to eldership curtailed may well be part of God's plan to further develop the candidate's character before he serves as an elder.

Of course, the elders' and congregation's lack of response and approval of a candidate may also be God's way of saying no to a man's desire for eldership. Of the aspiring pastor who has been turned down, Calvin says:

> And if it should turn out that they are not called in the way the order of the Church prescribes (*legitimo ordine*), then let them know that God willed it so, and not take it ill that others have been preferred to them. Those whose desire was only to serve God and who had no thought of themselves will take it in this way and will have enough modesty not to be envious if others are counted more worthy.[11]

We must remember, too, that for whatever reasons one is not accepted as an elder—whether they be temporary or permanent—eldership is not a requirement for serving, loving, or caring for the Lord's people. In God's eyes, such humble service is true greatness that He will richly reward. True faith, which is of great worth to God, patiently and prayerfully places all of life's injustices and disappointments into His care.

## NOTES

1. J.B. Lightfoot, *Saint Paul's Epistle to the Philippians* (New York: Macmillan and Co., 1894), page 193.
2. William Mitchell Ramsay, *St. Paul the Traveller and the Roman Citizen*, 3rd ed. (Grand Rapids: Baker Book House, 1951), page 121.
3. Frederick F. Bruce, *Answers to Questions* (Grand Rapids: Zondervan Publishing House, 1972), pages 29, 30.
4. Etymologically (the derivation of a word) *cheirotoneo* is made of two words, hand (Greek, *cheir*), and to stretch (Greek, *teino*), to stretch out the hand, and that for the purpose of voting. The word could, thus, mean to elect or vote.

   Isocrates, at the end of *Areopagiticus* (circa 355 B.C.) says, "but it is for you to weigh all that I have said and cast your votes according to your judgment of what is best for Athens." And Plutarch (45-120 A.D.), in his life of Phocion (34,34), writes, "But Hagnonides read aloud an edict which he had prepared, in accordance with which the people were to vote by show of hands whether they thought the men to be guilty, and the men, if the show of hands was against them, were to be put to death."

   But *cheirotoneo* was also used more generally to mean appoint or choose, without reference to the manner of choosing. In Luke's day, Philo, the Jewish philosopher (circa 20 B.C.-50 A.D.), uses the word without reference to voting: "Nor yet, when he [Joseph] was appointed to be the king's viceroy" (*On Joseph* 248); "a king appointed not by men but by nature" (*On Dreams* 2,243); "His wish to honor the ruler whom He [God] had appointed" (*Moses* 1,198). In the same way, Josephus (37 A.D.) used the word: "Samuel said to Saul, 'know that thou art king, elected of God to combat the Philistines'" (*Antiquities of the Jews* 6,54); "ask Claudius Caesar to give him [Herod] authority over the temple and the holy vessels and the selection of the high priests" (*Antiquities* 20:14).

   In the New Testament, the verb is used in a compound form, meaning chosen beforehand: "God raised Him up on the third day, and granted that He should become visible, not to all the people, but to witnesses who were chosen beforehand of God, that is, to us . . ." (Acts 10:40,41). And in 2 Corinthians 8:19, the only other place where the verb is used, the churches chose a well-known brother to travel with Paul: "and not only this, but he has also been appointed by the churches to travel with us. . . ." Although the procedure in choosing was undoubtedly different from that of Acts 14:23, the word itself does not indicate that.

   The point is, *cheirotoneo* can mean to elect or appoint. The context, not the etymology, determines its meaning. The context is perfectly clear that appoint is the only possible meaning here.

The first contextual indicator that appoint is the intended meaning of the verb is its subject, they. Plainly, the word *they* refers to Paul and Barnabas, not the disciples. If interpreters insist on the root meaning of the verb (they had stretched forth the hands), then the subject must be the voter, because the subject never is found presiding over the votes of others. The action is always predicated of the verb's subject. Therefore, only Paul and Barnabas raised their hands in voting, not the church. But such an interpretation doesn't make sense. Hebrew and Greek scholar Henry Craik remarks:

The verb *cheirotoneo* so far as I am aware, is nowhere else employed in the sense of electing or appointing by the votes of others. Had the historian told us that the members of the Christian communities chose their elders by vote, we should have necessarily understood him to mean that they themselves voted for his appointment. No such statement is made in the passage under review. I cannot, therefore, rest upon the passage as evidence for popular election (*New Testament Church Order*, Bristol: W. Mack, 1863, page 51).

Second, the pronoun *them*, following the verb, confirms this conclusion. Paul and Barnabas appointed elders *for* them (that is, the disciples, verse 22), not *by* them. In the words of Lake and Cadbury, "The implication of the phrase (especially when the *autois* following it is considered) is that the apostles appointed converts whom they thought best fit to be the presbyters of each church. The same is the natural meaning of Titus 1:5. In all these passages the idea of a choice by the church has to be inserted before it can be found" (Kirsopp Lake and Henry J. Cadbury, *The Beginnings of Christianity*, vol 4, *The Acts of the Apostles*, eds. Frederick John Foakes Jackson and Kirsopp Lake, Grand Rapids: Baker Book House, 1979, page 128).

Finally, this is the conclusion of leading Greek lexicons and dictionaries in their discussion of the word *cheirotoneo*:

*A Greek-English Lexicon*, 7th, ed.
*A Greek-English Lexicon of the new Testament.*
*Thayer's Greek-English Lexicon of the New Testament*, rev. ed.
*The Vocabulary of the Greek New Testament.*
*Theological Dictionary of the New Testament.*
*The New International Dictionary of New Testament Theology.*

5. John Peter Lange, ed., *A Commentary on the Holy Scriptures*, 25 vols., vol. 19: *The Acts of the Apostles*, by Gotthard Victor Lechler and Charles Gerok; trans., Philip Schaff and Charles F. Schaeffer (1867; reprint ed., Grand Rapids: Zondervan Publishing House, no date), page 272.
6. Henry Craik, *New Testament Church Order* (Bristol: W. Mack, 1863), pages 55, 56.

Craik's reference to Clement's statement about "the approval of the church" comes from *The Epistle of St. Clement to the Corinthians* (A.D. 96 or 97). Clement writes:

ACTS 14:23

And our Apostles knew through our Lord Jesus Christ that
there would be strife over the name of the bishop's office. For
this cause therefore, having received complete foreknowledge,
they appointed the aforesaid persons, and afterwards they
provided a continuance, that if these should fall asleep, other
approved men should succeed to their [the overseers]
ministration. Those therefore who were appointed by them, or
afterward by other men of repute with the consent of the whole
Church . . ." (Section 44, Brackets mine).

According to this letter, there was a plurality of overseers (bishops)
and deacons in the church at Corinth at the end of the first century.
The terms overseer and elder are synonymous. The apostles
appointed the first overseers and left the appointment of future
overseers in the hands of eminent men who had the consent of the
whole church. Note that the leading men (undoubtedly the overseers)
appointed other overseers with the congregation's approval.

7. Jon Zens, "The Major Concepts of Eldership in the New Testament,"
   *Baptist Reformation Review* 7 (Summer, 1978): 29.
8. Neil Summerton, *A Noble Task* (Exeter: The Paternoster Press,
   1987), page 31.
9. Bakht Singh, "The Rod that Budded," *The Hebron Messenger*
   4 (June, 1966): 3.
10. Phyllis Thompson, *D. E. Hoste "A Prince with God"* (London:
    China Inland Mission, 1947), page 160.
11. John Calvin, *The Second Epistle of Paul the Apostle to the
    Corinthians and the Epistles to Timothy, Titus and Philemon"* trans.
    T. A. Smail, Calvin's Commentaries (1964; reprint ed., Grand
    Rapids: Wm. B. Eerdmans Publishing Co., 1976), page 222.

# Chapter 7

# Guarding the Church from False Teachers

*And from Miletus he sent to Ephesus and called to him the elders of the church.*

Acts 20:17

*"Be on guard for yourselves and for all the flock, among which the Holy Spirit has made you overseers, to shepherd the church of God which He purchased with His own blood.*

*"I know that after my departure savage wolves will come in among you, not sparing the flock; and from among your own selves men will arise, speaking perverse things, to draw away the disciples after them.*

*"Therefore be on the alert, remembering that night and day for a period of three years I did not cease to admonish each one with tears.*

*"And now I commend you to God and to the word of His grace, which is able to build you up and to give you the inheritance among all those who are sanctified.*

*"I have coveted no one's silver or gold or clothes.*

*"You yourselves know that these hands ministered to my own needs and to the men who were with me.*

*"In everything I showed you that by working hard in this manner you must help the weak and remember the words of the Lord Jesus, that He Himself said, 'It is more blessed to give than to receive.'"*

*And when he had said these things, he knelt down and prayed with them all. And they began to weep aloud*

[85]

*and embraced Paul, and repeatedly kissed him, grieving
especially over the word which he had spoken, that they
should see his face no more. And they were accompanying
him to the ship.*

Acts 20:28-38

\*   \*   \*

Acts 20 is Paul's famous farewell message to the elders of the church at Ephesus. It is unique because it is the only record of Paul speaking directly to elders and because it is his final exhortation and warning to those responsible for the church during his absence. History demonstrates that the truth of Paul's message cannot be overstated or repeated too often. The appalling, centuries-long failure to stop false teachers from entering the churches can be traced to ignorance or disobedience of the Spirit's warning in Acts 20. Every new generation must grasp afresh the prophetic message to the Ephesian elders: wolves are coming!

"And from Miletus he sent to Ephesus and called to him the elders of the church." Note that Paul summoned for "the elders [plural] of the church [singular]," not for the minister, pastor, or elder of the church.[1] Since pastoral oversight of the local assembly belonged to the body of elders—not to one man—Paul "called to him the elders of the church."

It is interesting to note that Luke, the inspired historian and Paul's traveling companion, consistently uses the designation *elders* in both Jewish and Gentile contexts throughout his book. Only when Paul speaks directly to the elders does Luke use the term *overseers*. Most likely, elder was the more common designation for the body of church leaders.

At the beginning of Paul's ministry, he appointed elders in the churches (Acts 14:23). Now, at the end of his ministry in Asia Minor and the east, he bids farewell to the elders of the church at Ephesus, leaving the pastoral oversight of the church in their care (cf. Titus 1:5). Whenever possible, Paul committed the oversight of the church to a body of elders.

As the great missionary founder, apostle, and builder, Paul's departure was a critical moment for the church and for himself.

[86]

As he bids farewell, Paul reminds the whole church and its elders that they had received the full, authoritative message of God: "For I did not shrink from declaring to you the whole purpose of God" (Acts 20:27). Paul states this theme twice, in verses 20 and 27, to emphasize that he had thoroughly done his job as Christ's apostle. Thus, with his work done, Paul is free from responsibility for the congregation at Ephesus. With a clear conscience he must press on to new lands. The responsibility for what they had heard and received from God's messenger now belonged to the Ephesian elders. They were responsible to protect and build upon the foundation he had wisely laid.

### Be on Guard

The heart of Paul's exhortation is for the elders to guard themselves and all the flock. The verb "be on guard" is often used as a warning in the context of false teaching (Deuteronomy 12:30; Matthew 7:15; 16:6,12; Luke 20:46). It is an imperative verb and its tense indicates continuous action. So Paul actually means for the elders to keep a constant watch, continuously guarding themselves and all the flock.

*Guard yourselves.* The elders are first told to guard themselves. The enemy is fierce and will stop at nothing to destroy the flock. So dark times are ahead. The battle will rage. Since the Holy Spirit gave elders the responsibility to guard the flock, they will inevitably be in the center of the fight. As Richard Baxter notes in his classic work, *Reformed Pastor*, Satan first seeks to ruin the shepherds so the flock will be scattered:

Take heed to yourselves because the tempter will make his first and sharpest attack on you. . . . He knows what devastation he is likely to make among the rest if he can make the leaders fall before their eyes. He has long practiced fighting, neither against great nor small, comparatively, but against the shepherds—that he might scatter the flock. . . . Take heed, then, for the enemy has a special eye on you. You are sure to have his most subtle insinuations, incessant solicitations and violent assaults. Take heed to yourselves, lest he outwit you. The devil is a greater scholar than you are, and a more nimble disputant. . . . And whenever he prevails against you, he will make you the instrument of your own ruin. . . . Do not allow him to use you as the Philistines used Samson—first to deprive you of your strength, then put out your eyes, and finally to make you the subject of his triumph and derision.[2]

The instruction Paul gives the elders is the same he gives to Timothy: "Pay close attention to yourself and to your teaching; persevere in these things; for as you do this you will insure salvation both for yourself and for those who hear you" (1 Timothy 4:16). Thus, elders must protect themselves first. They, too, are vulnerable to dangerous attacks. They must not fall asleep. They must not let their souls drift from the truth or become indifferent. They must not neglect prayer and continuous Scripture reading and study. They must not (as many are) be blind to the dreadful danger of false teachers. They must not be unprepared (Ephesians 6:10-18) or make compromises for the sake of peace. Rather, elders must be attentive, alert to danger, and always prepared for battle.

*Guard all the flock.* In addition to protecting themselves from the evil one, elders are to continuously guard "the flock," which is a beautiful metaphor for the church. The inseparable relationship between the sheep and shepherd is an essential part of the flock metaphor. Throughout Scripture, a shepherdless flock is deplored and lamented.[3] Because sheep are defenseless, an unguarded flock is always in danger. The church is made up of followers—sheep who desire to be led and protected. The sheep/shepherd image demonstrates the church's need for leadership and protection from danger, and God has entrusted the elders with this guarding ministry.

The elders' guarding ministry primarily involves protecting the flock from the subtle attacks of false teachers. In this fallen world, the church is never free from danger. Thus, the elders' work always includes the negative aspect of guarding. Furthermore, the elders' work entails guarding the flock from debilitating problems such as the lack of spiritual food, internal fighting, and other unhealthy factors. Moreover, the elders must guard *all* the sheep, not just the favorites. Good shepherds care for *all* the sheep, not just a few. None must be neglected, for all are precious. In his own day, Paul continually fought off false teachers. But now, elders who have received the full apostolic message must do the same. History demonstrates that elders in every age need to remember to guard themselves and the whole flock. Elders all too easily forget and become indifferent, or become preoccupied with other matters, and neglect the flock's well-being. Protecting the church from danger is a major aspect of the elders' shepherding task. Because there are many weak, immature, and unstable believers, the elders must act as a wall of safety around the people, protecting them from the fearsome danger of savage wolves and other destructive influences. Although protection is a negative aspect of shepherding, it is absolutely essential to the flock's welfare. Phillip Keller illustrates, from his own experience as a shepherd, how unaware and vulnerable sheep can be in the face of danger, even their own inevitable death:

> It reminds me of the behavior of a band of sheep under attack from dogs, cougars, bears, or even wolves. Often in blind fear or stupid unawareness they will stand rooted to the spot watching their companions being cut to shreds. The predator will pounce upon one then another of the flock raking and tearing them with tooth and claw. Meanwhile, the other sheep may act as if they did not even hear or recognize the carnage going on around them. It is as though they were totally oblivious to the peril of their own precarious position.
>
> We see this principle at work even among Christians. We as God's people are continually coming under attack, either from without or within. Yet many are unable to detect danger among our number. It is as though we cannot hear or see or sense our peril. Often the predation is so crafty and cunning that fellow Christians are cut down before our eyes by the enemy of our souls.[4]

The history of the nation of Israel clearly demonstrates that spiritual leaders must constantly guard their people against the fierce and subtle attacks of false teaching and idolatry. From the days when Moses led the Israelites out of Egypt until they were carried away by the Assyrians and Babylonians, they repeatedly fell into idolatry. Just as many of Israel's elders failed to guard the people and led them into false religious practices, many Christian elders today follow the course of their Old Testament predecessors. Unaware, these shepherds do not even know that they are engaged in fierce spiritual conflict. As a result, their churches are open prey for predators. But this should not be, for Scripture explicitly instructs church elders to protect the flock from savage wolves. Thus the Spirit of God places the awesome responsibility of guarding the church from false teachers squarely upon the shoulders of local church elders. He does not place this responsibility upon seminaries or other worthy spiritual institutions.

*Overseers of the flock.* All that follows in verses 28 to 31 reinforces Paul's charge to guard the flock. Paul bolsters his exhortation by reminding the elders that "the Holy Spirit has made you overseers," not the church or anyone else. A divine obligation underlies Paul's exhortation to guard the church. The verb "made" (*set* or *placed*) conveys the idea that the Spirit sovereignly selected these men as elders (Acts 1:7; 13:47; 1 Corinthians 12:18, 28; 1 Timothy 1:12). Commenting on the use of this verb in 1 Corinthians 12:28, T. C. Edwards concludes that *etheto* means, "'placed for His own use.' The mid. voice and the signification of the verb . . . express the exact notion that these various functions depend on the sovereign will of God, who is source and end of all."[5] Although the means employed to publicly set the elders aside as overseers is not stated, knowing that a divine person sovereignly placed them as overseers to pastor God's flock should deeply move elders to diligently protect His flock.

Following the mention of elders in verse 17, we might expect Paul to say, "The Holy Spirit set you as *elders* to shepherd the church of God" (verse 28). But he doesn't. Instead, he uses the word "overseers." The *New American Standard Bible* accurately translates the Greek word, *episkopoi* as "overseers." Some English Bibles translate *episkopoi* as *bishops*, but this conveys concepts not present in Paul's thought and creates misunderstanding for modern readers.

In Greek society, overseer was a broad, generic term used to describe a wide variety of functionaries—from municipal officials to officers of various societies. The Greek Old Testament uses overseer in much the same way to refer to various officials: superintendents responsible for temple repair (2 Chronicles 24:12,17); army officers (Numbers 31:14); temple guardians (2 Kings 11:18); leaders over the people (Nehemiah 11:9); and tabernacle overseers (Numbers 4:16). At the root of the word (*epi-skopos* denotes over-seer, inspector or protector) is the idea of one who supervises, protects, guards, and keeps watch. So an overseer is a superintendent, guardian, manager, inspector, and protector. Indeed, the word's root concepts fit well in the present context. The kind of overseers Paul has in mind are shepherd-overseers (those who watch sheep), making the elders overseers of the local flock.

In this passage, the word overseer is applied to the elders of the church for the first time. Plainly, it is not used in the sense of a bishop presiding over the elders, deacons, and congregation, or over a body of churches. Nor is there a suggestion that only some of the Ephesian elders were "overseers [bishops]."

*Shepherding.* The Holy Spirit places elders in the flock "to shepherd the church of God," which entails feeding it the Word, leading it, caring for its many needs, and (particularly in this context) protecting it from danger. The latter task is the more dangerous aspect of the elders' work. Protection is the task that separates the hireling from the true shepherd: "I am the good shepherd; the good shepherd lays down his life for the sheep. He who is a hireling, and not a shepherd, who is not the owner of the sheep, beholds the wolf coming, and leaves the sheep, and flees, and the wolf snatches them, and scatters them" (John 10:11,12). Unfortunately, too many churches have hirelings for leaders—elders who run when the problems become too great.

The Holy Spirit, then, appoints elders to shepherd the local church. This point could not be stated more clearly! What will it take for Christian leaders, teachers, and scholars to acknowledge that elders are the ones appointed by God to pastor His church? Is God's Word not enough? Is not one word from God worth infinitely more than 2,000 years of tradition? Why do contemporary evangelical scholars consider the church leadership practices of the second and third centuries to be normative? Why is Ignatius' single overseer (bishop) of greater value to us than Paul's plurality of overseers (elders)? Let us return to the words of Christ's apostle, who taught that the Holy Spirit places elders as overseers to shepherd the church of God (Acts 20:28).

*Flock of great value.* The elders oversee no ordinary assembly of people. The flock they care for is of the greatest value because it is "the church of God." It is God's assembly—not the elders', the apostles', or any man's. God called His flock into being and cares for it, sustains it, and provides for it. What an honor it is to shepherd His church! The immeasurable worth of "the church of God" is further stated in verse 28 by the clause, "which He hath purchased with His own blood." Although disagreement exists over both the correct Greek text and the proper translation of this clause, these difficulties are not unresolvable. The best interpretation seems to be, "the church of God, which He obtained by means of the blood of His own One, Christ." However, do not permit the problem to detract from the statement's intent and impact. Whatever the correct solution is, the point is still the immense worth of God's church. The price one is willing to pay for an object demonstrates its value. How could God have paid more for the church? Can any man even begin to calculate its worth? How God must love the church! How much it must mean to Him when the elders care for and protect His dear ones! Do you see the church as God sees it? Do you value it as God does? Do you appreciate what He has done? When elders can answer these questions in the affirmative, the quality of their labor greatly increases. It is a serious matter for an elder to neglect the church's safety, yet this remains a problem. Understanding the great value of God's flock should challenge and revitalize elders to guard all the flock with all their strength.

To summarize verse 28, Paul charges the elders to guard the local church. Since the Holy Spirit has already set them as overseers to shepherd the church, the charge is in perfect harmony with the Spirit's purpose. The importance of this responsibility is shown by the immeasurable value of the church to God. Therefore, elders must guard themselves and all the flock.

### Wolves Are Coming

Paul's charge to guard the church is based on the sound knowledge of false teachers: "I know that after my departure savage wolves will come in among you." Paul's departure marked a crucial moment. For three years, Paul had thoroughly taught the gospel, but upon his departure he knew that false teachers would attack the flock and that false teachers would even arise from within its ranks. Paul's presence was a strong force against false doctrine. He fought against the intrusion of false teachers more strenuously and tirelessly than any of his contemporaries; his whole life was spent in defense of the gospel (Philippians 1:7). When it came to a question of the gospel's truth, Paul would not budge (Galatians 2:5). His most scathing anathema fell on anyone who attempted to distort Christ's gospel (Galatians 1:7-9).

Paul knew the power that false doctrine has over mind and soul (2 Corinthians 11:3; 2 Timothy 3:8) and knew that Satan himself—the chief of liars—was behind it (2 Corinthians 11:14,15).

In his letters, Paul continually warned the churches of false doctrine's destructive power. Because he knew the enemy so well, Paul could say, "I know . . . savage wolves will come." There was no question about it. It was going to happen.

Since the local church is figuratively called a flock, it follows that its enemies are "wolves," the proverbial predator of sheep. The false teachers are called "savage wolves" (a pack of large, savage wolves) because they will not spare the flock from destruction. As enemies of the flock and enemies of Christ, wolves have no part in God's church because they have not been purchased with His precious blood and do not know Him. Their presence can only bring death, confusion, and destruction.

But Paul predicts something even more subtle and frightening: that false teachers, "will arise," from within the congregation! Not only will wolves come in to destroy the flock, but men from within God's flock—professing Christians—will emerge as false teachers, too. Such men expose themselves by teaching false doctrine or, as Paul says, "perverse things." Paul means that they will teach perversions of God's holy truth—twisted, distorted, heretical doctrine. They will not out-and-out deny the truth of God's Word, for that would be too obvious and ineffective for Satan's purposes. Instead, they will pervert truth. As masters of subtlety and novelty, they will mix truth with error, reinterpret the truth, and change the meaning of words to give the illusion of truth.

Such false teachers desire recognition of their ingenious thoughts and seek followers to obey their authority. Their purpose is "to draw away the disciples" from the church. They do not merely want disciples, but want the Christians themselves. They seek to tear Christians from the flock to which they belong (and its Spirit-anointed overseers) and subject them to false teaching. These divisive men care nothing for the church's unity or safety. They care only for themselves. How different they are from Christ's true servants who preach Jesus Christ as Lord and consider themselves as the bondservants of His people (2 Corinthians 4:5)!

*Be alert.* After such alarming and frightening predictions, Paul charges the elders to be alert (verse 31), using another imperative command similar to verse 28: "Therefore be on the alert, remembering that night and day for a period of three years I did not cease to admonish each one with tears." The word "alert" (Greek *gregoreo*) means more than the absence of sleep. It implies a conscientious effort or discipline, a mental and spiritual attitude of alertness. The term is often used in the context of watching for the Lord's return, since we do not know when it will happen (Matthew 24:42). Here, it is used because one must be alert to the false teachers' constant, dangerous threat. Falling asleep could mean spiritual destruction.

To clearly emphasize his idea of watchfulness, Paul calls upon the elders to remember his example: "remembering that night and day for a period of three years I did not cease to admonish each one with tears." One who studies Paul studies watchfulness, vigilance, and alertness in action. Paul's alertness entailed a ministry of admonition (Greek, *noutheteo*). Although closely associated with teaching (Colossians 1:28; 3:16), admonishing is more than teaching. It conveys the concept that something is wrong and needs changing. It also implies a positive, caring aspect that seeks to correct what is wrong by a word of instruction or exhortation. In the present context, admonishing is warning believers of the persistent, dangerous attacks of false teachers and the human tendency to become inattentive to this danger. More than teaching, admonishing urges believers to respond to what they already know.

Paul's admonitions started when he first arrived in Ephesus. He did not wait until his departure to deal with false teachers. He admonished them "night and day," which is a figure of speech meaning all the time. Paul used every contact with them—not just official occasions—for admonition. Also, "tears" filled Paul's admonitions because the damage done by false teachers caused him much heartache: "For many walk, of whom I often told you, and now tell you even weeping, that they are enemies of the cross of Christ" (Philippians 3:18). Finally, Paul's admonition was inclusive over "a period of three years." His eye was on every single sheep. As the great overseer/shepherd, Paul never ceased "to admonish each one." Oh, that elders today might warn and equip the saints with such thoroughness and devotion!

*Blind watchmen and dumb dogs.* The Old Testament prophets cried out against the watchmen and shepherds of the people of Israel because they failed to protect the people from danger. They are vividly depicted as blind watchmen and dumb shepherd's dogs:

All you beasts of the field,
        All you beasts in the forest,
        Come to eat.

His watchmen are blind,
All of them know nothing.
All of them are dumb dogs unable to bark,
Dreamers lying down, who love to slumber;
And the dogs are greedy, they are not satisfied,
And they are shepherds who have no understanding;
They have all turned to their own way,
Each one to his unjust gain, to the last one.
"Come," they say, "let us get wine, and let us drink
    heavily of strong drink;
And tomorrow will be like today, only more so"
(Isaiah 56:9-12).

It is not easy to be watchful! The Old Testament proves that, for Israel fell into false religion time and time again. The natural human tendency is to become less alert, to become weary, unconcerned, and selfish. Alertness takes considerable time, thinking, energy, and work. It isn't easy to answer questions, speak to changing issues, answer criticism, stand against other people, and confront false teachers. At times, vigilance is wearisome. But it must be done!

So elders must watch. Elders must be wide awake to the possibility of what can happen to the flock. Elders must pray. Elders must be in contact with the people. Elders must continuously educate themselves in Scripture. And elders must be alert, ". . . for even Satan disguises himself as an angel of light. Therefore it is not surprising if his servants also disguise themselves as servants of righteousness . . ." (2 Corinthians 11:14,15). Elders must pray that God will give them keenness, strength, and—above all— courage, so that, like David, they will be steadfast against the lion and bear that come to ravish God's flock.

### Resting upon God and His Word

In this final section, Paul completes his task—entrusting the elders "to God and to the word of His grace." Paul entrusts the elders to no earthly authority or organization. Instead, the elders must look "to God and to the word of His grace" for help in everything.

Dependence upon God and His Word is a principle of first order. Paul was leaving, but God and His Word would remain. It was now time for the elders to trust God daily, to depend on Him in prayer and faith. Troubles and problems were to drive them to greater dependence and trust in Him, to a deeper and more intimate relationship with God, as Paul says he experienced: "indeed, we had the sentence of death within ourselves in order that we should not trust in ourselves, but in God who raises the dead" (2 Corinthians 1:9).

Paul also entrusts the elders to "the word of His grace." The Word has its own vital, living power. It can impart life (James 1:21; 1 Peter 1:23). It can cut into the soul of a man (Hebrews 4:12). It can empower and strengthen those who hear it in faith (1 Thessalonians 2:13; 2 Timothy 3:16,17). It can sanctify (John 17:17). It calls men to respond and obey, and is the power of God (1 Corinthians 1:18). Like a diamond, the Word has many facets. Here, Paul stresses the Word's "grace" which is one of his favorite subjects and is most needed in this case. With frightening predictions of wolves and divisions, the elders desperately need strength and help. Paul promises that "the word of His grace" will build them up; it will be food for strength and fuel for power.

"The word of His grace" was first heard through Paul's preaching, but today is Holy Scripture. In order to effectively guard the flock from wolves, then, elders must continually build upon the Word (1 Timothy 4:6). If elders neglect to read and study the Word, they will weaken and the flock will suffer. Only strong overseers can stand the pressure, and only the living power of the Word will build people up and—unlike anything else—protect them from false teachers.

### Caring for the Needy

Like Samuel before him (1 Samuel 12:3), Paul's farewell includes a disavowal of all greedy motives. Nothing is more apt to bring sinister charges against the Lord's servants than money, so Paul says he has "coveted no one's silver or gold or clothes." Few can honestly make such a blunt, open-hearted confession. Note that Paul did not say, "I took no one's gold." He did accept money from the saints. (The church in Philippi was especially faithful in sharing financially with Paul, as recorded in Philippians 1:5; 4:15,16, and 2 Corinthians 11:8,19.) By his statement, Paul is making a more profound comment. He is saying that greed had no control over him and he had no inner, secret desire for personal material profit from his converts.

Of course, anyone can say, "I have coveted no one's silver." (Greedy people are equally self-deceived.) But there was an unusual aspect to Paul's work to which he appeals in verse 34: "You yourselves know that these hands ministered to my own needs and to the men who were with me." By this, Paul reminds them that his normal practice was to provide his own lodging, food, and necessities by manual labor.[6] But even more amazing, Paul also supported his co-workers in the gospel by working as a tentmaker (Acts 18:3). Thus, working with his "hands" was no token gesture. It resulted in laboring night and day (1 Thessalonians 2:9; 2 Thessalonians 3:8). Like his Lord (Mark 3:20,21), Paul's life was characterized by arduous, ceaseless labor. Paul labored at his trade and his preaching. Truly, the phenomenal results of his service in the gospel were the Spirit's doing, not man's (1 Corinthians 3:5-9; 2 Corinthians 4:7). Such a life was proof enough that he had no desire for others' wealth.

It is important to note that in the qualifications for elders, Scripture requires that elders must be free from the love of money (1 Timothy 3:3). Unless an elder is above reproach in his finances, he will never gain the trust of those he shepherds.

Paul holds before the elders his own selfless example of hard work and generous support for the poor and needy: "In everything I showed you that by working hard in this manner you must help the weak." The elders must be examples of hard work so they will be able to care for the needy. The same idea of working in order to help the poor is mentioned in Ephesians 4:28: "Let him who steals steal no longer; but rather let him labor, performing with his own hands what is good, in order that he may have something to share with him who has need." The saints must display Christ's love in their care for the sick, poor, and needy. Paul was always concerned for the poor.[7] So the elders "must help the weak" in body and in material necessity, always remembering "the words of the Lord Jesus, that He Himself said, 'It is more blessed to give than to receive.'"

The elders, then, like Paul, will be characterized by hard work. They will be employed in order to support their families and help the needy. They will give considerable time to shepherding God's church. They will be examples to the congregation of the type of life God intends for all His people.

### Praying Together

What a touching scene Paul's departure was: "And they began to weep aloud and embraced Paul, and repeatedly kissed him." How the Ephesian elders loved him! What a bond of deep affection they shared in Christ! As brothers, co-laborers, and co-sufferers in Christ, they had experienced many wonderful victories for Christ.

Prayer, then, was the only fitting conclusion. As they "knelt down and prayed," they looked to God alone. As a man of prayer, Paul prayed for the spread of the gospel in Asia, for protection from false teachers, for the growth of the church, and for the Ephesian elders' labors and trials. Although Paul never commanded the Ephesian elders to pray, he set a clear example for them. It is God's intention that those who guard His flock utilize, as Paul did, persistent prayer—the greatest means of protection.

## *The Inspired Historian's Contribution*

Acts is crucial to the study of biblical eldership because of the historical background it provides. Luke is an accurate historian. Like any good historian, he carefully chose the material he recorded (Luke 1:1-4). So it is significant that Luke mentions the elders' importance in the churches as often as he does. Paul's lengthy farewell sermon to the Ephesian elders demonstrates the elders' prominence, particularly in regard to the local church's protection from false teachers in the apostles' absence. Undoubtedly, the Spirit of God considered this information to be quite valuable to the people of God.

Luke's historical account reveals that the first churches, under direct supervision of the apostles, established local pastoral oversight by the plurality of elders. The prime example of this is found in Paul's ministry. We read that Paul appointed a council of elders in each of his newly planted congregations (Acts 14:23). It is difficult to exaggerate the importance of this information. A proper understanding of the epistles and the first century churches depends upon it.

However, Luke never explains the appointment procedure for these early elders. He simply states that Paul and Barnabas appointed elders for the churches. He informs us, through Paul's sermon in Acts 20, that the Holy Spirit's sovereign activity placed these men in their positions.

The preferred designation in Acts for those appointed to the church's leadership body is *elders*. This is true for Jewish as well as Gentile congregations from Jerusalem to Ephesus. Luke uses the designation *overseers* (bishops) only once, and that appears in the context of Paul's words to the Ephesian elders. This is the clearest evidence that the terms *elder* and *overseer* are used interchangeably. Since the elders'/overseers' duty is to shepherd God's church, we

see all three terms (elders, overseers, shepherds) used in the same
context to refer to the same group of church leaders. Luke knew
nothing of the popular second century Ignatian bishop (overseer)
who presided over the elders, deacons, and congregation.
The importance of the early elders in the life of the church
is seen in the responsibilities they undertook: they provided
counsel for difficult problems, administered funds, handled all
major transactions and communications with other churches,
helped resolve doctrinal controversy, and in the general sense
shepherded God's church. Luke's record of Paul's mandate to the
entire body of elders to shepherd God's church is of profoundest
significance to the study of biblical eldership. If God's Spirit
originally placed a council of men in charge of shepherding each
local congregation, who are we to insist that only one man fulfill
this solemn mandate in our local congregations?

## NOTES

1. Paul did not call for the elders of the churches (plural), but for
the elders of the church. According to Acts, the local churches at
Jerusalem, Antioch, and Ephesus embraced all believers within each city.
There were thousands of believers in Jerusalem (Acts 4:4; 5:14;
6:1,7; 21:20), yet Luke speaks only of the church at Jerusalem, not
churches (Acts 5:11; 8:1,3; 11:22; 12:1,5; 15:4,22; 18:22). Acts pictures
the believers in Jerusalem as one large, united assembly (Acts 2:44,46;
5:12; 6:2) under the leadership of twelve apostles and later the elders
and James (Acts 2:42; 4:35,37; 5:2 ff; 6:2-4,6; 8:14-17; 9:27; 15:4 ff.).
Although they gathered in small groups in homes (Acts 2:46; 5:42;
12:12), they also all assembled together at Solomon's portico (Acts
5:12; 6:2). The Christians at Antioch are depicted also as one
congregation (Acts 11:26; 13:1; 14:27; 15:3,30). The same is true of
Ephesus (Acts 20:17; Revelation 2:1).
What was more natural for God's family than for all those in
geographical proximity (the city boundary being the most natural)
to assemble themselves together? What a wonderful outward display
of Christian unity! What a rebuke to the countless divisions among
God's true children today, which prevent them from meeting together.
Like Israel, Christians today are divided and at war with themselves
(1 Kings 12:16-33). How it should grieve and humble us all!
Two erroneous conclusions have been drawn from these facts.
First, that in Jerusalem (as well as in the other cities) a number
of separate churches existed, but that Luke referred to them together
as the church in Jerusalem, and this federation had a common governing
body of elders. This, however, is pure guesswork. No matter how

difficult it is to conceive the actual historical situation in Jerusalem, the only picture Scripture presents is of one congregation, with the apostles or elders as leaders. The truth is, there is very little information regarding the local organization of the Jerusalem community—far less than is commonly acknowledged.

Second, some have made a binding principle that a city can only have one local church. Although this is a glorious historical fact, it can never be made a legal requirement since no such instruction can be found anywhere in the epistles.

The elders, therefore, are the elders of the church in the city of Ephesus, for example. In the New Testament, elders are never depicted as overseeing several churches. Rather, they are leaders of an actual gathered community of believers.

2. Richard Baxter, *The Reformed Pastor* (Original publication date unknown; reprint ed., Grand Rapids: Sovereign Grace Publishers, 1971), page 7.
3. Numbers 27:17; 1 Kings 22:17; Zechariah 10:2; Matthew 9:36.
4. Phillip Keller, *A Shepherd Looks at the Great Shepherd and His Sheep* (Grand Rapids: Wm. B. Eerdmans Publishing Co., 1981), page 25.
5. Thomas Charles Edwards, *A Commentary on the First Epistle to the Corinthians* (London: Hamilton, Adams & Co., 1885), page 333.
6. 1 Corinthians 9:4-6; 2 Corinthians 11:7; 1 Thessalonians 2:9; 2 Thessalonians 3:8-10.
7. Acts 11:30; 2 Corinthians 8,9; Galatians 2:10.

# Chapter 8

# *Hard Working Men*

*But we request of you, brethren, that you appreciate those who diligently labor among you, and have charge over you in the Lord and give you instruction, and that you esteem them very highly in love because of their work. Live in peace with one another.*

*1 Thessalonians 5:12,13*

\* \* \*

Before studying our passage in 1 Thessalonians, we must first address an issue that is troublesome to many people. The issue is, Paul does not mention the term *elder* anywhere in his nine letters to the churches (Romans, 1 and 2 Corinthians, Galatians, Ephesians, Philippians, Colossians, and 1 and 2 Thessalonians). Yet Acts, 1 Timothy, and Titus reveal that Paul appointed elders, warned elders of their responsibility and the dangers they would face, and provided more detailed instruction about the eldership than any other New Testament writer.

As a result of this seeming discrepancy, many scholars conclude that Paul did not appoint elders. These scholars claim that Luke wrote his history to conform to later church practice and that Paul could not have written 1 Timothy or Titus. For example, Ernst Kasemann writes, "For we may assert without hesitation that the Pauline community had no presbytery during the Apostle's lifetime. Otherwise the silence on the subject in every Pauline epistle is quite incomprehensible."[1] Hans Kung also claims, "At all events Luke is making an unhistorical addition . . . when he maintains

that Paul and Barnabas 'appointed elders . . . in every church'"
(Acts 14:23; cf. especially 20:17-35), for this is not borne out by
the letters of Paul himself.[2] This type of reasoning has even
influenced more conservative biblical scholars.[3]

However, to claim that Luke is unhistorical denies the doctrine
of divine inspiration, which states: "All Scripture is inspired by
God and profitable for teaching, for reproof, for correction, for
training in righteousness; that the man of God may be adequate,
equipped for every good work." (2 Timothy 3:16,17). If Luke made
historical assertions that Paul appointed and spoke to the elders
(Acts 14:23; 20:17 ff.)—when in truth Paul did not—then Luke's
account is unprofitable, totally misleading, and detrimental to
the truth, the Scripture, and God's people. Until one resolves the
question of inspiration, there is no solution to the problem. Only
by accepting the entire New Testament canon as God's inspired
and authoritative Word can one rest in Scripture's sufficiency.
As always, the problem here lies with unbelieving man, not with
Scripture. Jesus Himself once asked, ". . . 'Is this not the reason
you are mistaken, that you do not understand the Scriptures, or
the power of God?'" (Mark 12:24).

### Paul's Manner of Addressing the Churches

The solution to this seeming discrepancy lies in Paul's lofty
view of God's Spirit-indwelt people, and his manner of addressing
them. God's Spirit reveals that Paul and Barnabas appointed a
body of elders in all the churches of Psidian Antioch, Iconium,
Lystra, and Derbe on their first missionary journey. Yet in his
letter to these churches, Paul does not once address the elders
(assuming that the churches of Acts 13:14-14:21 are the same
as those of Galatians 1:2). This is because it was Paul's practice
to address the entire congregation, not just the elders or leaders.

For example, disorder and sin in the church at Corinth had
to be dealt with, but Paul calls upon no one person or group to
resolve the problem. Was there no one to call upon? Of course
there was! Paul could have called upon the dedicated Stephanas
(1 Corinthians 16:15-18); Gaius, in whose home the church met
(Romans 16:23); Erastus, the city treasurer (Romans 16:23); Crispus,
a converted chief ruler of the synagogue (Acts 18:8); or a number
of other gifted men and prophets (1 Corinthians 1:5,7). He could
easily have addressed a responsible brother (or brothers) to help

the congregation work through its problems, but he addresses—as always—the entire assembly of believers.

In 1 Thessalonians 5:12,13, Paul calls upon the church to highly esteem those who give instruction and have charge over the congregation. So we know that some men provided leadership for the people. But in his two letters to the Thessalonians, Paul never calls upon these leading men to correct problems within the congregation. Instead, he says, "Therefore encourage one another, and build up one another, just as you also are doing" (1 Thessalonians 5:11).

Paul's letter to the Philippians is the best example of his practice of exhorting the entire congregation, not just the officials: "Paul and Timothy, bond-servants of Christ Jesus, to all the saints in Christ Jesus who are in Philippi, including the overseers and deacons" (Philippians 1:1). This is the only letter of its kind in which Paul directly greets the overseers. If not for this brief comment, there would be no indication that there were overseers and deacons at Philippi. Nevertheless, the presence of overseers and deacons does not change Paul's customary writing procedure. The rest of the letter, except for 4:2,3, is addressed to the entire company of believers. Peter, James, and John follow Paul's practice, too. Each one writes to congregations that have recognized elders, but they always address the entire congregation, not just the officials (James 5:14; 1 Peter 5:1; Revelation 2:1-7).

Paul's failure to specifically address the elders in his letters to the churches doesn't imply an absence of elders. Rather, it demonstrates the profoundest truth of the gospel and the new creation, the Church.[4] That is, all members of the congregation must be addressed because they equally share a lofty, glorious, new status in Christ and must share in the responsibilities, privileges, and obligations of their new position. Responsibility does not lie solely with the community leaders. So, no contradiction exists between Acts, 1 Timothy, Titus, and Paul's letters to the churches—only three different perspectives, all of which are essential to fully understand the truth. Acts presents the historical viewpoint (what Paul did), while Timothy and Titus contain instruction to an apostolic delegate in the apostle's absence (instruction directed to dealing with various groups within the church). The letters to the churches contain direct teaching for the entire congregation; hence, everyone is accountable, not just the leaders.

# 1 THESSALONIANS 5:12,13

**The Hard Working Leaders at Thessalonica**

Although the term *elder* doesn't appear in Thessalonians, those referred to as leaders were either officially appointed elders or prototype elders who would later qualify for apostolic appointment. The probable situation is that Paul had not yet officially appointed elders for this newly planted congregation, which was only a few months old.

Paul had stayed in Thessalonica only a short time, perhaps a month (Acts 17:2), and had planned to return soon (1 Thessalonians 2:17,18). In accordance with Acts 14:23 and Titus 1:5, Paul would have appointed elders upon his return visit to Thessalonica, or after some lapse of time. It appears that able brothers emerged as conscientious leaders during Paul's absence. Clearly, one did not need apostolic appointment to sacrificially serve God's people. Apparently Paul felt it important for the congregation to recognize its responsibility toward its leaders, even if he had not officially appointed them as elders.

*Know your leaders.* The Greek text of 1 Thessalonians 5:12 reads: "But we ask you brethren to know those who work hard among you." "To know" seems like an odd request. Would not Christians naturally have knowledge of those who led and admonished them? Because of this unusual request, most translators and commentators think Paul uses the term "know" (Greek, *oida*) with an unusual shade of meaning—to respect, acknowledge, or as the *New American Standard Bible* says, "appreciate." The thought behind such an interpretation would be to recognize the leaders' importance and properly appreciate them. The translation *know*, however (which is the term's constant meaning throughout the New Testament), makes perfectly good sense when we closely consider the circumstances in Thessalonica:

• When 1 Thessalonians was written, the church was only three to six months old. Paul had only stayed with the Thessalonians about a month (Acts 17:2). All was new, and the believers themselves were new babes in Christ, newly saved out of a pagan background (1 Thessalonians 1:9; 4:1 ff.).

• There was no distinction between clergy and laity, no officialism, and no priestly garments distinguished certain members. Nor should we assume that anyone was supported full time in the assembly's service. Therefore, the humble, servant leaders who built others up within the congregation could easily be overlooked.

- As the plural verbs indicate, a number of brothers were doing the leadership work, not merely one man. (Paul requests that the Christians know "those" who labor, not he who labors.)
- As the letters indicate, certain gifted men or prophets may have received more public attention than those laboring at less spectacular duties (1 Thessalonians 5:19,20). Moreover, false laborers, busybodies, and would-be teachers (2 Thessalonians 3:6-15) were active. So, it required some effort for the congregation to know all those who truly labored at leading and admonishing.
- The human race harbors a basic dullness and ingratitude for those who humbly serve and care for others (Luke 17:11-19). But this should not be the case among Christian brethren. Consequently, Paul urges every member of the congregation (not just a few) to know and esteem all who humbly take the lead and instruct.

In light of these considerations, it seems likely that Paul was calling upon the congregation at Thessalonica to make the necessary effort *to know* their leaders so the leaders might receive the esteem and love they fully deserve. Such advice is well suited for congregations governed by elders today.

*Diligent labor.* The first quality to note about the leading men of Thessalonica is that they worked very hard. Paul describes them as "those who diligently labor." The word "labor" (Greek *kopiao*) is a strong word denoting strenuous work that results in weariness and fatigue. Trench describes diligent labor as, "being not so much the actual exertion which a man makes, as the lassitude or weariness which follows on this straining of all his powers to the utmost."[5] As a term used to describe manual labor (1 Corinthians 4:12; Ephesians 4:28), it is another example of the New Testament's use of common, lowly, servant words to describe one's spiritual service.

The labor Paul refers to here is service rendered to the brethren ("labor among you"), not labor for personal employment. The Thessalonian brethren were exerting themselves, working hard, and wearying themselves for the sake of the church's welfare. Indeed, caring for the Lord's people is strenuous work, and how desperately our churches need committed men to labor sacrificially among God's people.

On the surface, it appears that this passage refers to three separate classes of individuals: those who labor diligently among the congregation, those who direct the congregation, and those who give instruction. However, the structure of the clause indicates that Paul is referring to a single class of men who discharge three functions. In his commentary, A. L. Moore writes: ". . . as there is one definite article and three participles, Paul is indicating a group of people and not three particular officers. He first describes their work as labour, then expounds what this entails in two other participles."[6] Note, the plural forms of these three participles should not be overlooked. A team of men labored at leading and instructing. James Denney observes: "At Thessalonica there was not a single president, a minister in our sense, possessing to a certain extent an exclusive responsibility; the presidency was in the hands of a plurality of men."[7]

In the words, "diligently labor among you," we discover a vitally important aspect of a biblical eldership: hard work. Biblical eldership is not a church board that conducts its business for an hour or two a month—it is a hard working pastoral body! One reason there are so few elders or good Christian elderships is that, generally speaking, men are spiritually lazy.

Spiritual laziness is an enormous problem in the worldwide Christian community. *Spiritual laziness is a major reason why most churches will never establish a biblical eldership.* Men are more than willing to let someone else fulfill their spiritual responsibilities. Biblical eldership cannot function without committed, self-disciplined, hard working men, who love the flock and are willing to sacrifice for it. Thank God a group of men at Thessalonica labored strenuously for the church: leading their community of faith as God intended them to do.

Many people say, "You can't expect men to raise their families, work all day, and provide leadership for the local church." But that is simply not true. Many people raise families, work, and give hours of time to community service, clubs, or religious institutions. The cults have built up large lay movements that survive almost solely on the volunteer time of its members. We evangelicals are becoming a lazy, soft, pay-for-it-to-be-done group of Christians. It is positively amazing how much people can accomplish when they are motivated to work, when they love something. I've seen people build and remodel houses in their spare time. I've also seen men discipline themselves to gain a phenomenal knowledge of the Scriptures. What joy this brings to God's heart! Furthermore, God's power works through our human limitations and weaknesses. God would not ask

## 1 THESSALONIANS 5:12,13

men to raise their families, provide their own bread, and lead the household of God if doing so would hurt the church, the men, or their families. And remember the work of eldership is to be shared by a group of men, not done by one person. The real problem, then, is not with men's limited time and energy, but with false ideas about work, Christian living, and especially, Christian ministry.

So how do men serve the church yet maintain family life and employment? They do it by self-sacrifice, self-discipline, faith, perseverance, hard work, and the power of the Holy Spirit. Listen to the wise counsel of R. Paul Stevens:

And for tentmakers to survive three full-time jobs (work, family and ministry), they must also adopt a sacrificial lifestyle. Tentmakers must live a pruned life and literally find leisure and rest in the rhythm of serving Christ (Mat. 11:28). They must be willing to forego a measure of career achievement and private leisure for the privilege of gaining the prize (Phil. 3:14). Many would like to be tentmakers if they could be wealthy and live a leisurely and cultured lifestyle. But the truth is that a significant ministry in the church and the community can come only by sacrifice.[8]

*Taking the lead.* The brethren mentioned in this passage worked very hard to provide leadership. The words, "have charge over," represent a general Greek term (*prohistemi*) for leading, managing, guiding, or caring for. In accordance with the root meaning and common use for this word, a better English rendering would be: "those who take the lead among you in the Lord," or "direct you," or "guide you." Arthur Moore comments on this term:

. . . the Greek verb used here, *prohistemi*, has a variety of meanings but its basic sense is "to set over." It could be used of voluntary, informal leadership (which is the sense accepted here by those scholars who think there were at this time no elders), but it could also denote an official leader or office-bearer. The word, in this sense, is not altogether devoid of a note of superiority, which is probably why Paul adds to this participle "in the Lord," giving to the secular word a unique quality.[9]

Paul used *lead* in its broad, general sense. In its verbal form, lead describes what these brothers do—their activity. The corresponding Greek noun, *prostates*, is not used here, so lead is not used as an official title, i.e., president.

Most important, we must remember that because of our Lord's

[107]

teaching, the generic word *lead* must have a distinct, Christian meaning. As our Lord repeatedly taught, those who take the lead in His kingdom must not be like the secular or religious rulers of His day who, for their own advantage, selfishly lorded their authority and status over others. Instead, humility, servanthood, love, and sacrifice characterize Christian leadership. That is why we cannot identify leaders, as defined by later ecclesiastical practice, at Thessalonica. Humble, Christ-like leaders do not parade in special clothes or lust after superior titles and status. Instead, the advantage and well-being of others is paramount to Christ-like leaders.

Leading is a spiritual gift. Using the same terminology as here, Paul writes, in Romans 12:6-8, "And since we have gifts that differ according to the grace given to us, let each exercise them accordingly . . . he who leads [*prohistemi*], with diligence. . . ." Undoubtedly, some of the Thessalonians had the gift of leadership and were using it for the advantage of the whole church.

Of real importance to our study of elders is the fact that Paul uses the same term for leading here that he uses to describe the elders' work in 1 Timothy 5:17: "Let the elders who rule well [*prohistemi*] be considered worthy of double honor. . . ." Since the work of elders is to lead (*prohistemi*), the Thessalonian leaders were either already elders or potential elders whom Paul would later have appointed.

Because the phrase, "in the Lord," is added only to the verb lead, some clarification is needed. We must not misunderstand this particularly delicate area of service. Some men are assigned "in the Lord" to take the lead for the well-being of the Lord's people. The phrase circumscribes the leaders' sphere of labor—a sphere that all share and enjoy together, but is distinctly God's (not any one man's) and where all must be in harmony with His ways.

*Instruction (Admonition).* These brethren also labor hard in instructing the church. "Instruction" translates the Greek word *noutheteo*, which has no exact English equivalent. (Admonish is actually a better translation than instruct. See the commentary on Acts 20:31.) Most often, *noutheteo* is used by Paul in the sense of admonishing or warning, as in Acts 20:31, where Paul says, "I did not cease to admonish each one with tears." To instruct in the sense of admonishing means to give a needed, corrective word or seek to change wrong behavior, thoughts, or direction through proper instruction. In a sinful world, admonishing is necessary both on individual and congregational levels for the people's protection and proper development.

### Esteeming Your Leaders

Paul exhorts every member to first know all who labor hard at leading and admonishing, and second, to "esteem them very highly in love." The magnitude in which believers are to esteem their elders is expressed in the intensive adverb "very highly." G. G. Findlay speaks of this exuberant word as "the strongest intensive possible to the language. So deep and warm should be the affection uniting pastors and their flocks."[10] William Hendriksen adds this masterly comment: "Note the piling up of prefixes in this word: the ocean of esteem having reached its outermost perimeter, reaches even higher and begins to flow outward, overflowing its banks."[11] Thus, Christians must esteem their leaders superabundantly and most exceedingly. When elders are honored in this manner, it greatly enhances their effectiveness in leadership and inspires young men to prepare for this noble task.

God cares about how people treat those who are in authority. The Bible exhorts us not only to obey, but to honor our rulers (Romans 13:7; 1 Peter 2:17). When Paul, for example, realized he had spoken rudely to the high priest, Ananias, he apologized by saying, ". . .'I was not aware, brethren, that he was high priest; for it is written, "You shall not speak evil of a ruler of your people"'" (Acts 23:5). If people's thoughtlessness, disobedience, and ingratitude towards their civil leaders deeply concerns God, imagine how much greater concern He has that His people properly honor church elders!

The term *elder* describes one who is honored and respected in the community. In the Old Testament, disregard for elders was one sign of a nation's ruin (Lamentations 4:16; 5:12). The New Testament makes it plain that church elders are fully deserving of their fellow brethren's honor: "Let the elders who rule well be considered worthy of double honor, especially those who work hard at preaching and teaching." (1 Timothy 5:17). Few people are able to bear the weighty responsibility of leadership. Those who bear the yoke of leadership in God's house bear even greater responsibility and accountability than their counterparts in society. To be servant-leaders of God's people is an arduous and noble task. Therefore the elders thoroughly deserve the congregation's honor and love. As John Calvin writes, "The excellence and dignity of this work are inestimable: hence those whom God makes ministers in connection with so great a matter, ought to be held by us in great esteem."[12]

Our natural tendency, however, is to take elders for granted, forget what they have done for us, complain rather than be thankful, accentuate the bad, and disregard the good. For example, God gave Israel some of the greatest leaders in history—men like Moses and David. Yet during difficult times, the people were ready in a moment to stone both Moses and David to death. Knowing man's basic ingratitude and complaining spirit, the Spirit exhorts us to highly honor all who shepherd the flock.

Paul also adds the beautiful and comprehensive phrase, "in love," to his injunction: "esteem them very highly in love because of their work." Leon Morris captures the idea of this passage when he writes: "A special kind of love within the brotherhood is love for the leaders; they are to be loved because of their work, not necessarily because of their personal qualities."[13] There is always some degree of tension between the elders and the people. Difficult situations arise in which the elders cannot avoid displeasing or angering part of the congregation. Indeed, conflict between elders and church members can become very severe and trying. As Bricknell observes, "The exercise of authority is always apt to provoke resentment. . . . Hence natural human resentment at admonition is to be overcome by the positive attitude of love."[14]

Ultimately, however, God uses these heart-breaking situations to show us our pride, selfishness, and lovelessness. These conflicts reveal what is really in our hearts and what principles actually operate within the church. Conflicts also reveal whether we are living life as Christ would have us live, or living in the flesh. Conflicts reveal our need—as a corporate body—to confess and repent of sin and lovelessness. Paul Billheimer is right in noting that the local church—with all its problems, stresses, and conflicts— is actually a testing ground for growth in love and preparation for the future:

> The local church, therefore, may be viewed as a spiritual workshop for the development of agape love. Thus the stresses and strains of a spiritual fellowship offer the ideal situation for the testing and maturing of the all-important qualification for sovereignty. . . .

Most controversies in local congregations are produced, not primarily by differences over essentials, but by unsanctified human ambitions, jealousy, and personality clashes. The real root of many such situations is spiritual dearth in individual believers, revealing lamentable immaturity in love. Therefore the local congregation is one of the very best laboratories in which individual believers may discover their real spiritual emptiness and begin to grow in agape love. This is done by true repentance, humbly confessing the sins of jealousy, envy, resentment, etc., and begging forgiveness from one another. This approach will result in real growth in the love that covers.[15]

Love is the divine glue that holds the elders and congregation together through conflict and disagreement. No council of elders is perfect. All elders have problems, weaknesses, and faults, and each believer has a unique perspective on how elders should operate. As a result, even the best elders are inevitably accused of pride, wrong judgment, doing too much or too little, moving too slowly or too quickly, changing too much or not enough, and being too harsh or too passive. But love (and only love) suffers long (1 Corinthians 13:4,6). Love unites, heals, and builds up the church. And love covers a multitude of sins (1 Peter 4:8). Believers who love their shepherds will have greater understanding and tolerance for their shepherds' mistakes. In love, believers will view difficult situations in the best possible light. In love, believers will be less critical and more responsive to the elders' instruction and admonition.

The best thing a congregation can do for its elders is love them. Only then will believers and elders be able to live in peace as Paul directs in 1 Thessalonians 5:13. If the Corinthians had only loved Paul the way they should have, the awful strife and misunderstanding that marred their relationship would not have occurred. Many troubles at Corinth were due to a lack of Christian love. Likewise, the majority of problems in evangelical churches today are due to a lack of love.

Elders deserve this high regard and love "because of their work." They are not to be highly regarded because they are older men, hold titles, have received an apostolic appointment, or have friendly personalities. Rather, they deserve "esteem" and "love" solely because of their "work" on behalf of the congregation. We frequently direct our esteem towards those leaders we personally like or agree with, but that is wrong. All who diligently labor on behalf of the congregation are to be esteemed most highly in love, even those we may not easily be compatible with.

### Live in Peace.

Paul's use of the present, imperative verb of command, *keep on maintaining peace*, indicates that the Thessalonian church was at peace and must continue to maintain it. The entire congregation, including the leaders, is addressed and involved in the effort to "live in peace." It is no easy matter for people to "live in peace." Satan does all he can to create warfare and division among God's people, and Christians often help him succeed by acting in the ways of the old life (1 Corinthians 3:3,4; 2 Corinthians 12:20). In fact, so many churches are marked by fighting, quarreling, and bitterness that a church at peace is an oasis in the desert.

In the context of leaders and followers, Paul's exhortation to live in peace has special, practical relevance. The relationship between a congregation and its leaders involves a delicate tension that can easily create division or ill feeling (Acts 6:1), such as that between Moses and the people of Israel. Both elders and followers must be fully aware of potential conflict and their solemn duty to conscientiously work for peace. The New Testament repeatedly reminds us of the importance of peacemaking:

- "'Blessed are the peacemakers . . .'" (Matthew 5:9).
- "'. . . be at peace with one another'" (Mark 9:50).
- "So then let us pursue the things which make for peace . . ." (Romans 14:19).
- ". . . live in peace . . ." (2 Corinthians 13:11).
- "being diligent to preserve the unity of the Spirit in the bond of peace" (Ephesians 4:3).
- "And let the peace of Christ rule in your hearts . . ." (Colossians 3:15).
- "Now may the Lord of peace Himself continually grant you peace in every circumstance . . ." (2 Thessalonians 3:16).
- "And the seed whose fruit is righteousness is sown in peace by those who make peace" (James 3:18).
- "'. . . Let him seek peace and pursue it'" (1 Peter 3:11).

This emphasis on peace has been observed by F. J. A. Hort, who writes that Paul: "is giving instruction on the very essence of membership when in each of the nine Epistles addressed to Ecclesiae he makes the peace of God to be the supreme standard for them to aim at, and the perpetual self-surrender of love the comprehensive means of attaining it."[16] The testimony and spiritual growth of a church is intricately tied to the measure of peace it enjoys. Yet genuine peace, so vital to the welfare of the local assembly, is exceedingly difficult to maintain. Harry Ironside provides practical counsel to help us maintain peace among ourselves:

> We have an added word which we as Christians need to remember always, "And be at peace among yourselves." It is so easy to allow little things to set one Christian against another, and thus bring in strife and a spirit of quarrelsomeness among God's people. When we realize that anything like this is in our hearts we should take it immediately to the Lord in humiliation and self-judgment, and seek grace not to say or do anything willfully that is likely to cause contention among God's children.[17]

*Summary*

Despite certain debatable details, the main point of Paul's exhortation to the Thessalonians is perfectly clear and must not be neglected. Paul is making an apostolic plea to the congregation to know and highly esteem in love those brethren who work hard caring for the church. Furthermore, his plea goes out to all members of God's household (leaders and congregation alike) to work for peace—divine instruction all too easily forgotten in the pressures, hurts, and conflicts of life. Referring to the need to obey this inspired exhortation, John Eadie writes, "On obedience to it depended, in no small measure, the peace and the spiritual prosperity of the church."[18]

**NOTES**

1. Ernst Kasemann, *Essays on New Testament Themes* (Naperville, Illinois: Alec R. Allenson, Inc., 1964), page 86.
2. Hans Kung, *The Church* (New York: Sheed and Ward, 1967), page 405.
3. James D. G. Dunn, *Jesus and the Spirit* (Philadelphia: Westminster Press, 1975), page 182.
4. Neil Summerton writes:
    This biblical relationship is brought more sharply into focus by considering the high position accorded in scripture to the

congregation itself. Despite the existence of priestly and Levitical castes, and later of kings, that position can already be perceived in shadow in the Old Testament. The old covenant was with people rather than simply with leaders and under it a certain egalitarianism can be perceived in the relation between people and their covenant God: the superior status, as distinct from authority, later accorded to the monarch in Israel obviously derived from the hardness of the people's heart rather than the primitive purpose of God (see 1 *Samuel* 8:10-18; *Hosea* 8:4, 13-14).

The promise is comprehensively fulfilled in the New Testament. There we see a new covenant with a new people which embraces the youngest to the oldest. All receive the sign and guarantee of the covenant—the Holy Spirit; from that Spirit all have knowledge of God and all have the heart of flesh to obey God; all are kings and priests to God; and each receives (from young to old) spiritual gifts, severally according to the will of God, for the mutual upbuilding of the church. The old Israel was dependent usually on a few leaders; in the new, spiritual insight, spiritual power, spiritual character and spiritual standing are now much more widely disseminated through the whole body.

Consistent with this teaching, the New Testament accords a much higher status and role to the congregation at large than has often been accepted and practised in the experience of the church—though it should be noted that in times of revival and renewal there has been a constant tendency to rectify matters (*A Noble Task,* Exeter: The Paternoster Press, 1987, pages 98, 99).

5. Richard Chenevix Trench, *Synonyms of the New Testament*, 9th ed. (Grand Rapids: Wm. B. Eerdmans Publishing Co.,1969), page 378.
6. Arthur Lewis Moore, *1 and 2 Thessalonians*, The Century Bible (Greenwood, South Carolina: The Attic Press, Inc., 1969), page 80.
7. James Denney, *The Epistles to the Thessalonians*, The Expositors' Bible, (Cincinnati: Jennings & Graham, no date), page 205.
8. R. Paul Stevens, *Liberating the Laity*, (Downers Grove: Inter Varsity Press, 1985), page 147.
9. Moore, *1 and 2 Thessalonians*, page 80.
10. G. G. Findlay, ed., *The Epistles to the Thessalonians*, The Cambridge Bible for Schools and Colleges (Cambridge: Cambridge University Press, 1908), page 87, 117.
11. William Hendriksen, *Exposition of I and II Thessalonians*, New Testament Commentary (Grand Rapids: Baker Book House, 1955), page 135.
12. John Calvin, *Commentary on the First Epistle to the Thessalonians*, trans. John Pringle, Calvin's Commentaries (Reprint ed., Grand Rapids: Baker Book House, 1979), page 292.
13. Leon Morris, *Testaments of Love* (Grand Rapids: William B. Eerdmans Publishing Co., 1981), page 205.

14. E. J. Bricknell, *The First and Second Epistles to the Thessalonians*, Westminster Commentaries, (London: Methuen & Co. Ltd., 1932), page 59.
15. Paul E. Billheimer, *Love Covers* (Fort Washington, PA: Christian Literature Crusade, 1981), page 34.
16. Fenton John Anthony Hort, *The Christian Ecclesia* (1897; reprint ed., London: Macmillan and Co., Limited, 1914), page 123.
17. Henry Allan Ironside, *Addresses on the First and Second Epistles of Thessalonians* (Neptune, New Jersey: Loizeaux, 1947), page 66.
18. John Eadie, *A Commentary on the Greek Text of the Epistles of Paul to the Thessalonians*, ed. William Young (1877; reprint ed., Minneapolis: James Publications, 1976), page 196.

# Chapter 9

# *The Relationship Between Elders and Congregation*

*Live in peace with one another.*

1 Thessalonians 5:13

\*   \*   \*

The final exhortation of 1 Thessalonians 5:12,13 is to "live in peace with one another." These words are addressed to both the congregation and its leaders. In our rebellious world, maintaining peace among people and their leaders can be very trying. At heart, people do not want to submit to authority, especially when it is against their interest or desire. On the other hand, leaders can easily abuse their authority or act insensitively toward the feelings and needs of the people they lead. So we all need constant reminders to keep on working to maintain peace. Our purpose in this chapter is to examine the delicate relationship between elders and congregation. Hopefully, by gaining a better understanding of our mutual roles, we can all live together in greater peace and oneness to the praise of God.

### *Understanding the Congregation's Responsibility*

The New Testament emphasizes the congregation's responsibility to esteem, love, and honor its elders. Scripture teaches that the congregation is to obey and submit to the elders' guidance,

[116]

protection, and care (Hebrews 13:17). It is all too easy to forget that the elders are Christ's undershepherds. God has given them the solemn responsibility to shepherd His flock, and will hold them accountable for that responsibility. Spiritually minded Christians will not only submit, but will earnestly seek to be led by those God has placed in leadership. There is no place in the local church for anarchy—self-will; lawlessness; disobedience; stubbornness; or willful, independent behavior. Sinful disobedience is part of the unregenerated life style that Christians have died to in Christ (Romans 1:30; Ephesians 2:2). When Christ enters a person's life, He produces the good fruit of submission and obedience to God and one's fellow man.

Unless all brothers and sisters submit themselves to the governing authority of the elders, the Christian community will not enjoy the unity, peace, love, and truth that are to characterize the life of the church. If the sheep wander and chafe under the shepherd's direction and protection, the shepherds will be unable to do their work effectively. All will suffer. Elders are dependent, then, on the people's submission for the progress, vitality, and safety of the church.

Submission is always difficult. Our hearts are stubborn, prideful, and rebellious. Also, in a fallen world, situations arise in which submission to elders may be a genuine violation of conscience and truth. In such perplexing and agonizing situations, we must patiently pray for God's wisdom to guide us in all our ways (James 1:5). Remembering that we are all called to submit—even in trying and disagreeable situations—children must submit to imperfect parents, wives to difficult husbands, and employees to harsh employers. Likewise, the congregation is required to submit to and obey the elders, even if the elders have weaknesses and faults. (Indeed, most elders are quite imperfect, so those who are disobedient can always find reason to revolt.) Remember too, that the things we may interpret to be the elders' misjudgments or errors may be our own. It is often difficult to understand our leaders' perspectives because we can't see things from their vantage point. So we should not be hasty to disregard or question the judgment of those God has placed in church leadership, for theirs is a most trying job.

Of course this does not suggest blind, mindless, irrational submission. Nor does it suggest that elders are above questioning or immune from doing wrong. In fact, Christians must strive to improve and change difficult leaders/follower-related situations. But Christians must do so through persevering prayer, studying the Word, humble and loving entreaty, and by viewing the difficulties as a means of glorifying God and refining one's faith. As Christians we must understand that submission to the church shepherds is for our own growth and protection. God has placed elders in the congregation for the spiritual profit and protection of all the saints. Hence, a diligent eldership will be of great blessing to the saints' welfare and growth. As explained in Hebrews 13:17, disobedience and a lack of submission to the elders will be to one's disadvantage: ". . . Let them do this with joy and not with grief, for this would be unprofitable for you." As we see repeatedly throughout Israel's history, disregard for the spiritual watchmen's pleas may result in spiritual shipwreck. Disobedient Christians who cause the elders much pain and loss of effectiveness hurt themselves far more. So it is to each Christian's spiritual blessing, protection, growth, and advantage to heed the elders properly.

*Equal vote for everyone.* Yet in many churches, a congregational structure of government exists in which each member has an equal vote in making community decisions. The elders have no more authority in voting than anyone else. Robert Saucy, a congregationalist, describes congregational government this way: "In the ultimate sense, officers have no more ecclesiastical authority than any other member. Each has but one vote on any issue."[1]

Certain democratic theories of government may insist on an equal vote for every member, but this is not scriptural. The church is not bound by such democratic, governmental theories. True wisdom does not require giving every member an equal vote in discerning God's will for the church. Why, for example, should a member who attends church four or five times a year have a vote equal to that of a wise, experienced elder who knows the facts and wants only God's best for the church? When asked about the disadvantages of congregational church government, Haddon Robinson, president of a Baptist theological seminary, said, "One is that everyone has one vote . . . and therefore you're assuming that all of them have spiritual maturity and insight, as compared to a board of elders who should be chosen for their spiritual maturity and therefore are generally better qualified to make many of the decisions."[2]

People often appeal to Acts 6:1-6 to defend congregational church structure, but their defense stems from a misunderstanding of the text. According to Luke, the twelve apostles—the acting body of overseers—took the lead in presenting a specific, problem-solving plan to the congregation. The apostles wisely asked the congregation to select seven men from the assembly. The apostles set the qualifications for the seven men. And the apostles—not the congregation—appointed the men the people selected. Acts 6, like Acts 15, is a good example of the congregation and leaders working together in brotherly cooperation—not an example of congregational rule. (See also the exposition of Acts 14:23.)

Many democratic ideas conflict with New Testament principles of church government. For example, modern democracy (at least in theory) allows women equal share in society's leadership. But Paul, under divine inspiration, teaches that a woman must not exercise authority over men in the church (1 Timothy 2:9-15). So the church is not a democracy as we perceive it today, although it is very democratic. In the local Christian community, all men who desire and qualify may take part in governing the community, which must be done in close, brotherly cooperation with the whole community. All are equally under the authority and rule of Christ and His Word.

Due to fear that the elders (or pastors) may extend their authority too far over the congregation—a legitimate fear—men have devised church structures that only create further problems by extending the congregation's authority too far. For example, a good shepherd who seeks to help people mature and who confronts sin and problems may quickly become unpopular and be voted out of office. But according to Scripture, which is the rule of God's house, an elder cannot be removed from his God-given task by the whim of a majority vote.

In voting, people do not have to give biblical reasons or answers for their actions. They just vote. But in God's household, we are all answerable and accountable for our actions and decisions. If anyone thinks a man should be removed from a church office, he or she must show scriptural reasons for disqualification. We are all under the authority of God's Word. More than any other form of church government, congregationalism breeds fighting and divisions because it gives troublesome—even wicked—people an equal vote in directing God's household. The New Testament does not teach that every Christian has an equal vote in discerning God's will for the body.

In addition to saying nothing about every member having one vote, Scripture says nothing about absolute majority rule or total unanimity. Scripture insists on unity and peace in the congregation, but to allow one or two people to veto the whole assembly in a decision is unwise at best. Such a practice certainly doesn't create peace or unity. Instead, it places the congregation and its elders at the mercy of the assembly's most incompetent, hard-headed, and rebellious members. It will inevitably frustrate the rest of the congregation, create bad feelings, and thwart the church's progress.

However, denying the notions that every member has one vote, or that final church authority rests wholly in the congregation, does not imply that the congregation is to be passive or uninvolved in church decisions. Absolutely not! Each member is a gifted servant (minister), priest, and saint with appropriate responsibilities and obligations in the body. All members are necessary to the church's life and growth. All have a voice in assuring that what is done is done according to Scripture's truth. So, all members of the body participate, although not all lead and teach.

### Understanding the Elders' Responsibility

According to Scripture, God's Holy Spirit has placed elders in His flock as overseers to shepherd His church (Acts 20:28). This emphasis is found in 1 Peter, where the elders are urged to do the work of shepherding God's flock (1 Peter 5:2). It is also seen in Paul's reminder to the elders that they are God's stewards (Titus 1:7), that they are to take the lead in the church (1 Timothy 5:17), and that they are to care for God's church (1 Timothy 3:5). God has established government in every area of life. In the family, the husband is the head. In the church, all believers are priests and ministers (servants), but not all are leaders, pastors, and teachers. Elders are the church leaders—overseers, stewards, and shepherds. These terms imply that the elders have authority to direct the church, protect it from evil, and care for its overall welfare.

The elders are not mere figureheads or temporary, elected board members; they are God's stewards and Spirit-placed overseers. Yet many Christians act as if they lead, oversee, and shepherd the elders! Too often, Christians think they know better than their elder. In the church, Jesus Christ is Head, Shepherd, and

Lord. He is the final authority, and Scripture—God's voice—is the final and sufficient authority to which all must conform and submit. Since the elders are Christ's undershepherds, they have been given the authority to guide and protect the flock by means of His precious Word. But having stated that, we have not yet completed the biblical picture of church leadership.

The New Testament's real emphasis is on the way in which church leaders operate among God's people. First and foremost, church leaders are to be humble, loving, servant leaders. This is the teaching of Jesus Christ that is of great concern to God. Peter, for example, warns the elders against shepherding the church in a lordly and domineering manner (1 Peter 5:3). Paul, too, insists that no self-willed man can be an elder (Titus 1:7). This is because a self-willed man oppresses others; he is unyielding, headstrong, and blind to others' feelings. The quick-tempered and quarrelsome man also cannot be an elder since he will butcher and scatter the sheep (Titus 1:7). God requires an elder to be gentle and forebearing so the sheep can properly develop and live in harmony and peace together (1 Timothy 3:3). The Christian leader's greatest power to lead God's flock is his godly example of service and love for God and His Word (1 Peter 5:3).

Elders are not to be authoritarian rulers. Instead, they are to be humble, servant leaders among their brethren. Consequently, they must always guard against creating a repressive atmosphere within the church. In a repressive environment people cannot mature or develop their gifts and abilities. Paul is a good example of a leader who never sought to dominate his converts' faith (2 Corinthians 1:24; 10:1). Like Paul, elders must insist on the broad liberty and freedom that all members possess through the gospel of Jesus Christ. Elders must be cautious of extending their leadership authority into areas in which believers have the right to disagree and be different. In 1 Thessalonians 5:12, Paul uses three participles in reference to church leaders: those laboring hard, those taking the lead, and those admonishing the assembly. What is of particular interest to us is that Paul added the phrase, "in the Lord," to the second participle, taking the lead. Only this second designation needed the added clarification of the phrase, "in the Lord." It is as if to say that church leaders deal with matters that pertain to the Lord, not every sphere of the people's lives. Jon Zens comments: "The elders are responsible for the spiritual welfare of the church, but have no business dictating—either subtly or openly—the personal affairs of the saints. The elders may have some sound advice in many areas which the saints should take into consideration. But it is only advice, not a mandatory direction, unless there is a 'thus saith the Lord' from Scripture attached to it."³

The elders protect the church from false teachers, teach the Word, discipline members, and guide the congregation in making decisions and solving problems. At the same time, the elders must respect each saint's liberty in Christ and conscience in light of Scripture's truth. However, when a question of moral evil arises, the elders (as well as all responsible Christians) must act and judge. But there is a large area of Christian living in which believers are free to seek the guidance and help they need from their heavenly Father. The elders must never usurp the unique place that Christ and the Father enjoy over each believer (Matthew 23:7-12).

Only if elders exercise their authority and responsibility in a humble, servant-like manner, can they ever hope to shepherd the church in a way that maintains maximum peace, unity, and brotherly love. God longs for His flock to experience peace, love, and unity. This desire is mentioned many times in the New Testament:

• Love—"And beyond all these things put on love, which is the perfect bond of unity" (Colossians 3:14; cf. John 13:34,35; Romans 12:10; 13:8; 1 Corinthians 16:14; Galatians 5:13; Ephesians 5:2; Philippians 1:9; 1 Thessalonians 3:12; 4:9,10; James 2:8; 1 Peter 1:22; 4:8; 1 John 3:16; 4:7,11).

• Peace—"And let the peace of Christ rule in your hearts, to which indeed you were called in one body . . ." (Colossians 3:15; cf. Romans 12:18; 15:13; 1 Corinthians 7:15; 2 Corinthians 13:11; Ephesians 6:23; 1 Thessalonians 5:13; 2 Thessalonians 3:16; Hebrews 12:14; James 3:17,18).

• Oneness—". . . standing firm in one spirit, with one mind striving together for the faith of the gospel" (Philippians 1:27; cf. John 17:1-23; Acts 4:32; 6:5; 15:22,25; Romans 15:5,6; 1 Corinthians 1:10,11; 2 Corinthians 7:13,15; 13:11; Ephesians 4:1 ff; 1 Peter 3:8).

Since this is God's longing for His people, elders must guide the local flock through the storms of conflict, change, and decision making in peace and unity. That is no easy task! In our own strength it is impossible. But through prayer, patient waiting upon the Lord's timing, a humble spirit, and open communication, the inevitable conflicts that arise can be successfully resolved. The congregation and its elders can reach decisions in full agreement without bitterness, strife, and division.

However, in the course of their work, elders are often caught in the midst of contention. As Charles Swindoll observes, "It is impossible to lead anyone without facing opposition. The leader must learn to take the heat. He will face opposition—it's an occupational hazard of every leader."[4] In contentious situations, elders need to remember that they must provide the example of how true Christians handle problems and disagreements. They must exhibit the principles of love, humility, and servanthood. This does not mean that they passively wait until the storms pass, for that is the worst possible action, and is the source of endless unresolved problems. Art Glasser is right when he says, "Passivity is an enemy."[5] Instead of closing their eyes to problems, elders must work hard to protect the flock from internal fighting. They must warn and rebuke malicious behavior. They must provide counsel for contending parties. They must actively guide the flock by laboring together in prayer, searching the Word, patiently teaching, providing open and free discussion (Acts 15:5-29), and lovingly admonishing (and even rebuking) stubborn members. Throughout the process of resolving church conflict, elders must provide the example of brotherly love, forgiveness, submission, understanding, yieldedness, humility, and servanthood.

In making decisions as an eldership, remember that it is always Christ's will and direction that the elders, as His undershepherds, must seek. He is the "Senior Pastor." He is not only interested in the final decision but is most concerned about the way in which we deal with one another and seek His will. So in all major decisions, the elders should seek unanimity among themselves. In minor decisions or proposals, a complete unanimity would not have to be insisted upon.[6] Each elder should seek to advance and encourage one another's plans and interest. This is what loving, humble servanthood demands. If the elders, who are to be wise men, cannot decide if an issue is major or minor (and there are major and minor issues), then they should consider it major and seek total unanimity.

## The Elder-Congregation Relationship

The relationship between elders and congregation is essential to the peace, unity, and discernment of the Lord's will for His people. This requires a great deal of free and open communication between the elders and congregation. So Christian elders must fully innoculate themselves against aloofness, secrecy, or independently seeking their own direction.

Over the years, I have observed church elders who do not allow their brothers and sisters to have any involvement in the church's decision-making process. These elders wrongly act as the ruling oligarchy of the church. Good elders should not be satisfied with a passive congregation. Good elders want an educated, involved, and mature congregation. The vibrant health of the eldership (and the church) lies in its sensitivity to its fellow brethren, its flexibility, and its desire to involve every member of the body in the art of living together in peace.

The eldership must always seek the counsel and mind of those they lead. No clergy-laity division exists between elders and congregation. Instead, there is a tightly knit, delicate, and reciprocal relationship. In the local church, there are no rulers who sit above or subjects who stand below. All are equal brethren. However, there are leaders and followers in a horizontal relationship. The intimate, horizontal relationship between elders and congregation is implied by the biblical shepherd-sheep imagery. John J. Davis vividly brings this imagery to life:

> One of the amazing discoveries of my days with Palestinian shepherds was the ability of these men to lead their flocks through the most difficult places. They always seemed to know the safety of the trail and the best and most efficient way to get to pastures and adequate water supplies. It is well known, of course, that Palestinian shepherds normally lead their sheep rather than drive them. The intimate relationship sustained between shepherd and sheep makes this possible. Herein lies a big difference between ranching techniques of the West and the personalized intimate relationship established in the Oriental East.[7]

One important aspect of the elders' work is to lead the congregation in seeking the Lord's will whenever it needs direction or must make decisions. In all major church decisions, especially the expulsion of a member (Matthew 18:17-20), the goal of the elders and congregation must be to speak and act as one united church body. At times this will require that the overseers call the whole church together in council. When assembled, the elders lead the church in seeking the Lord's mind and assessing the Lord's will.

A beautiful example of elders and congregation working together in peace and unity is the council at Jerusalem, recorded in Acts 15:22,28: "Then it seemed good to the apostles and the elders, with the whole church, to choose men from among them to send to Antioch. . . . 'For it seemed good to the Holy Spirit and to us to lay upon you no greater burden than these essentials.'" The apostles, elders, and congregation harmoniously joined together in a crucial decision affecting the doctrine and well-being of the first century churches. If the elders and congregation sense a division among godly members, decisions may need to be postponed for further discussion and prayer. However, in situations of false teaching, evil discord, or immorality, the elders must exercise their authority as shepherd-overseers and make decisions against the contending brethren, false teachers, or immoral behavior.

In most situations where there is genuine disagreement between godly brethren, the best policy is to wait on God in patient prayer before making a decision. Does not God often use these difficult situations to test our humility, love, and trust in Him? Only by exercising humility and a servant disposition can Christians achieve the oneness and brotherly love God desires for His people. Pride will surely ruin any hope for peace and unity in the holy brotherhood. In this area, D. E. Hoste's counsel has been an enormous blessing to many:

> In a Mission (China Inland Mission) like ours, those guiding its affairs must be prepared to put up with waywardness and opposition and be able to desist from courses of action which, though they may be intrinsically sound and beneficial, are not approved by some of those affected. I shall never forget the impression made upon me by Mr. Taylor in connection with these affairs. Again and again, he was obliged either greatly to modify or lay aside projects which are sound and helpful, but met with determined opposition, and so tended to create greater evils than those which might have been removed or mitigated by the changes in question. Later on, in answer to patient continuance in prayer, many of such

projects were given effect to. Patient persevering prayer plays a more vital practical part in the development of the Mission's work than most people have any idea of.[8]

In the end, no ultimate cures, formulas, or constitutional procedures for decision-making will safeguard the church's peace and unity. Only humble, wise, servant shepherds can lead the flock through decisions and conflict in love, peace, and unity. Both the elders and congregation play a vital role in this process, and neither should ever be downplayed, overlooked, or elevated beyond the biblical design.

## NOTES

1. Robert Saucy, *The Church in God's Program* (Chicago: Moody Press, 1972), page 114.
2. "Leadership Forum: Power, Preaching, and Priorities," *Leadership* 1 (Winter, 1980): 14.
3. Jon Zens, "The Major Concepts of Eldership in the New Testament," *Baptist Reformation Review* 7 (Summer 1978): 31, 32.
4. Charles R. Swindoll, *Hand Me Another Brick* (Nashville: Thomas Nelson Inc., Publishers, 1978), page 78.
5. *Ibid.*, page 202.
6. Carefully consider Neil Summerton's excellent comments:
     The first may be expressed as *consensus* on major issues and *agreement to differ* on minor ones.
     It is not practicable to suppose that upon major matters affecting the life and work of the congregation an eldership could proceed other than on the principle of substantial agreement, if not unanimity. Persistent disagreement in such matters would be bound to be debilitating to the elders and to threaten the credibility of their leadership.
     In such matters, it is important that each elder should conduct himself within the group with *integrity:* in making clear to his colleagues his position and any reservations which he may have; and in avoiding any secret politicking with individual colleagues, or any appearance of it. Openness must be the watchword. Granted this, the elders must learn to handle their differences in an acceptable fashion: this requires patience and the willingness to spend time exploring them and the underlying reasons for them. Above all, time should be spent in prayer and perhaps fasting, in order to seek the mind of the Lord so as to establish a spiritually inspired consensus among elders and congregation alike.
     In lesser matters, it should be possible for individuals *to allow their preferences to be over-ridden by the majority* without

feeling that some great personal or theological cause has been sacrificed. Nor should this impair the effectiveness and credibility of the group. But such a principle does call for discretion on the part of the elder concerned. There are strict limits within which it is possible on major and minor matters for the elder to make public his dissent, especially if it is in a manner which casts doubt on the wisdom of colleagues. Plural eldership implies collective responsibility, which in turn implies solidarity with fellow-elders even when they are taking a course with which the individual may personally disagree. (Integrity may of course demand that, when members of the congregation ask about the matter, they should be referred discreetly to other elders for explanations.) If disagreement on important matters is persistent, it may be that the individual should consider resigning in order to relieve himself from an ambiguous position (*A Noble Task*, Exeter: The Paternoster Press, 1987, pages 83, 84).

7. John J. Davis, *The Perfect Shepherd* (Grand Rapids: Baker Book House, 1979), page 48.

8. Phyllis Thompson, *D. E. Hoste "A Prince with God"* (London: China Inland Mission, 1947), pages 158, 159.

# Chapter 10

# *Shared Brotherly Leadership*

*Paul and Timothy, bond-servants of Christ Jesus, to all the saints in Christ Jesus who are in Philippi, including the overseers and deacons.*

*Philippians 1:1*

\*   \*   \*

One of the great joys of my life has been to share the pastoral oversight of a church with a team of dedicated men. Over the years we have experienced many problems, heartaches, tears, conflicts, and—let me assure you—failures. But we have also experienced victory, joy, laughter, friendship, and deeper love for one another. As partners in the work of shepherding the flock of God for many years, we have sharpened, balanced, comforted, protected, strengthened, and supported one another. Ultimately, this shared responsibility has provided better, longer-lasting care for the Lord's people and for ourselves.

But far more important than my experience, or that of any-one else, is what God's Word says about participation in church leadership. According to the New Testament, the leadership, or pastoral oversight, of the local church is to be shared by all men in the community who qualify and desire the work. Hence, church leadership is a team effort—not the sole responsibility of one "professional" religious leader.

[128]

Paul's greeting to the "overseers and deacons" at Philippi plainly demonstrates the plurality of overseers within a local church: "... to all the saints in Christ Jesus who are in Philippi, including the overseers and deacons." This greeting also provides other highly significant information for our study; it is Paul's only letter to the first century churches that mentions both overseers and deacons. Without this brief reference, there would be no way to know, either from Acts or the rest of the letter, that the Philippian church had recognized overseers and deacons. Indeed, this passage is a vital link between Acts and Paul's letters to Timothy and Titus. So, Philippians 1:1 sheds a welcome light over the whole subject of apostolic church leadership structure.

Although Paul singles out "overseers and deacons" for special mention in this greeting, they are given no separate, elevated position above the congregation. The letter is written "to all the saints . . . in Philippi," and the terms, "overseers and deacons," are subjoined to this phrase. All the members at Philippi are truly elevated in God's sight. "The overseers and deacons" are associated with "all the saints" and, as leaders, are distinguished from the congregation within the greeting, but for uncertain reasons. A. T. Robertson comments: ". . . Paul does not ignore the officers of the saints or church, though they occupy a secondary place in his mind. The officers are important, but not primary. The individual saint is primary. Church officers are made out of saints. . . . Paul does not draw a line of separation between clergy and laity. He rather emphasizes the bond of union by the use of 'together with.'"[1]

Although "the overseers and deacons" are mentioned in the greeting, Paul speaks to the entire company of saints in the rest of the letter, as he does in all of his letters to the churches.

The terms overseers and deacons are used here as official designations for recognized church leadership positions. Some commentators insist, however, that the two terms are only used functionally to designate those who generally superintend and serve the saints. They support this interpretation by the absence of the definite article before "overseers and deacons."

But the absence of the definite article in Greek is insufficient to assign a purely functional sense to these terms, for the context makes these terms definite. After addressing all the saints, Paul clearly gives special mention to two distinct groups. This context makes them definite. In addition, the word *episkopos* gives further clarification, as Ernest Best points out: "I say 'officials' because *episkopos* at any rate could not have been used in any other way than as a designation of an office. . . . a first century Greek could not have used it in a purely functional sense without suggesting that the person who exercised oversight held 'official' status."[2] Moreover, there is an obvious similarity in the joint use of the words "overseers and deacons," in this passage and 1 Timothy 3:1-13. Both letters were written in the early to middle sixties, so there were officially recognized overseers/elders and deacons at both Philippi and Ephesus. The interpretation that assigns these words to anyone in the community who supervises or serves is confusing and meaningless.

Furthermore, only two distinct groups of officials—"overseers and deacons"—appeared at Philippi, not the three offices (overseer, elders, and deacons) commonly found in the second century. Fifty years later, in Polycarp's letter to the Philippian church (circa A.D. 70-155 or 160), there are still only two distinct bodies of officials. Polycarp writes, "Wherefore it is right to abstain from all these things, submitting yourselves to the presbyters and deacons as to God and Christ."[3]

### Overseers and Elders

This is the first occasion that the word overseers is used directly as an official designation for a body of leaders. One must ask, then, what relationship the overseers have to the elders. A number of New Testament passages make it obvious that the two terms refer to one and the same group and are used interchangeably:

*Acts 20:17,28.* Luke writes that Paul sent for the elders of the church at Ephesus. But in the sermon to the same elders, Paul says that the Holy Spirit has placed them as overseers. This is the plainest indication that elders and overseers represent the same body of people.

*Titus 1:5,7.* In verse five, Paul directs Titus to appoint elders in every city. In verse six, he begins listing the elders' qualifications, but as he continues the list in verse seven, he uses the word overseer. (See comments on Titus 1:7.)

*1 Peter 5:1,2.* Peter exhorts the elders to oversee the church. Since the elders oversee the local church, they are also the overseers.

*1 Timothy 3:1-13; 5:17-25.* In 1 Timothy 5:17-25, Paul speaks of the leading role and great value of "elders who rule well . . .

especially those who work hard at preaching and teaching." But in 1 Timothy 3:1-13, he speaks of the qualifications of overseers and deacons, making no mention of elders. All questions are resolved when one understands that the word *overseer* in 3:1 is a generic, singular form for overseers, and that the word *overseers* is used interchangeably for elders (Philippians 1:1; Acts 20:17,28). Thus, 1 Timothy 3 and 5 refer to two groups of men—elders and deacons—not three.

*Philippians 1:1.* At Philippi, only two corporate bodies are designated: "overseers and deacons." It is improbable that there was a body of overseers in addition to a body of elders. It is equally improbable that Paul would greet "overseers and deacons" but omit the elders who held an essential place in early church leadership. Thus, one must conclude that overseers and elders are one and the same.

*Polycarp's letter to the church at Philippi.* Written some 50 years after Paul's letter to Philippi, Polycarp refers only to two bodies of leaders—elders and deacons.[4]

Unfortunately, the terms elders and overseer, which were used interchangeably in the New Testament, came to refer to two different officials in the second century—the overseer (bishop) who was the superior, and the body of elders. Even so, by the fourth century, Jerome made the startling and bold assertion—to the consternation of the Catholic Church—that bishops and elders were originally the same.

> A presbyter and a bishop are the same . . . the churches were governed by a joint council of the presbyters. . . . If it be supposed that it is merely our opinion and without scriptural support that bishop and presbyter are one. . . . examine again the words the apostle addressed to the Philippians. . . . Now Philippi is but one city in Macedonia, and certainly in one city there could not have been numerous bishops. It is simply that at that time the same persons were called either bishops or presbyters.[5]

Today, Jerome's observation would not be considered eccentric. Over 100 years ago, J. B. Lightfoot wrote, "It is a fact now generally recognized by theologians of all shades of opinion, that in the language of the New Testament the same officer in the Church is called indifferently 'bishop' (*episkopos*) and 'elder' or 'presbyter' (*presbyteros*)."[6] Although the two terms apply to the same body of men, elder reflects the Jewish heritage that stresses dignity, maturity, honor, and wisdom, while overseer reflects a Greek-speaking origin that stresses the work of oversight.

## Collegiality

Philippi had a plurality of overseers. The use of "overseers" (plural) has profound implications. In one stroke, the plural form utterly confounds later false theories of church government. How could a number of bishops reside in one local church? (Philippians 4:15,16 proves that it was one church, not several.) No single overseer governed the assembly at Philippi. Instead, a team of overseers jointly directed the assembly. This again reinforces the doctrine of multiple leadership. John Eadie brings the radical leadership changes that took place in the second century to our attention: "The mention of *episkopoi* in the plural, and the naming of both classes of office-bearers after the general body of members, indicate a state of things which did not exist in the second century."[7]

The practice of shared leadership is plainly evident throughout the New Testament. It is first observed in the leadership example of the twelve apostles who, in a most beautiful way, jointly led and taught the first Christian community. What a marvelous example of unity, humble cooperation, and brotherly love they provide! Corporate oversight is also seen among the seven who were chosen to relieve the apostles (Acts 6:3-6). There is no scriptural indication that one of the seven almoners was the head, with the others serving as his assistants. As a body of servants, they together did their work on behalf of the community. Shared leadership is also practiced in the deaconship (Philippians 1:1; 1 Timothy 3:8-13) and in the eldership. In addition, other examples of multiple leadership exist throughout the New Testament (Acts 13:1; 15:35; 1 Corinthians 16:15,16; 1 Thessalonians 5:12,13; Hebrews 13:7,17,24).

Interestingly enough, no one has seriously challenged the plurality of deacons in an effort to create a singular deacon, yet that is precisely what many scholars have tried to do with elders. However, shared pastoral leadership through a body of elders needs to be preserved just as much as a plural deaconship because the apostles gave the mandate to pastor the church of God to a *plurality* of elders (Acts 20:28; 1 Peter 5:1,2). Although often overlooked, this significant and decisive fact must be reckoned with.

Some scholars have tried to plead the case for the traditional singular pastorate by using the New Testament examples of Timothy, Epaphras, James, or the angels of the churches of Revelation. These attempts, however, have proven quite unsuccessful.[8] It is generally agreed that Timothy was an apostolic delegate, Paul's co-worker in spreading the gospel and strengthening the churches Paul planted. Epaphras was perhaps the original evangelist of the church at Colossae. James was an apostle ministering uniquely to the Jews in Jerusalem. And, if the angels of the churches of Revelation were men (and that is doubtful), we are uninformed as to who they actually might have been.

In spite of various objections to shared pastoral leadership, a growing number of Christian teachers have recognized Scripture's solid testimony concerning shared pastoral leadership and its obvious lack of support for the one-man pastor system. John MacArthur, Jr., for example, writes:

Clearly, all the biblical data indicates that the pastorate is a team effort. It is significant that every place in the New Testament where the term *presbuteros* is used, it is plural, except where the Apostle John uses it of himself in 2 and 3 John, and where Peter uses it of himself in 1 Peter 5:1. The norm in the New Testament church was a plurality of elders. There is no reference in all the New Testament to a one-pastor congregation.[9]

Bible commentator and teacher, James M. Boice observes:

The church did not install merely one person to do this job but several. In fact, there is no reference anywhere in the New Testament to the appointment of only one elder or one deacon to a work. We would tend to appoint one leader, but God's wisdom is greater than our own at this point. In appointing several persons to work together, the church at God's direction provided for mutual encouragement among those who shared in the work as well as lessened the chance for pride or tyranny in office.[10]

Gene Getz, in his book, *Sharpening the Focus of the Church*, comments:

. . . multiple leadership in the church is a New Testament principle. The "one man" ministry is a violation of this important guideline. The Scriptures frequently stress the "mutuality of the ministry." No local church in the New Testament was ruled and managed by one person. Plurality of elders appears as the norm.[11]

Jon Zens writes:

> In the light of the emphasis today on a single pastor, it is significant that in the New Testament it is always assumed that the brethren are in submission to a plurality of spiritual oversight. . . . Nowhere in the New Testament will you find "obey *him* who has the rule over you." . . . in the early days of the church it was the normal state of affairs for brethren to have a plurality of elders over them in the Lord. Again, it is our abnormal (and subnormal) situation that makes this concept seem strange to our ears.[12]

In the book, *The Team Concept*, Bruce Stabbert explores all the passages used for and against shared leadership and concludes:

> It is concluded after examining all the passages which mention local church leadership on the pastoral level, that the New Testament presents a united teaching on this subject and that it is on the side of plurality. This is based on the evidence of the seven clear passages which teach the existence of plural elders in single local assemblies. These passages should be allowed to carry hermeneutical weight over the eight other plural passages which teach neither singularity or plurality. This is a case where the clear passages must be permitted to set the interpretation for the obscure. Thus, of the eighteen passages which speak of church leadership, fifteen of them are plural. Of these fifteen, seven of them most definitely speak of a single congregation. Only three passages talk about church leadership in singular terms, and in each passage the singular may be seen as fully compatible with plurality. In all these passages, there is not one passage which describes a church being governed by one pastor.[13]

So, the New Testament witness to the practice of joint pastoral leadership is clear, and the characterization of this practice as "a new and subversive concept that threatens the very life of the church" is totally unfounded.[14]

### Reasons for Shared Leadership

We have seen that corporate leadership was practiced in the New Testament era, but why was that so? Certainly it is no accident that the apostles and early Christians did not appoint a "ruler of the synagogue" to lead their newly planted churches. Such leadership was an integral part of their Jewish heritage and would have been quite natural to adopt, but it was not done. Although Acts 18:8 says, "And Crispus, the leader of the synagogue, believed in the Lord . . .", there is not the slightest indication that he, or anyone else, was placed in charge as the chief ruler of the Christian assembly at Corinth.

The most likely reason for choosing plurality of leadership was that the early Christians knew that Christ, in the power of the Holy Spirit (Matthew 18:20), was uniquely present with them as Head, Lord, Pastor, and Overseer. This was no theoretical idea to the early Christians—it was reality. In Christ alone was all they needed to be in full fellowship with God and one another. Christ's person and work was so infinitely great, final, and complete, that nothing—even in appearance—was to diminish the centrality of His presence and sufficiency for His people.

So, in the first century, no Christian would dare take the position or title of head, overseer, pastor, or leader of the church. We are so accustomed to speaking of "the pastor" that we do not stop to realize that Scripture does not. There is profound significance in this fact, and we must not permit customary practice to shield our minds from divine truth. In the church only Christ is the Head and Pastor. Quoting Neander's *Church History*, Alexander Hay points out how the improper elevation of one man within the church obscures the centrality of Christ and the people's perception of themselves:

> The monarchical form of government was in no way suited to the Christian community of spirit. The preeminence of a single individual at the head of the whole was too likely to operate as a check on the free development of the life of the Church and the free action of the different organs, in whom it was necessary to keep alive a consciousness of mutual independence. The individual on whom everything would in such a constitution be made to depend, might acquire too great an importance for the rest, and, consequently, become the centre around which all would gather, in such a manner as to obscure the sense of their common relation to the One Who ought to be the centre of all.[15]

History abundantly demonstrates the human tendency to exalt men in the church to a status that belongs only to Christ. For example, at the beginning of the second century, Ignatius, the bishop of Antioch, wrote of the local church bishop, "Plainly therefore we ought to regard the bishop as the Lord Himself."[16] Elsewhere he says, ". . . respect the bishop as being a type of the Father and the presbyters as the council of God and as the college of Apostles. Apart from these there is not even the name of a church."[17]

A second important reason for shared leadership is that Jesus continually warned His followers against pride and self-elevation over their brethren. He explicitly forbade them from assuming special titles and seeking honored places for themselves. He knew that those in leadership positions are especially susceptible to the pride of position and status. Charles Edward Jefferson singles out some of the temptations toward self-elevation a pastor faces: "Covetousness and ambition, inordinate desire to possess for personal gratification and an unlawful love of advancement, prominence and authority. Christian history makes it clear that these are the cardinal sins which ever lie like crouching beasts at the shepherd's door."[18]

In contrast to one-man leadership, shared leadership, I am convinced, helps to develop and mature leaders in the chief virtues of brotherly love, humility, and servanthood. It also helps curb the tendency towards superiority, independence, and aloofness. Indeed, the modern concept that the pastor is the lonely, trained professional—the sacred person who can never really become a part of his congregation—is utterly unscriptural. Not only is this concept unscriptural, it is unhealthy. Radmacher, himself a president of a Baptist theological seminary, contrasts what happens when church administration is left largely in the hands of one pastor to the wholesomeness of multiple elders:

> Laymen . . . are indifferent because they are so busy. They have no time to bother with church affairs. Church administration is left, therefore, largely in the hands of the pastor. This is bad for him, and it is bad also for the church. It makes it easier for the minister to build up in himself a dictatorial disposition and to nourish in his heart the love of autocratic power.
>
> It is my conviction that God has provided a hedge against these powerful temptations by the concept of multiple elders. The check and balance that is provided by men of equal authority is most wholesome and helps to bring about the desired attitude expressed by Peter to the plurality of elders: ". . . shepherd the flock of God among you, not under compulsion, but voluntarily, according to the will of God; and not for sordid gain, but with eagerness; nor yet as lording

it over those allotted to your charge, but proving to be examples to the flock" (1 Peter 5:2,3).[19]
Third, the Christian congregation is to be characterized by brotherliness; mutuality; interdependence; strong community interaction and participation; and humble, loving service to one another. Joint leadership allows all able brothers—not just one man—to share equally in the oversight of the brotherhood. Thus, shared leadership provides a living model of how the whole congregation is to live and work in mutual accord.

### Some Practical Benefits of Shared Leadership

Because of the tendency to adopt one-man rule, and the fact that many people who criticize shared leadership really do not understand it, it is necessary to explain some of the distinct advantages of leadership by a council of qualified, dedicated, Spirit-placed equals.

*Sharing the burden.* The heavy burdens, conflicts, complaints, and problems of church leadership are shared equally by a team of shepherding elders—not by one, over-burdened pastor. Of course, some pastors can do everything. They can preach, teach, exhort, counsel, administer, organize, visit, write, lead, and bear the whole load of the church themselves. Thank God for men like these! Often God uses them for great works. But such super-talented men are few and far between. In reality, most pastors are not multi-gifted or exceptionally strong. A pastor may be an excellent teacher, but a poor administrator and counselor.

As a result, many pastors cannot adequately bear the full burden of their work. Other pastors are continually criticized for not being perfect. The churches in which these pastors serve face the serious problem of repeatedly replacing their "short-term" pastors every three or four years. However, because it takes years for a pastor to know the people in his congregation and set the right example for them, leadership by short-term pastors ultimately damages the local church.

But when a team of elders shares the leadership responsibility, each man contributes his special abilities to the leadership of the congregation and helps bear the work. This lightens the load, making it bearable for all. In his wisdom, Solomon speaks of the blessings of partnership: "Two are better than one because they have a good return for their labor. For if either of them falls, the one will lift up his companion. But woe to the one who falls when there is not another to lift him up. Furthermore, if two lie down together they keep warm, but how can one be warm alone? And if one can overpower him who is alone, two can resist him. A cord of three strands is not quickly torn apart" (Ecclesiastes 4:9-12).

Please note that I am not claiming shared leadership is problem free. Indeed, joint leadership can be painfully difficult and absolutely aggravating. As D. E. Hoste said, "Colleagueship calls for an orientation and method different from the direct rule over juniors and subordinates."[20] Joint leadership demands much greater patience, prayer, humility, and consideration of others' gifts and perspectives. That is why most men prefer to work alone or with a staff under them. In the final analysis, however, the joy, comfort, and satisfaction of working together for the Lord in a team effort far outweigh the difficulties.

*Balancing weaknesses and strengths.* Shared leadership balances each leader's individual weaknesses and strengths. Earl Radmacher insightfully points this out: "Human leaders, even Christian ones, are sinners and they only accomplish God's will imperfectly. Multiple leaders, therefore, will serve as a 'check and balance' on each other and serve as a safeguard against the very human tendency to play God over other people."[21] Balance is one of man's biggest problems, and this is especially true of gifted, prominent men. Many great men have destroyed themselves because they had no peers to confront and balance them. Among colleagues who equally share leadership responsibilities, there is a greater sense of accountability, more open interaction and criticism, and greater potential for balancing each individual's strengths and weaknesses. This balancing of one another normally does not occur when men are subordinate to one man at the top of an organization. As Robert Greenleaf observes, "When someone is moved atop a pyramid, that person no longer has colleagues, only subordinates. Even the frankest and bravest of subordinates do not talk with their boss in the same way that they talk with colleagues who are equals, and normal communication patterns become warped."[22] Erroll Hulse explains in more practical terms how joint leadership helps and balances fellow colleagues:

> An eldership which goes wrong can be harmful. But where the biblical procedures are prayerfully and carefully followed there is far more by way of inbuilt precaution against things

going wrong in an eldership than in a one-man oversight. In a plurality of elders if one elder gets spiritually sick the others are there to help him recover. If one is prostrated for a time by the burdens laid upon him the others can lighten those burdens and help him through. Within an eldership extreme ideas are tempered, harsh judgments moderated and doctrinal imbalances corrected. If one elder shows prejudice toward, or personal dislike for any person, in or outside the church, the others can correct that and insist on fair play and justice. If one elder is in a fierce mood over some offender that offender has others to whom he can appeal.[23]

*Increased participation.* Joint leadership permits a greater number of capable, dedicated men to share fully in the leadership of the church community to which they belong and love. This means greater participation in the oversight and teaching of the community. The single pastorate, on the other hand, permits only one man to teach and pastor, although others in the church may be equally or even more talented. Often, men of equal spiritual maturity and ability are a threat to the pastor's position rather than the blessing they should be. Since the single pastorate allows only one man to be the pastor, it is a poor utilization of manpower and spiritual gifts.

By allowing a greater number of capable men to share equally in leadership, communication and sharing of information from different perspectives—especially between the young and old—is enhanced. Shared leadership increases interaction, which sharpens both decision making and character and provides true corporate wisdom by those who are wisest: ". . . in abundance of counselors there is victory" (Proverbs 11:14). In the end, shared leadership produces better community leadership than is possible when a lone pastor is forced to assume all responsibility.

**NOTES**

1. Archibald Thomas Robertson, *Paul's Joy in Christ* (1917; reprint ed., Grand Rapids: Baker Book House, 1979), page 43.
2. E. Best, "Bishops and Deacons: Philippians 1:1," in *Studia Evangelica*, ed. F. L. Cross (Berlin: Akademia Verlag, 1968) 4:371.
3. Polycarp, Philippians 5.
4. Polycarp, Philippians 5,6,11.
5. W. A. Jurgens, ed. and trans., *The Faith of the Early Fathers*, 3 vols.

PHILIPPIANS 1:1

(Collegeville, Minnesota: The Liturgical Press, 1979), 2:194.
6. J. B. Lightfoot, *Saint Paul's Epistle to the Philippians*, 4th ed. (reprint ed., New York: Macmillan and Co., 1894), page 95.
7. John Eadie, *A Commentary on the Greek Text of the Epistles of Paul to the Thessalonians*, ed. William Young (1877; reprint ed., Minneapolis: James Publications 1976), page 4.
8. Bruce Stabbert, *The Team Concept* (Tacoma: Hegg Bros. Printing, 1982), pages 27-44.

Answering those who seek to use Epaphras, Timothy, James, and others as evidence for a singular pastorate, Stabbert replies (pages 30, 35, 37, 43):

It seems that the evidence points to an evangelist's ministry for Epaphras, rather than a pastoral one. Even if we should call Epaphras a pastor . . . , we would still have no proof that Epaphras was the only pastor or the chief pastor of the Colossian flock. . . . There is in the end nothing which demands taking Epaphras as the pastor of Colosse. . . .

. . . Since Timothy is so regularly called a partner and co-worker with Paul, could it be that his duties merely reflect the ministries of an apostolic representative? Actually, the only semi-official titles given to Timothy would lead us to believe that he was not a pastor at all, but rather an evangelist-missionary who worked with Paul. Timothy is called "God's fellow-worker in the gospel of Christ" (1 Thessalonians 3:2). . . .

Apparently, Timothy's specialty was to go back to a church that had been founded earlier in order to encourage and strengthen them. His was a follow-up ministry. . . .

. . . it is not peculiar to see James in leadership over the Jerusalem church. . . . As a resident apostle, who took care of Jerusalem matters while the other apostles apparently traveled (implied perhaps in Galatians 1:18,19), it is natural that he would superintend the affairs there. Yet, in no instance is James called an elder; nor does his peculiar ministry at Jerusalem need to reflect anything more unusual than that of another apostle of the order of Paul. The singular bishop is still unproven in James.

Answering those who seek to use the angels of the churches in Revelation as proof for the one-pastor system, Stabbert states (pages 31-33):

The main problems with the pastor view is that every other time that John uses "angel" he means a celestial being. . . .

. . . But the term "angel" never elsewhere is a title for church leaders. . . .

What has really been solved even if we could all be agreed that these angels were men? . . . Lange's commentary poses the question well: "No opinion is expressed as to whether by the angel is meant a single prelate, a bench of presbyters, or the moderator of a presbytery. . . . These are questions which

[140]

are not determinable from the passage before us, and which can
be determined only from a discussion of the entire scriptural
teaching on the subject of church order . . ." (Rev. p. 108).
What we usually find is that men tend to find in these angel-
leaders a justification for whatever view of church leadership
they had at the start of their investigation.
Bruce Stabbert concludes by saying, "The scripture is clear in this
respect, it consistently presents plurality as the pattern for local
church leadership. Plurality is biblical!"

9. John F. MacArthur, Jr., *Answering the Key Questions About Elders*
(Panorama City: Word of Grace Communications, 1984), page 27.
10. James M. Boice, *Foundations of the Christian Faith* (Downers
Grove: Inter-Varsity Press, 1986), page 632.
11. Gene Getz, *Sharpening the Focus of the Church* (Chicago:
Moody Press, 1974), page 121.
12. Jon Zens, "The Major Concepts of Eldership in the New Testament,"
*Baptist Reformation Review* 7 (Summer, 1978): 28.
13. Stabbert, *The Team Concept*, pages 25, 26.
14. MacArthur, *Answering Key Questions*, page 1.
15. Alexander Rattray Hay, *The New Testament Order for Church and
Missionary* (Audubon, New Jersey: New Testament Missionary
Union, 1947), page 284.
16. Ignatius, Ephesians 6.
17. Ignatius, Trallians 3.
18. Earl D. Radmacher, *The Question of Elders* (Portland: Western
Baptist Press, 1977), page 9.
19. *Ibid.*, page 11.
20. Phyllis Thompson, *D. E. Hoste "A Prince with God"* (London:
China Inland Mission, 1947), page 119.
21. Radmacher, *Question of Elders*, page 7.
22. Robert Greenleaf, *Servant Leadership* (New York: Paulist Press,
1977), page 63.
23. Erroll Hulse, "The Authority of Elders," *Reformation Today* 44
(July-August, 1978): 5.

# Chapter 11

# *The Elders' Work, Attitudes, and Rewards*

> *Therefore, I exhort the elders among you, as your fellow elder and witness of the sufferings of Christ, and a partaker also of the glory that is to be revealed, shepherd the flock of God among you, exercising oversight not under compulsion, but voluntarily, according to the will of God; and not for sordid gain, but with eagerness; nor yet as lording it over those allotted to your charge, but proving to be examples to the flock. And when the Chief Shepherd appears, you will receive the unfading crown of glory. You younger men, likewise, be subject to your elders; and all of you, clothe yourselves with humility toward one another, for God is opposed to the proud, but gives grace to the humble.*
>
> *1 Peter 5:1-5*

\* \* \*

### *The Elders' Work*

The biblical image of a shepherd caring for his flock—standing long hours watching over its safety, leading it to fresh pasture, carrying the weak, seeking the lost, healing the wounded and sick—is precious. The whole image of shepherding is characterized by intimacy, tenderness, skill, hard work, and love. The shepherd-sheep relationship is so rich and beautiful that God uses it to describe the way He cares for His people. He also uses it to describe His people and those who care for them. Here, in 1 Peter 5, the Spirit of God passionately charges the elders of the churches of Asia to shepherd the flock of God. This exhortation carries an extremely relevant and needed message for today's spiritual leaders.

First Peter 5 is unique because it is the only passage in a New Testament letter that singles out elders from the rest of the believers for direct exhortation. The only other example of direct exhortation to elders is found in Paul's message to the Ephesian elders (Acts 20:17 ff.). In fact, the Acts and 1 Peter passages are very similar. Peter's message, however, is different in that it appeals to the elders to shepherd God's flock in the proper Christian manner, and promises a reward for those who shepherd the Lord's people.

Peter—like Luke, Paul, and James—refers to local church leaders as, "elders." There were recognized elders in each Christian community throughout all five of the Roman provinces Peter addresses: Pontus, Galatia, Cappadocia, Asia, and Bithynia (1 Peter 1:1). The type of leadership and organization implied in this passage corresponds to what we saw in Acts and Paul's letters. Peter writes from the viewpoint that each congregation had an official body of elders (plural) to whom he directs his exhortation. It is obvious that he knows of no singular overseer (bishop) who rules the local congregation as was the case in the second century. However, despite the overwhelming evidence, scholars today almost totally deny the uniformity in church government seen throughout the epistles and book of Acts.

It is interesting to note that Peter uses the designation, "elders," rather than *overseers* in writing to these predominately Gentile churches. *Elder* was most likely the more common term used to describe the local church leadership body. It is to these elders that Peter directs the mandate to "shepherd the flock of God."

*Fellow elder, sufferer, and partaker of the glory.* The earnestness of Peter's exhortation to the Asian elders is displayed by his threefold personal identification as a fellow elder, a witness of Christ's sufferings, and a partaker of the glory to come (1 Peter 5:1). No other group in the letter receives such a persuasive personal appeal, so we cannot be indifferent to what Peter says. The well-being of God's flock is at stake.

When Peter appeals to the Asian elders as a "fellow elder," he places himself on the same level as those he is addressing. His identification as a fellow elder is not a pious platitude. Peter was at one time a local elder, so he can fully sympathize with the problems and dangers the elders face. Peter left his responsibilities in Jerusalem in the hands of James and the body of elders, but he never forgot the lessons he learned while an elder. Even though the twelve apostles probably never carried the name *elder*, they were the Jerusalem community's acting elders during its initial years. Since the term *elder* is flexible enough to apply to any community leader, Peter, as an apostle, was in a real sense an elder to the whole Christian community—even at the time he wrote his letter. He had every right to refer to himself as a fellow elder, and made his appeal from a wealth of related experiences.

Not only is Peter a fellow elder, he is also a fellow sufferer with the Asian elders because he, too, witnessed Christ's sufferings (1 Peter 4:13). He can testify to suffering just as much as they can. In accordance with such suffering he, too, shares in the joyous anticipation of the future glory that will be revealed when Christ appears. These credentials show how qualified Peter is to make his exhortation to the Asian elders. Peter had shared in the pressures, joys, and sorrows of eldership. His intent in this rather lengthy personal identification is to draw the elders closer to himself in order to more effectively inspire them to heed his urgent appeal to properly shepherd God's flock.

### Shepherding

After establishing his credibility, Peter charges the Asian elders to "shepherd the flock of God among you." Peter's command demands urgent attention. He uses an aorist imperative verb—"shepherd the flock." Peter's charge (derived from the Greek word, *poimaino*, meaning to shepherd or tend) is not just limited to feeding the flock, but includes the full shepherding responsibility—the overall care of God's flock. Peter is, in effect, commanding the elders to be what good shepherds should be, or, as Lenski says, to "do everything that shepherding requires."[1] Solomon also expresses this same thought: "Know well the condition of your flocks, And pay attention to your herds" (Proverbs 27:23).

Again, the mandate to pastor the local church is given to the entire body of elders, not to one man. Peter's exhortation is to "the elders," so there is no lone pastor, only pastors. These elders, then, are the ones whom Peter charges to be everything a shepherd (pastor) should be and do everything a shepherd should do.

Peter's message is urgently important. The Bible teaches that people are like sheep. Sheep cannot be left unattended. Their well-being depends on a great deal of care and attention. They must be constantly fed, guided, protected, and nurtured in many practical ways. As God's sheep, people need to be fed God's Word, protected from false teachers, and protected from internal clashes. They need constant encouragement, comfort, guidance, prayer, correction, and a listening ear. As a result, the elder's life is one of devoted work, long hours, and skillful management. At times, it is even a life of danger, as was the case for the Asian elders who were endangered by prevailing persecution.

Unfortunately, many people today have a different concept of the task church elders are called to do. In most churches, elders meet with the pastor to develop and administer church programs and approve budgets. Such elders are policymakers and administrators, not shepherds. They make sure the church institution keeps running but have little involvement in the people's personal lives. Stephen B. Clark observes that true community life in many churches has therefore been lost.

> However, in most churches in the Western world, the institutional elements predominate over communal elements . . .

> . . . the leaders of most modern churches concern themselves more directly with the institution than with the people, and their leadership consists primarily of administration, decision-making, and opinion-forming. The people's lives are a private matter. The leader will counsel someone upon request. The leader will run a program for those who want something enough to sign up and participate. The leader thus provides services for some individuals when they express a personal interest. The authority of church leaders extends over the institution—the common activities—but not the lives of the church members.[2]

Instead of being a living community then, most churches have become institutions where the staff and elders serve as administrators. This, however, is not how God intends His people to operate. In the Old Testament, people went directly to the elders for personal help and counsel. As community leaders, the elders judged the most intimate family matters.

Likewise, the New Testament elders are charged to shepherd the local church. They are to lead the people, protect them from false teaching, admonish them, teach them, counsel them, rebuke them, care for them, and even go to their bedsides to pray. The elders are much more like shepherds or fathers than corporate board members. Of course, as overseers of the church, elders must supervise budgets and programs, but that task is secondary to caring for the people. Deacons or church committees can also administer finances and programs.

Because the work of shepherding the Lord's people is so demanding, few men actually desire it. Unfortunately, those who do must often be exhorted, as Peter does here, to be conscientious in their work. Inattentive, non-functioning elders are a serious problem. It is easy for an elder to be sidetracked with other tasks. An elder may excuse his inattentiveness, but he will be out of touch with the people and they will suffer. An elder may watch only a small part of the flock (his favorites), neglecting others who need attention. Or, an elder may only perform one aspect of his work, forgetting that healthy sheep need to be led, fed, protected, and cared for in many practical ways.

To take the awesome responsibility of pastoring God's flock lightly is a serious matter. Yet taking the work of eldership lightly is the most common fault of elders and the greatest frustration for God's people. In many cases, elders who are elders in name only cause this frustration. They are "Sunday morning" elders. Six days a week, these elders feed and care for no one. They have no heart or skill in the work of shepherding. They wear shepherds' clothes but refuse to go into the fields with the sheep. They want the title, but not the work. No wonder the sheep of such shepherds feel aimless, weak, and unloved! The solution to the problem of elders' inattentiveness and sloth is their renewed obedience to the Holy Spirit's urgent, imperative command for elders to be all that a shepherd should be in caring for God's flock.

In complete harmony with his shepherd imagery, Peter refers to those the elders tend as "the flock of God among you." This metaphor stresses the fact that the congregation is God's precious possession—the sheep He loves and cares for—and enhances the elders' urgent responsibility to care for God's flock. Elders must remember that the flock is not their own, but God's, and His flock is of infinite worth to Him. The flock metaphor also shows the church's dependence, weakness, helplessness, and need for feeding, protection, and care. Other metaphors demonstrate the church's strength and splendor, but the shepherd/flock metaphor illustrates its dependence and ownership (Luke 12:29-32).

The image of the local church as a flock, however, must not stand in opposition to other biblical truths about the church. Improper use of the shepherd/flock image has resulted in serious error and abuse. For example, many of the Lord's people have been reduced to an inferior status and become totally dependent upon a shepherd despot. This is not what Scripture intends.

We must remember that each metaphor emphasizes a particular truth regarding a different aspect of God's church. Each metaphor is limited in its ability to portray all dimensions of the church. But when these diverse images are placed together, one sees a balanced and glorious picture of the church's privileges and responsibilities.

*Overseeing.* Immediately before Peter elaborates on the proper manner of shepherding God's flock, he adds the participle exercising oversight (Greek, *episkopeo*, the corresponding verb to *episkopos*, overseer).[3] He writes, "exercising oversight not under compulsion, but voluntarily." The terms *shepherding* and *overseeing* are so closely associated that Peter can use one or the other without confusion (cf. 1 Peter 2:25).[4] Shepherding is the vivid, figurative expression for governing, while overseeing is the literal term, which can be used to explain the work of the first; to shepherd the flock entails the general overall supervision and oversight of the entire company of saints. As in Acts 20, all three terms—elder, shepherd, and overseer—are used in the same context with respect to the same body of church leaders.

In Acts 20:28, Paul reminds the Ephesian elders that the Holy Spirit placed them in the church as overseers, specifically to shepherd the flock of God. Peter charges the elders to shepherd the flock of God, adding that they must oversee the church in the proper spirit. So the kind of overseers that Paul and Peter have in mind are shepherd-overseers.

Of the two terms, shepherding more fully describes the elders' work. In fact, in the only two places in Scripture where elders are addressed directly (Acts 20:28; 1 Peter 5:2), they are charged to shepherd the flock of God. (In each of these two accounts, the

church is specifically referred to as the flock of God.) Furthermore, the figurative term shepherding conveys a richer, more vivid
image than the literal term overseeing. There is an amazing like-
ness between real shepherds and real sheep, and God's shepherds
and His people. The shepherd-flock vocabulary communicates
the skillful, loving, sacrificial image of the leader-follower relationship that befits the Christian community and its leaders.
Shepherding or overseeing entails the overall spiritual care of
God's flock, the local Christian church. Thus, the elders' basic
responsibility can be described as the general pastoral oversight
of the local church.

The Old Testament provides many enlightening examples of
the elders' general community oversight. Briefly, the elders of
the community are men who sit as wise counselors at the city
gate to protect, administer justice, and govern the people. The
book of Acts reveals several examples of the New Testament elders'
general church supervision. In the assembly at Jerusalem, the
elders officially administered funds sent by Antioch for the poor
(Acts 11:30); handled all major transactions, problems, and communication with other churches (Acts 11:15; 21:17-26); and provided
counsel in difficult situations (Acts 21:20-25).

Furthermore, the elders' oversight of the community extends
to the practical care of its people. This is beautifully illustrated
in the New Testament by the elders' prayers for the physically
sick (James 5:13,14), their economic care for the poor (Acts 11:30;
20:33-35), their hospitality (1 Timothy 3:2; Titus 1:8), and the laying
on of hands (1 Timothy 4:14). Job's life impressively illustrates
what an elder's concern for the people's practical cares should
be (Job 29:7). In several touching passages, Job epitomizes the
ideal elder—a man of wisdom and justice who loves the community:
"Behold, you have admonished many,
And you have strengthened weak hands.
"Your words have helped the tottering to stand,
And you have strengthened feeble knees"
(Job 4:3,4).

Because I delivered the poor who cried for help,
And the orphan who had no helper.
"The blessing of the one ready to perish came upon me,
And I made the widow's heart sing for joy.

[148]

"I put on righteousness, and it clothed me;
My justice was like a robe and a turban.
"I was eyes to the blind,
And feet to the lame.
"I was a father to the needy,
And I investigated the case which I did not know.
"And I broke the jaws of the wicked,
And snatched the prey from his teeth"
(Job 29:12-17).

"Have I not wept for the one whose life is hard?
Was not my soul grieved for the needy?"
(Job 30:25).

Elders today would do well to use Job as a true model of practical pastoral care.

Aside from the general shepherding responsibilities explained above, the New Testament gives little detailed information regarding elders' duties. This frustrates some elders who would like a more detailed job description. Yet the New Testament explains the elders' work in general terms for at least two reasons. First, what local elders do depends largely on the size of the congregation (Acts 4:32-37; 6:1-6), the people's cultural and educational level (Acts 17:11), the elders themselves, and the gifts and abilities within the congregation. Among the New Testament churches one finds considerable diversity in the character, gifts, spiritual life, and maturity of the people. (Consider the differences between the congregations at Philippi, Corinth, Thessalonica, and Berea, for example.)

Second, and this is essential to grasp, the elders of the church do not do everything for the church. They are not the total ministry of the church. Ministry is the work of the whole congregation, with each Christian promoting the welfare and growth of others. Therefore, it is vitally important to understand that the elders are dependent upon the gifts and devotion of others for the proper growth and well-being of the body. As good stewards and supervisors, the elders want all members of the body to actively function according to their gifts. The local church is not merely a flock; it is also a body of Spirit-alive people. As long as the elders provide necessary pastoral oversight, a great deal of flexibility and freedom concerning church organization and work exists.

We must not lose sight of this God-given freedom and flexibility and impose rigid human regulations and traditions on the eldership.

### *The Proper Attitudes*

But how are the elders to oversee and shepherd God's flock? This is Peter's main subject. God is intensely concerned about the manner in which the elders shepherd His people. It's natural to shepherd the church in a worldly, selfish, unchristian manner. But elders must carry out the charge to shepherd God's flock in a distinctly Christian way. This is Peter's theme in the rest of verse two, and verse three. Jesus repeatedly taught His disciples to act in a humble, sacrificial, servant-like way. Peter reiterates this teaching, using the same terminology Jesus selected when He described the Gentile rulers as those who *lord it over* others (Matthew 20:25; Mark 10:42). Peter says the elders are to willingly and freely shepherd the flock through their godly example. Unwillingness to serve, using others for personal profit, and authoritarianism should never characterize the Christian way to lead God's flock. The three following adverbial contrasts indicate the improper and proper ways to oversee God's flock:

- "not under compulsion, but voluntarily"
- "not for sordid gain, but with eagerness"
- "nor yet as lording it over . . . but proving to be examples"

*Not under compulsion, but voluntarily.* According to Scripture, a divine compulsion for service is both necessary and good (1 Corinthians 9:16). However, in this instance, Peter uses "compulsion" in the negative sense, meaning without a true God-given desire and without proper human motivation (2 Corinthians 9:7; Philemon 14). Peter knows the elders' work will never be done properly if it is done by someone who feels forced to serve. It is far too difficult a task, with too many problems, dangers, and demands. Elders who minister begrudgingly, under constraint, are incapable of genuine care for people. Such elders will be unhappy, impatient, guilty, and ineffective overseers. In contrast, God demands that an elder have a willing heart, a true desire, and make a voluntary choice. Those who oversee the church "voluntarily" do it because they have a heartfelt burden for the Lord's people. They are willing to bear others' grief, sorrow, and cares. They are good shepherds who are willing to lay down their lives for the sheep.

The phrase, "according to the will of God," suggests that voluntary service is God's standard, God's way (1 Peter 1:15; 4:6). Just as God loves a cheerful giver—not a forced giver (2 Corinthians 9:7)—He demands willing shepherds to oversee His flock, not shepherds who serve under constraint.

*Not for sordid gain, but with eagerness.* Apparently temptation was close at hand for some of the early elders because Peter warns them against greed and using their position for financial profit. Evidently some of the elders received financial assistance (1 Timothy 5:17,18) or administered the community funds (Acts 11:30). Otherwise, there would be no need for Peter's warning. "Sordid gain" means dishonest gain resulting from greediness for money that rightfully belongs to someone else. Paul also lists the same stipulation as a qualification for eldership. This does not mean, however, that elders cannot receive financial provision from the church. What Peter condemns is a base, avaricious motive that only desires financial gain and uses people for personal profit. A man who shepherds the flock merely for financial reasons is, in the Bible's word, a hireling. He will not hold up under problems or persecutions (John 10:12,13), and will desert the people in the hour of trial.

Instead of shepherding for one's own profit, an elder is to oversee "with eagerness"—which means readily or with devoted zeal. Unlike the word, "voluntarily," which Peter uses in his first contrast, the term used here stresses enthusiasm, zeal, joy, and a readiness to serve. But like the word, "voluntarily," the term also expresses the heart's true desire. Hence, personal sacrifice or gain is no matter of concern for a good elder. Elders who serve with an eager spirit go beyond minimal duty, self-interest, and money. They are creative and seek to give their best.

*Nor yet as lording it over . . . but proving to be examples.* The final contrast addresses a more subtle temptation than that of greed. It addresses the lust for power, control, and authority over others. Elders lead, admonish, supervise, teach, and shepherd, all of which require leadership and authority. Therefore, elders face the temptation to control and dominate others, which for some is a greater temptation than the lust for money.

"Lording it over" others conveys the idea of gaining power or dominion over others. It is an authoritarian-type rule—the antithesis of the Christian way to lead God's flock—that has no place in God's household. When problems and conflicts increase, many leaders tend to become more domineering and authoritarian. But that is not God's way. Both Jesus Christ and Peter prohibit any individual or group within the church from lording it over their brethren like worldly leaders. In a brotherhood that is to be characterized by mutual love (1 Peter 1:22; 3:8; 4:8; 5:14), submission, and humility (1 Peter 2:13,14,18; 3:1; 5:5), there is absolutely no place for lordly rulers, or, as Peter says, ones who lord it over those in their care. In spite of these demands, churches began to adopt the world's lordly structures of rule, habitually fighting over power, status, and authority only a few centuries after Peter's death. How different church history would have been if men had only obeyed Christ instead of their own prideful thoughts and schemes!

The phrase, "those allotted to your charge," is difficult to understand. In Greek, only one word (*kleroi*) is used, which means lots, portions, or shares. So the clause literally reads, "nor as exercising lordship over the portions." What does Peter mean by this plural word? The prevailing view interprets the phrase to mean portions of the whole flock, or various congregations assigned by God to different groups of elders. If this view is correct, then God has sovereignly placed a specific group of people under the care of a specific body of elders. So elders have no right to lord it over what God has assigned to them.

In contrast to "lording it over those allotted to your charge," elders are to oversee the church by being "examples to the flock." Elders are not to drive the sheep, but are to lead them by the personal example of a godly walk in Christ. They lead by their example of Christian living; by their spiritual, moral, and godly character; by their obedience to God's Word; and by sacrificial service to the flock.

The greatest way to inspire and influence people's behavior and thinking for God is through personal example. Character and deed influence people, not official position or title. As Samuel Brengle has said, "The final estimate of men shows that history cares not an iota for the rank or title a man has borne, or the office he has held, but only the quality of his deeds and the character of his mind and heart."[5] In truth, elders who demonstrate love for God and service to His people are the ones who actually influence and change others for God. John Brown writes,

"What a blessed influence is the holy character and conduct of Christian elders calculated to diffuse through the church."[6]

The Spirit of God places a desire in the hearts of obedient people to seek godly examples to follow. Much of the Bible is biographical, giving examples of how (and how not) to live for God. Jesus is the greatest example of all (1 Peter 2:21). Paul practiced modeling Christ, and expected people to follow (1 Corinthians 4:16,17; 11:1; Galatians 4:12; Philippians 3:17; 1 Thessalonians 1:5,6; 2:1; 2 Thessalonians 3:7,9; 1 Timothy 4:12; Titus 2:7). Since elders are not sheep drivers or lords and rulers who reign over others, they are to lead the church of God by the living, visual power of example (1 Peter 5:3). Thus, the elders stand out among their brethren as those the community desires to follow and obey because of their irreproachable lives; their humble, loving service to others; and their sacrifice and suffering. In fact, the shepherd's power to lead depends largely on the reality of his character and service. The failure of elders to provide genuine examples of Christian living has been one of the greatest hindrances to Christian growth.

Today, men and women urgently search for living examples of true Christianity. Who can better provide the week-by-week, long-term examples of family life, business life, and church life than local church elders? Throughout this epistle, Peter emphasizes the importance of humility and submission (1 Peter 2:13-3:12; 5:5). If elders are petty tyrants who lord their authority over the church, others will follow their example, abusing and fighting one another for power and recognition. If the elders are examples of absolute fidelity to Scripture, then the congregation will be loyal to Scripture. If the elders trust in God, the people will trust God. If the elders love God and His people, the people will love. If the elders are peaceful, gentle, loving, and prayerful, the church (for the most part) will emulate their pattern of life. Finally, if the elders are humble, the people will be humble, avoiding much contention. If the elders are servant leaders, then the church will be marked by humble servanthood.

### Elders' Rewards

In verse 4, Peter adds a glorious promise to his solemn charge: "And when the Chief Shepherd appears, you will receive the unfading crown of glory." What could be more encouraging for faithful shepherds who face trials and persecutions than to think of Christ's return and His reward? When elders think of Christ as "the Chief Shepherd," their present work is enhanced and His return becomes even more personal. This characterization of Christ as "the Chief Shepherd," or shall we say, "Senior Pastor," also reminds the elders that they are His undershepherds and co-laborers. It also repeats the message of John 10:16 where Jesus says, "and they shall become one flock with one shepherd."

The truth that Christ is "the Chief Shepherd" also teaches that the elders *are men under authority* — the authority and rule of Jesus Christ. Thus, everything the elders teach and do must be in complete harmony with Christ's teaching and work. The elders are not free to speak or lead the people in any way they wish, for they must answer to the Master Shepherd. Everything the elders do will be judged on the basis of faithfulness to Christ, "the Chief Shepherd."

Someday Christ will appear. At that time, His undershepherds will receive an "unfading crown of glory." This does not mean elders will receive a glorious crown, but a "crown" of divine glory. (The adjective, "glory," is a genitive of apposition; the "glory" itself is the "crown.") Since it is a heavenly "crown of glory," it will never fade as earthly rewards do. What a time of victory and joy Christ's appearance will bring to elders who have faithfully shepherded God's flock! At that moment, their sacrificial work will be worth it all. Elders who by faith set their sights on the heavenly glory will experience less discouragement and fear. The promise of heavenly glory will also motivate elders to act on Peter's charge to pastor God's flock voluntarily, eagerly, and as examples worthy to be followed.

### Younger Men and the Elders

Following his exhortation to the elders, Peter turns to the younger men and says, "You younger men, likewise, be subject to your elders; and all of you, clothe yourselves with humility toward one another, for God is opposed to the proud, but gives grace to the humble." Possibly Peter means the "younger men" should submit to the older ones. If so, this is simply a general statement regarding proper Christian relationships between age groups, similar to 1 Timothy 5:1,2. However, because of the context and the connective, "likewise," it seems more likely that there is a close link in thought between verses one and four. In this view, the "younger men" are contrasted with the "elders." The "younger men" of the church, particularly those who are diligently working—eager for change and further service—are the most likely group to conflict with the church elders. If the eldership is stagnant or ineffective, the younger men are most likely to be discontent. Peter has just exhorted the elders not to lord it over the people, but he is also compelled to encourage the younger men to act responsibly and subject themselves to the elders so harmony will rule in the church.

Polycarp, in his letter to the Philippian church some 50 years later, also encourages the younger men to submit to the overseers: "Wherefore it is right to abstain from all these things, submitting yourselves to the presbyters and deacons as to God and Christ."[7] The best training a young man can have is to submit himself to the judgment of those the Lord places over him. He can learn a wealth of valuable wisdom through the experience of older, godly men. Someday he too will be sought out by younger men.

With this directive to younger men, Peter closes his exhortation to elders. In light of the existing persecution, everyone—especially the elders—needed Peter's encouragement and counsel. As a fellow elder, Peter knew that the elders' work is exceedingly difficult and becomes even more so in times of persecution. These persecuted Christians didn't need authoritarian leadership; they needed a shepherd's loving, tender leadership. That's why Peter exhorts the elders to shepherd God's flock in God's manner.

Yet even the best shepherds will inevitably be accused of a lordly spirit. Moses, for example, was falsely accused of lording it over the other leading men of the nation: ". . . 'You have gone far enough . . . why do you exalt yourselves above the assembly of the Lord?'" (Numbers 16:3). Because there is just as much conflict and misunderstanding in churches today as then, Peter offers a final word of advice. He says, "all of you, clothe yourselves with humility toward one another, for God is opposed to the proud, but gives grace to the humble." Only when everyone wears the garments of humility will peace and unity prevail.

**NOTES**
1. R. C. H. Lenski, *The Interpretation of the Epistles of St. Peter, St. John and St. Jude* (Minneapolis: Augsburg Publishing House, 1966), page 217.

2. Stephen B. Clark, *Man and Woman in Christ* (Ann Arbor: Servant Books, 1980), page 124.
3. The mid-fourth century Greek manuscript, Codex Vaticanus (B) omits the word, *oversight*, as does Codex Sinaiticus ( ℵ ), the eleventh century Codex Colbertinus (33), and Coptic Sahidac (the oldest Egyptian version). But oversight is included in the oldest, and perhaps best, manuscript (**P**⁷²) as well as in the Codex Sinaiticus by a later corrector, Codex Alexandrinus (A), Codex Leicestrensis (69), Codex Athous Laure (1739), the Latin Vulgate, the Coptic Bohairic, and all later manuscripts.

    I believe the evidence favors the inclusion of *oversight* in the text for the following reasons: first, the term *overseer* is superfluous. The text makes good sense without it, so it is difficult to see why someone would add it. It is not a characteristic interpolation. Second, the widespread belief that bishops and elders are different, and that elders do not do the work of bishops stands against it being included by later scribes. Third, the word *overseer* is a participle, and this agrees with Peter's frequent use of it. Fourth, Peter has already used the combination of shepherd and overseer in 2:25.
4. Numbers 27:16,17; Jeremiah 23:2; Ezekiel 34:11,12; Zechariah 11:16; Acts 20:28; 1 Peter 2:25; 5:2.
5. J. Oswald Sanders, *Spiritual Leadership* (Chicago: Moody Press, 1967) page 13.
6. John Brown, *Expository Discourses on 1 Peter*, 2 vols. (1848; reprint ed., Carlisle, Pennsylvania: The Banner of Truth Trust, 1975), 2:453.
7. Polycarp, Philippians 5.

# Chapter 12

# *Congregational Submission*

*Obey your leaders, and submit to them; for they keep*
*watch over your souls, as those who will give an account.*
*Let them do this with joy and not with grief, for this*
*would be unprofitable for you.*

*Hebrews 13:17*

\* \* \*

Contemporary personal values and attitudes about authority are
radically different from those taught in the Bible. Modern man,
for the most part, rejects the authority of Scripture, denies objective
standards of right and wrong, and refuses to accept the moral
absolutes of good and evil. As J. I. Packer points out, there is
growing contempt for all forms of authority: "Undisguised contempt
for restrictions and directions, and truculent defiance which bucks
all systems when it is not busy exploiting them, have become almost
conventional, and anyone who respects authority stands out as odd."[1]
In his usual lucid style, Chuck Swindoll further describes our age
as one in which:

> Not even the President of our nation carries the clout he once
> did. Ours is a talk-back, fight-back, get-even society that is
> ready to resist—and sue—at the slightest provocation. Instead
> of the obedient Minute Man representing our national image,
> a new statue with a curled upper lip, an open mouth screaming

obscenities, and both fists in the air could better describe our times. Defiance, resistance, violence, and retaliation are now our "style."[2]

For twentieth century Western people, values and authority have become relative and arbitrary. One of the perverse results of this moral relativism and loss of divine truth is modern man's obsession with personal rights, freedom, and self-fulfillment. Our age is characterized by an all-consuming selfishness. In his discussion of biblical authority, John D. Woodbridge has perceptively characterized our "me-first" society:

> . . . one of the principal reasons for today's onslaughts against biblical authority has to do with a previous point: many Americans want to live their lives according to their own fancies. A "Gospel of Self-Fulfillment" swept through the United States in the 1970's and helped nurture the spirit of a perverse narcissism. Anne David, professor of sociology . . . puts the matter bluntly: "Our culture promotes a type of pathological (disturbed) narcissism. . . . We have a lot of grown-up two year olds out there expecting to be happy now." Millions of Americans heed the siren-like message of the "Gospel of Self-Fulfillment." Now they sense that obeying the Bible's teachings would rain on their narcissistic parade.[3]

Thus, modern man has little understanding of community life, responsibility, obligation, or moral accountability. Even the family no longer has the power to hold itself together.

Because our modern secular society lacks a consensus on personal values, people demand that governments and religious institutions keep out of their personal lives and choices. It is common to hear that abortion, homosexuality, and divorce are private matters in which no one has the right to interfere. Therefore, few contemporary-minded people agree with the Bible's emphatic command to obey and submit to church leaders (Hebrews 13:17). Nor do they understand that Christians are accountable to one another and that church elders have the responsibility to involve themselves in people's personal lives. Contemporary people then, cannot understand church discipline, whether it be for doctrinal or moral reasons. They do not easily grasp that church overseers teach and enforce God's eternal values and laws, as revealed in the objective standard of God's Word.

In this age of perverse narcissism and rebellion against

authority, it is especially urgent to not only understand the elders' proper place and role in the church, but to thoroughly understand the congregation's proper response to its leaders. The tragedy, however, is that many evangelical churches operate more like secular society than God's community of saints. Church leaders often do not involve themselves in people's personal lives, nor do the people expect them to. People in the congregation divorce for unbiblical reasons, have abortions, and fight one another. Yet the church takes little or no action. Leaders and congregational members alike believe that these sins are private matters, when in fact they are community matters that demand attention. In stark contrast to this unfortunate mind set, being a member of a Christian community means placing oneself first under the authority of God's Word and second under the community leaders' authority. The Bible clearly teaches that elders are to shepherd, oversee, care for, lead, and admonish the people, and that the people are to submit, honor, and love their leaders.

### *The Congregation Is to Obey and Submit to Its Leaders*

It is tremendously important that Christians know what God says about submission and obedience to church leaders. Such knowledge is necessary for one's spiritual protection, growth, and blessing. Hebrews 13:17, more than any other New Testament passage, addresses the issue of the believer's responsibility to the church shepherds: "Obey your leaders, and submit to them."

The author's inspired exhortation calls for obedience and submission to the church's spiritual leaders. By using two imperative verbs of command, "obey" and "submit," the writer intensifies his charge. Thus, his message is conveyed as a matter of utmost importance. Although it is difficult to distinguish between the meaning of these two verbs, "submit" is the broader term. By using the word, *submit*, the author indicates that Christians are not only to "obey" their leaders, but are to "submit," that is, yield, give way, or defer to them. This includes obedience to their authority and directives, as well as a disposition of deference, respect, and subjection to the elders even when there are differences of opinion.

A spirit of obedience and submission is a key principle for right Christian living and service (Romans 16:19; 2 Corinthians 2:9; Philippians 2:12; Philemon 21; 1 Peter 1:2,14). Submission is the fruit of genuine humility and faith. So, first and foremost, the Bible says,

"Submit therefore to God . . ." (James 4:7). True submission to God, however, naturally expresses itself in obedience and submission to earthly authority. Genuine submission to God and His Word expresses itself in obedience and submission in the home, in marriage, at work, in society, and in the local assembly of believers. Submitting to others is a mark of the Spirit-filled life (Ephesians 5:18-6:9).

Children, for example, are commanded to obey their parents (Ephesians 6:1; Colossians 3:20). Christians are exhorted to submit to the rules and rulers of society (Romans 13:1; Titus 3:1; 1 Peter 2:17). Wives are to submit to their husbands (Ephesians 5:22; Colossians 3:18; Titus 2:5; 1 Peter 3:1,6). All Christian employees are to submit to their employers (Ephesians 6:5; Colossians 3:22; Titus 2:9; 1 Peter 2:18). Christians are also commanded to submit to their spiritual leaders: the apostles and their delegates (2 Corinthians 2:9; 7:15; 10:6; Philippians 2:12; 2 Thessalonians 3:10); all who devote themselves to the care of the saints (1 Corinthians 16:15,16); the elders (1 Peter 5:5); and all other church leaders (Hebrews 13:17). God, then, is truly concerned about how His people treat one another, particularly how they treat those in positions of authority. Submission to authority is absolutely necessary for the proper ordering of society, and the church of God is no exception. Indeed, submission to authority is often a test of our submission to God.

The effectiveness of any body of elders is measurably affected by the response of the people they lead. Look, for example, at the nation of Israel. Because of the people's awful rebellion and endless complaining, Moses, Aaron, the seventy elders, and all of the people involved were unable to enter the promised land. All were hurt by sins of rebellion and unbelief. Today, when God's people are proud, stubborn, or neglectful of their leaders, there is little progress, peace, or joy in the local church. The tragedy is that many churches are characterized by a fighting and uncooperative spirit, thereby dishonoring the name of Jesus Christ—the most humble servant of all. Only when believers properly submit to and honor their leaders will the peace and cooperation needed to grow and rejoice as a body of believers exist.

### The Elders Are to Watch Over the Souls of God's People
Although the term *elder* does not appear here, the exhortation for believers to obey and submit to church leaders would certainly

include the elders who lead the church (1 Timothy 5:17). In the early Christian congregations there were recognized leaders, designated in this passage by the Greek term, *hegoumenoi*, which is a general term used to describe various types of leaders. For example, in the Greek Old Testament, *hegoumenoi* refers to heads of tribes (Deuteronomy 5:23), a commander of an army (Judges 11:11), the ruler of the nation Israel (2 Samuel 5:2, 7:8), a superintendent of the treasury (1 Chronicles 26:24), and the chief priest (2 Chronicles 19:11). The early Christian leaders, however, must always be thought of in the context of Jesus Christ's teaching on leadership. They would not have been like some of the worldly rulers to whom this term is also applied.

Jesus also used the term *hegoumenos* to refer to leaders. In a paradoxical statement, Jesus says, ". . . let him who is the greatest among you become as the youngest, and the leader as the servant" (Luke 22:26). Clearly, Jesus defines leaders of His kingdom in terms of humility and servanthood, and Christians must understand leadership in the Christian community in the same manner. So, servant leaders—men who humbly use their gifts and abilities to serve the interests and meet the needs of those they lead—are the kind of leaders referred to in this passage. Obedience and submission to such leaders isn't a burdensome task.

The type of leadership mentioned here is shared leadership (*hegoumenoi* is plural) which is in perfect harmony with the rest of the New Testament's portrayal of the apostolic congregations. There is no question that early church leadership was multiple leadership. Guarding the spiritual welfare of the saints was the task of a team of shepherd-leaders.

Church leaders fully deserve to be obeyed because of their extremely important and self-sacrificing work. As shepherds and watchmen over the "souls" of God's people, they bear an awesome responsibility. (The rendering of "souls" for *psyche*, in the sense of spiritual well-being, seems preferable to the personal pronoun *you* that is found in some translations.) God will someday hold the elders accountable for those He placed under their care. The congregation's care has been entrusted to the elders, and they will be judged for their stewardship. So, obedience and submission to the elders is in perfect harmony with their God-given responsibility to watch over the souls of those entrusted to them. One who refuses to submit to God's watchmen may face spiritual disaster.

Elders are to "keep watch over" the souls of those under their care. The verb, "keep watch" (Greek, *agrypneo*), conveys the idea of vigilance, tireless effort, self-discipline, great care, and concern that could even lead to the loss of sleep. The concept of keeping watch may apply to city watchmen or the shepherds/overseers of a flock. Like city watchmen or shepherds, the elders must always be keenly alert. Watching over the souls of the Lord's people is a task that, if taken lightly, could result in serious harm to the ones requiring attention. Watching over others' safety and growth is a highly responsible and essential task. Since false teachers and spiritual pitfalls abound, since all Christians start out as newborn babes in Christ, and since some Christians are perpetually weak in faith, leaders who watch over the church's well-being are absolutely essential.

The book of Hebrews itself illustrates the critical need for spiritual watchmen. Some of the Hebrew Christians seriously neglected the truth, were spiritually apathetic, compromised with Judaism's old ways, feared hardship, were bitter, became backsliders, and disregarded God's undershepherds. So, the shepherds who cared for this needy flock faced situations requiring vigilant attention. If the elders were the ones who alerted the writer of Hebrews to the congregation's problems, then they are an excellent example of watchfulness. They were undoubtedly stable, mature Christians in whom the author had complete confidence. However, they needed the obedience and submission of those under their care in order to protect the congregation so it would experience vitality and growth.

*Accountability*. The writer of Hebrews greatly intensifies the solemn responsibility of watching over the Lord's people by adding the phrase, "as those who will give an account." As undershepherds or watchmen, the elders must "give an account" of their stewardship to the Master. God will ask, "What have you done?" And the elders will have to answer Him. In the Old Testament, God promised that He would call the watchman into account for his holy responsibility:

"When I say to the wicked, 'You shall surely die'; and you do not warn him or speak out to warn the wicked from his wicked way that he may live, that wicked man shall die in his iniquity, but his blood I will require at your hand.

"Yet if you have warned the wicked, and he does not turn from his wickedness or from his wicked way, he shall die in his iniquity; but you have delivered yourself" (Ezekiel 3:18,19).

Paul, too, viewed himself as a watchman accountable to God for those entrusted to his care: "'Therefore I testify to you this day, that I am innocent of the blood of all men. For I did not shrink from declaring to you the whole purpose of God'" (Acts 20:26,27). Along with the leader's greater privileges come greater responsibilities to one's fellow man and to God. Scripture says that teachers will receive a more severe judgment because of their influence and responsibility (James 3:1). Since positions of teaching and leadership require greater responsibility and accountability, a wise individual will never rush into leadership for his own self-glory. Such action will only bring judgment and reproach on the individual and those he leads.

The elders' accountability to God should greatly affect the quality of their leadership. Indeed, elders who have a deep sense of their accountability to the Lord will inevitably do a more conscientious job. Paul is a good example of this. He knew the certainty of God's evaluation of his labor, and diligently sought God's approval (1 Corinthians 4:1-5; 9:27; 2 Corinthians 5:9-11; 2 Timothy 2:15; 4:7,8). When we, as God's people, understand that our leaders must give an account to God for their leadership, we will be much more tolerant, understanding, and appreciative of their actions. We will be more willing to yield and submit to them.

*Make the work a joy for your leaders.* There is inexpressible joy in caring for the Lord's people. In fact, few greater joys exist than seeing lives changed by the gospel—watching people grow in Christ, heed correction and warning, bear fruit, and live in loving harmony with others. John, the apostle, felt such joy: "I have no greater joy than this, to hear of my children walking in the truth" (3 John 4). But that joy, which every leader has a right to expect (2 Corinthians 2:3), is possible only when the people truly submit to their leaders. So Scripture counsels believers to let the difficult work of watching over the Lord's people become a joyous work by obeying and submitting to their leaders.

When there is disobedience, rebellion, and self-will, the joy of leadership vanishes. When Christians refuse to heed the watchmen's warning, the watchmen groan in sorrow. That's why the author of Hebrews exhorts his readers to let their leaders do their work without "grief," or literally without groaning, sighing, or moaning. He writes, "let them do this with joy, and not with grief."

The word *grief* expresses a strong inward emotion—an emotion that words are unable to articulate (Mark 7:34; Romans 8:23,26). In this context, the word expresses deep sorrow and longing for better conditions. "Grief" will be present in leaders' hearts whenever their warnings go unheeded, whenever there is rebellion and disobedience, and whenever the spiritual condition of the people wanes.

Godly elders are deeply concerned about the flock. They sigh over sheep that willfully wander after false teaching. They groan in sorrow over others who refuse to grow, learn, change, or receive correction. The flock's coldness of heart, indifference to truth, senseless fighting, and resistance to help takes its toll on the shepherds. Moses is a good example of a leader who suffered because of the people's disobedience and stubbornness. At one time in his life, the situation became so intolerable that Moses called on God to take his life: "I alone am not able to carry all this people, because it is too burdensome for me. So if Thou art going to deal thus with me, please kill me at once, if I have found favor in Thy sight, and do not let me see my wretchedness" (Numbers 11:14,15).

Paul also suffered many heartaches because of his converts' disobedience. Anyone who watches over the spiritual lives of people will eventually experience deep sorrow over their disobedience, waywardness, and stubbornness. Because people willfully rebel and endlessly complain, many good elders eventually resign from their work; they become too weary to carry the people's burdens. In the end, everyone in the congregation suffers from the disobedience of wayward members.

*Spiritual disaster.* God appoints elders for the spiritual profit of His people, but the elders' success in a large measure depends on the people's response. All the shepherds' good efforts are fruitless if the sheep disobey or run away. While disobedience distresses church leaders, it has an even more serious impact on the wayward believer. Ultimately, the disobedient believer is hurt, or as the writer to the Hebrews says, "this would be unprofitable for you."

The author's remark is an intentional understatement. It is a literary device, called a *litotes*, in which a milder, negative statement is used instead of a strong, affirmative statement. It is the opposite of an hyperbole. (For example, instead of saying, "really great work," we might say, "not bad work.") The expression causes the reader to stop, think, and fill in the fuller meaning. Stated positively, this clause would read, "that is harmful to you," or "that is disasterous for you." God may severely chastise the disobedient believer (Hebrews 12:5-11; 1 Corinthians 11:29-34), the devil may delude the mind (2 Corinthians 11:3), or a bitter spirit may set in, halting all growth and maturity. When this happens, all the God-given benefits of the shepherding ministry are lost. To cut oneself off from God's watchmen is dangerous business. Yet tragically that is precisely how many Christians handle their sin and their conflicts. To refuse to heed the cries and pleas of those in authority within the church may result in spiritual catastrophe. Look, for example, at the awful consequences of Israel's disobedience and rebellion; the people suffered far greater harm than Moses. Consider also the child who causes his parents deep sorrow because of disobedience, and eventually ruins himself. Christians can avoid much heartache, confusion and suffering if they will heed Scripture's exhortation to obey and submit to their leaders. While it may sound harsh, this injunction benefits and protects Christians. It is a strong command, but if obeyed it will greatly strengthen the household of faith.

**NOTES**
1. J. I. Packer, *Freedom and Authority* (Oakland: International Council on Biblical Inerrancy, 1981), page 7.
2. Charles Swindoll, *Strengthening Your Grip* (Waco: Word Books, 1982), page 238.
3. John D. Woodbridge, "Recent Interpretations of Biblical Authority Part I: A Neo-orthodox Historiography under Siege," *Bibliotheca Sacra* 142 (January-March, 1985): 4, 5.

# Chapter 13

# *Only Qualified Men Can Serve as Elders*

> *For this reason I left you in Crete, that you might set in order what remains, and appoint elders in every city as I directed you, namely, if any man be above reproach, the husband of one wife, having children who believe, not accused of dissipation or rebellion. For the overseer must be above reproach as God's steward, not self-willed, not quick-tempered, not addicted to wine, not pugnacious, not fond of sordid gain, but hospitable, loving what is good, sensible, just, devout, self-controlled, holding fast the faithful word which is in accordance with the teaching, that he may be able both to exhort in sound doctrine and to refute those who contradict.*
>
> *Titus 1:5-9*

\*   \*   \*

A leading evangelical journal in America courageously brought together five divorced ministers and asked them to share their feelings, experiences, and views on divorce and the ministry.[1] The ministers' thoughts were presented in the journal through an open forum format. The journal's staff published the forum because they believed the growing problem of divorce among ministers needed to be faced honestly. In fact, the article claimed that a recent survey of divorce rates by profession in the United States showed that ministers had the third highest divorce rate, exceeded only by that of medical doctors and policemen![2] Along with the forum, the journal published seven well-known evangelical leaders' responses to the divorced ministers' comments. What is monumentally significant about the article is that not one of the seven leaders mentioned the biblical qualifications for pastors (elders)! This article reveals a widespread ignorance within the Christian community of Scripture's vigorous statements concerning qualifications for local church leaders. From the New Testament's perspective, the five divorced pastors do not even qualify to be deacons, let alone pastors (elders) of churches.

### Insisting upon God's Requirements

On the matter of qualification for eldership, the New Testament is emphatic—only spiritually and morally qualified men can be elders. On this point there is no debate. Not just anyone who wants to be an elder can become one. Only those men who meet God's qualifications can become part of the pastoral leadership of the congregation.

Twice the New Testament insists that an overseer be properly qualified (1 Timothy 3:1-7; Titus 1:5-9). Proper qualification is a scriptural imperative, objective requirement, moral obligation, indispensable standard, and absolute necessity for those who would serve as leaders in the church. The New Testament gives more instruction regarding the elders' qualifications than on any other aspect of eldership. In fact, an individual's qualifications must be carefully examined before he is allowed to serve as either an elder or deacon (1 Timothy 3:10). It's interesting to note that these qualifications are not required of gifted teachers or evangelists. One may be gifted as an evangelist and used of God in that capacity, yet be unqualified to be an elder. For example, an individual may be an evangelist immediately after conversion. But a new convert, Scripture says, cannot be an elder (1 Timothy 3:6).

In spite of the clear statements in Scripture regarding the elders' qualifications, people often take one of two extreme positions regarding the qualification of elders. The first is to ignore the full range of scriptural qualifications, thus permitting unqualified men to fill a crucial position of leadership. "Too often," Bruce Stabbert says, "men of money and secular influence or of good looks and eloquence are elected to church boards with little regard for their spiritual qualities."³ Ultimately this practice weakens and lowers the congregation's spiritual life. The other extreme is to add qualifications or restrictions that God doesn't demand, thus excluding needed and qualified men from church leadership. Roland Allen describes the situation this way:

> We are so enamoured of those qualifications which we have added to the apostolic that we deny the qualifications of anyone who possesses only the apostolic, whilst we think a man fully qualified who possesses only ours. A young student fresh from a theological college lacks many of those qualifications which the apostle deemed necessary for a leader in the house of God, the age, the experience, the established position and reputation, even if he possesses all the others. Him we do not think unqualified. The man who possesses all the apostolic qualifications is said to be unqualified, because he cannot go back to school and pass an examination.⁴

Such practices only serve to hold a congregation back from reaching its full potential. The only solution is to demand nothing less, or more, than God's standards for elders and deacons, a solution Francis Schaeffer implored Christians to follow: "The church has no right to diminish these standards for the officers of the Church, nor does it have any right to elevate any other as though they are then equal to these which are commanded by God himself. These and only these stand as absolute."⁵ What God prizes among the leaders of His people is not education, wealth, social status, success, or even great spiritual gifts. Rather, He values personal moral and spiritual character, requiring that those who lead His people be just, devout, self-controlled, peaceable, and forbearing with others. They must also be loyal husbands, good fathers, and men who are firmly committed to His Word. In other words, God requires the overseers of His people to be spiritually mature men. The kind of personal character that God requires of elders is revealed in the following separate lists of qualifications:

| 1 Timothy 3:2-7 | Titus 1:6-9 |
|---|---|
| 1. Above reproach | 1. Above reproach |
| 2. The husband of one wife | 2. The husband of one wife |
| 3. Temperate | 3. Having children who believe |
| 4. Prudent | 4. Not self-willed |
| 5. Respectable | |

| | |
|---|---|
| 6. Hospitable | 5. Not quick-tempered |
| 7. Able to teach | 6. Not addicted to wine |
| 8. Not addicted to wine | 7. Not pugnacious |
| 9. Not pugnacious | 8. Not fond of sordid gain |
| 10. Gentle | 9. Hospitable |
| 11. Uncontentious | 10. Lover of what is good |
| 12. Free from the love | 11. Sensible |
| of money | 12. Just |
| 13. Manages his | 13. Devout |
| household well | 14. Self-controlled |
| 14. Not a new convert | 15. Holding fast the faithful |
| 15. A good reputation with | Word—both to exhort |
| those outside the church | and refute |

Much of the weakness and waywardness of our churches today is directly due to our failure to insist that church leaders meet God's qualifications for leadership. Simple obedience to God's Word is the only solution to this problem. The main point of Titus 1:5-9 is this: only morally and spiritually qualified men can be appointed to the church eldership. If we want the local church to be spiritually fit, then we must insist that its leaders meet God's qualifications.

### Paul's Directive to Titus

Paul and Titus had been together on the island of Crete, but Paul left Titus behind to finish some uncompleted work: "For this reason I left you in Crete, that you might set in order what remains, and appoint elders in every city as I directed you" (Titus 1:5). Paul had preached the gospel on Crete and perhaps founded a number of churches there, although the historical record remains unclear. If Paul was the founder of these congregations, Titus was expected to establish elders in these newly planted communities, just as Paul had done on his first missionary journey (Acts 14:21-23). Evidently Titus was Paul's special temporary representative (Titus 3:12), and not the bishop of Crete as later tradition would have us believe.

Shortly after Paul's departure, he wrote to Titus and repeated his instructions. In a manner similar to his first letter to Timothy, Paul addresses his readers as their apostle and teacher, expecting them to obey his personal envoy, Titus. There is no indication that Titus was unfaithful or that Paul had lost confidence in him. Rather, the letter more formally and fully authorized Titus' task. Titus would have read the letter as he performed various functions of his ministry such as teaching and appointing elders. Thus, as explained in Titus 2:15, Titus administered Paul's own instructions: "These things speak and exhort and reprove with all authority. Let no one disregard you."

Paul immediately states his reason for leaving Titus in Crete: "that you might set in order what remains." The apostle was saying that unfinished matters still needed to be set right within the churches on Crete. The congregations on Crete lacked proper order and instruction, and Paul was not able to complete the job of setting them in order. So Titus was left behind to complete what Paul had started. The kind of setting in order Paul has in mind is specifically conveyed by his statement, "appoint elders in every city as I directed you." This is a significant and important message. It teaches us that a church is not fully and properly established until elders are appointed. Setting churches in order means to establish a body of qualified elders in each church.

Of course churches can exist without elders, as we saw in Acts 14:23. Indeed, if Paul, as many think, was not the founder of the congregations on Crete, then these churches existed without elders for a long time. But, a church must have elders if it is to be properly structured and strengthened. As an apostle and teacher, Paul set these immature gatherings of Christians in order by appointing elders, much as he had done in Acts 14:21-23.

Regardless of the historical situation, Paul clearly directed Titus to "appoint elders." The Greek word for "appoint" (*kathistemi*), means to "appoint, especially to an office or position."[6] Since there were no elders in these churches, Titus was to appoint qualified men to eldership. Paul's terminology, however, suggests nothing about the actual procedure of appointing these elders (cf. Acts 14:23). The phrase, "in every city," means in every church, since the New Testament churches embraced all believers within a particular city (see endnote on Acts 20:17). It was imperative that Titus make his appointments according to Paul's directive: "appoint elders in every city as I directed you." Since the "I" is emphatic in the original language, Paul was making an authoritative, apostolic charge or directive. Paul gave specific orders on this vital matter so neither Titus his representative, nor the local Christians, could do as they pleased. Elders were only to be appointed according to God's directive.

But what exactly is Paul's directive? The answer to this question focuses on a crucial point: not just anyone can be an elder, nor can anyone set up his own standards for appointment to eldership. Elders must be appointed according to the directive of God's Spirit, given to us in Titus 1:6-9: "Namely, if any man be above reproach." Paul's thought is abbreviated here, so in order to understand what he is saying, we need to expand his words in a manner such as this: "Appoint elders as I had directed you, that is, consider only the kind of man who is above reproach in moral character for appointment to eldership." F. F. Bruce's paraphrase conveys Paul's meaning quite well:

> The reason I left you behind in Crete was this: I wanted you to set right the things that remained to be dealt with, and in particular to appoint elders in each city, in accordance with my directions.
>
> You remember those directions of mine about the kind of man who is fit to be appointed as an elder—one who is beyond reproach. . . . The man who exercises pastoral leadership must be beyond reproach because that befits a steward in God's house.[7]

At an earlier time, Paul told Titus that an elder must be morally above reproach and reminds him of the fact again. As in 1 Timothy 3:1-7, the basis for appointment to the eldership is moral character, not education, gift, age, status, need, or talent. This is God's criterion that no man or organization has the right to change. Elders "must be" morally qualified. Notice that Paul does not change subjects in verse six, although he does change from the plural, "elders," to the singular, "any man." Paul is still speaking about elders, so only those who are "above reproach" can qualify for the body of elders.

*Above reproach.* The term "above reproach" (*anegkletos*, meaning unaccused) indicates one whose character and conduct has not been called into question, or one who is free from accusation. The synonym in 1 Timothy 3:2 emphasizes that nothing in the person would cause an opponent to make a damaging charge against him, thus the person is irreproachable or unassailable. The first qualification in Titus, as in 1 Timothy, stands out as the fundamental qualification under which all other qualifications are subsumed. An elder must be "above reproach" in all his affairs. This means that a Christian elder must be a man with a good moral and spiritual reputation who lives an irreproachable life in the sight of other people. An elder must be free from any offensive or damaging blight of character or conduct so critics cannot discredit his beliefs or prove him unfit to be a community leader.

Job was undoubtedly an elder among his people (Job 29:7). His upright character, above all else, qualified him to be a man God delighted in. In Job 1:1, we read a description of Job's character: "There was a man in the land of Uz, whose name was Job, and that man was blameless, upright, fearing God, and turning away from evil." God insists on irreproachable character because an elder is God's steward (Titus 1:7). An elder represents God. He is entrusted with God's household, God's possessions, God's treasures, and God's riches. He acts on behalf of God's interests. An elder is accountable and responsible to God. No earthly monarch would dare think of using an immoral, uncontrolled, or unfaithful person to manage his estate. Likewise, God demands that those entrusted with the supervision of His house be morally and spiritually fit. A noble occupation thus demands a noble character (1 Timothy 3:1,2).

The very nature of the church also requires leaders of high moral character. The local church is made up of saints or holy ones who form a temple of God (1 Corinthians 3:16,17). God calls His redeemed saints to live holy and righteous lives in a chaotic and sinful world. So it is understandable that those among the saints who are called to leadership be morally fit.

The elders, as Peter says, are examples to the people (1 Peter 5:3). Therefore, they must represent what God desires every member of the congregation to be in character and conduct. Those inside as well as outside the church first look to those who stand as leaders. It is understandable if a new or struggling believer falls prey to sin or hyprocrisy, but when one who leads the congregation is found in reproach, the world blasphemes the teaching of the gospel, and saints within the church become disillusioned—some even turning away from the church. For these reasons, the stewards of God's household must be above reproach.

Furthermore, local congregations tend to mold themselves according to their leaders—a tendency clearly seen throughout the Old Testament. When Israel had a bad king, for example, the people were sinful. When Israel had a good king, the people followed the Lord. Because people are like sheep, their shepherds have a profound impact on their direction and spiritual well-being. Therefore:

• If an elder has a contentious spirit, the people will inevitably become contentious. So, a man with a contentious disposition is not qualified for eldership—even if he has the greatest teaching gift in the world (1 Timothy 3:3; Titus 1:7).

• If an elder is not hospitable, the people will be unfriendly and cold (1 Timothy 3:2; Titus 1:8).

• If an elder loves money, he will subtly use the people and work for his own ends (1 Timothy 3:3). Following his example, the people, too, will become lovers of money.

• If an elder is not just and devout, he will be unable to rightly discern critical issues and problems (Titus 1:8), causing the people to become unjust and disloyal to the truth.

• If an elder is not sensible, balanced, and self-controlled, his judgments will be characterized by disorganization, aimlessness, and ugly extremes—as will the judgments of the entire congregation (1 Timothy 3:1,2; Titus 1:8).

• If an elder is not a faithful, one-woman husband, he will ultimately encourage others to be unfaithful (1 Timothy 3:2; Titus 1:6).

• If an elder does not faithfully hold to the Word, the people will not. Such an elder will be unable to guide the church through the fierce storms of Satanic error (Titus 1:9).

What the churches of Jesus Christ need in the way of leadership is men of deep inner spiritual and moral character. The best systems, laws, and constitutions are impotent without men who are just, devout, lovers of what is good, sensible, self-controlled, forbearing, free from the love of money, uncontentious, and faithful keepers of God's Word. These are precisely the qualities that God requires of those who lead His people.

*The husband of one wife.* See comments on 1 Timothy 3:2.

*A father who controls his children properly.* Not only is an elder to be a one-woman man, he must have proper control of his children (see 1 Timothy 3:4). The translation, "having children who believe, not accused of dissipation or rebellion," is better rendered as having *faithful children*, which is its rendering in the *King James Version*. This translation renders the Greek word, *pistos*, in a passive sense meaning faithful, loyal, trustworthy, trusted, or dutiful (1 Corinthians 4:17), which better suits the strong contrast with "dissipation or rebellion" that follows. In other words, Paul does not set up a contrast between believing and unbelieving children. Even the best Christian fathers cannot guarantee that all their children will really believe. To say this passage means believing Christian children places an impossible standard upon a father. Salvation is a supernatural act of God. God, not good parents (although they are used of God), ultimately brings salvation (John 1:12,13).

While the characterization of a prospective elder's children as faithful does not mean they must be believers, it implies that they must be responsible and faithful family members. This requirement is similar to that of 1 Timothy 3:4,5, where an elder's children are expected to be submissive and under his control. Here, though, the qualification is stated in a more positive way—the elder must have children who are loyal and dutiful, good citizens, or—as we might say today—responsible children.

In contrast to faithful children, an elder must not have children who are "accused of dissipation or rebellion." These are very strong words. "Dissipation" means debauchery, profligacy, or wild, immoral living (cf. 1 Peter 4:3,4; Luke 15:13). Nigel Turner describes dissipation this way: "It is more than wastefulness, worse than prodigality, and nothing short of immoral debauchery and excessive lewdness."[8] "Rebellion" means to not be subject to control, to be disobedient, unruly, or insubordinate. Such children not only bring disgrace and shame upon their father, as Eli's children did (1 Samuel 2-3), but bring disqualification from leadership upon him. An elder must be a model father. Wild and disobedient children are a bad reflection on the home, especially on the father's lack of discipline and inability to guide others. If one who aspires to eldership lacks such ability, he will never be able to manage God's family.

*God's stewards.* The necessity for proper qualification is further stressed by the interruption of Paul's thought in verse seven. After beginning to list the domestic requirements for elders, Paul suddenly adds a profound reason for the necessity of these qualifications. An elder is "God's steward," and "must be" morally and spiritually qualified to manage God's invaluable possessions. There can be no debate upon this point. A "steward" (Greek, *oikonomos,* literally means house-manager) is a manager, an administrator, and a trustee of someone else's household, property, or business.

A steward acts on behalf of another's interests. He is accountable and responsible to another for what has been entrusted to his care. "Steward" is an appropriate name for elders/overseers. Since the local church is called the household of God (1 Timothy 3:15), the elder/overseer who manages it can be called, "God's steward." So in this passage Paul emphasizes that an elder must be above reproach because he is "God's steward." The emphasis is on "God" as the steward's owner. Thus God demands that those entrusted with supervising His house be morally and spiritually fit.

*Overseer.* In the context of his instruction to elders, Paul also says, "For the overseer must be above reproach as God's steward." Paul uses the designation "overseer" as a generic singular (cf. 1 Timothy 3:2). Commenting on this generic singular, William Hendriksen writes, "Though it is true that the text has the singular 'the overseer,' this 'the' is generic, one member representing the entire class viewed from the point of view of a definite characteristic. . . ."[9] No doctrine justifying a single overseer (pastor) can adequately be built on the use of the singular in this case. Paul already switched from the plural to the singular in verse six, so we should not be surprised at his use of the singular here.

Note, too, that the change of terms from "elders" to "overseer" does not mean a change of persons or subject. If verse seven begins a list of qualifications for someone other than the elders of verse five—such as someone superior to the elders (the bishop, for example)—it is a most confusing and awkward subject change. Such a change makes complete nonsense out of the transitional word "for" used in verse seven. If Paul meant that "the overseer" was different from the elders, he would have said, "I left you in Crete to appoint elders and a bishop in every city, as I directed." "Overseer," therefore, is nothing more than another term for elder.

*Not self-willed.* Paul continues his list of requirements— negative and positive—by saying that "God's steward" must not be "self-willed." A self-willed man wants his own way regardless of others (self-willed literally means self-pleasing). He is stubborn, arrogant, and inconsiderate of others' opinions, feelings, and desires. A self-willed man is headstrong, independent, self-assertive, and ungracious toward those of a different opinion. A self-willed person is not a team player, which in the shared leadership of the eldership will cause much contention and division. Furthermore, a self-willed man will scatter the sheep because he is unyielding, overbearing, and blind to others' feelings and opinions. Such a man must not be permitted to be an elder.

*Not quick-tempered.* The Bible warns against the perils of an angry man in Proverbs 29:22, "An angry man stirs up strife, And a hot-tempered man abounds in transgression." The fierce looks and harsh words of a quick-tempered man tear people apart emotionally, leave people sick, destroy the spirit, and turn people away from God's family. Man's anger is a hindrance to the work of God, "for the anger of a man does not achieve the righteousness of God" (James 1:20).

One of God's beautiful attributes is that He is slow to anger. So His stewards must also be slow to anger. Since an elder must deal with people and their problems, a "hothead" will find much fuel to provoke his anger. With his ugly, angry words, a quick-tempered man will destroy the peace and unity the Lord desires for His people. Of course, everyone experiences anger, and leaders often experience a great deal of anger because they must deal with contentious situations. Hudson Taylor confesssed his own problem with anger: "My greatest temptation is to lose my temper over the slackness and inefficiency so disappointing in those on whom I depended. It is no use to lose my temper—only kindness. But oh, it is such a trial."[10]

Paul isn't so much concerned about the fact of anger in the life of an elder as he is about whether or not that anger is properly controlled and channeled. The issue here is whether an individual aspiring to the office of overseer is uncontrolled in *expressing* his anger. If he is, he does not qualify for the position.

*Not addicted to wine.* See comments on 1 Timothy 3:3.

*Not pugnacious.* See comments on 1 Timothy 3:3.

*Not fond of sordid gain.* The chief religious leaders of Jesus' day provide the perfect example of those who are "fond of sordid gain." They turned God's house into a merchandise mart for their own profit (Mark 11:15-17). Jesus was so enraged by their misconduct as leaders of God's chosen people that he began to cast the buyers and sellers out of the temple and overturn the money changers' tables. Other New Testament examples of those who lusted after "sordid gain" are Judas, who betrayed our Lord for a few pieces of silver (John 12:6), and the many false teachers who were lured into God's church by the sight of other people's money

(2 Corinthians 2:17; 1 Thessalonians 2:5; 1 Timothy 6:5; Titus 1:11; 2 Peter 2:13,14; Jude 11,12).

The temptation to use one's position or prestige to gain an unfair financial advantage lurks at every prominent leader's door. A perfect example of this is Valens, an elder of the second century church at Philippi who disgraced himself and the church by an obvious greedy act. Polycarp bemoans this fact in his letter to the Philippians:

> I was exceedingly grieved for Valens, who aforetime was a presbyter among you, because he is so ignorant of the office which was given unto him. I warn you therefore that ye refrain from covetousness, and that ye be pure and truthful. . . . If a man refrain not from covetousness, he shall be defiled by idolatry. . . . Therefore I am exceedingly grieved for him and for his wife, unto whom may the Lord grant true repentance. Be ye therefore yourselves also sober herein. . . ."

The stewards of God's household must not seek what rightfully belongs to others. They should not be "fond of sordid gain." This does not mean that overseers cannot receive financial provision, however. What the Bible condemns is the base, avaricious motive that desires what rightfully belongs to someone else. Hence, it is sordid, base gain, or disgraceful profit. Elders must be free from all shameful greed.

*But hospitable.* See comments on 1 Timothy 3:2.

*Loving what is good.* Not only must the overseer be "hospitable" (literally, a lover of strangers), he must be known for "loving what is good." This requirement is derived from the word *philagathos,* which Hermann Cremer defines as "one who willingly and *with self-denial* does good, or is kind."[12] Hendriksen explains the word as, "ready to do what is beneficial to others."[13] Grundmann says, "According to the interpretation of the early Church it relates to the unwearying activity of love."[14] King David was a lover of goodness. He spared his enemy Saul, who admitted to David's goodness: "'And you have declared today that you have done good to me, that the Lord delivered me into your hand and yet you did not kill me. For if a man finds his enemy, will he let him go away safely?'" (1 Samuel 24:18,19a). David sought to show kindness to his deceased friend, Jonathan—Saul's son—by taking Jonathan's crippled son, Mephibosheth, into his own house (2 Samuel 9). Job also loved goodness: "Behold, you have admonished many, And you have strengthened weak hands. Your words have helped the tottering to stand, And you have strengthened feeble knees" (Job 4:3,4).

An elder who loves goodness will always seek to do helpful things for all people. He will be loving, generous, and kind towards all and will never sink to evil, retaliatory behavior (Acts 11:24; Romans 12:21; 15:2; Galatians 6:10; 1 Thessalonians 5:15; 1 Peter 3:13). Men such as these, however, will be more and more difficult to find as time goes on. Paul prophesied (2 Timothy 3:3) that people in the last days will be unloving, irreconcilable, malicious gossips, without self-control, brutal, and haters of good. Thus, the society led by lovers of good, rather than haters of good, is truly blessed.

*Sensible.* See comments on the word "prudent" in 1 Timothy 3:2. For some reason, the *New American Standard* translates the same Greek term as "prudent" in 1 Timothy 3:2, and "sensible" in Titus 1:8.

*Just.* God's steward must also be "just," that is, an upright, righteous man who conducts himself in accordance with the principles of divine truth. Such a man can be counted on to make wise, fair, and righteous judgments for the community (Proverbs 29:7). Job is a good example of a just community leader.

> There was a man in the land of Uz, whose name was Job, and that man was blameless, upright, fearing God, and turning away from evil (Job1:1).
> "I put on righteousness, and it clothed me;
> My justice was like a robe and a turban.
> "I was eyes to the blind,
> And feet to the lame.
> "I was a father to the needy,
> And I investigated the case which I did not know.
> "And I broke the jaws of the wicked,
> And snatched the prey from his teeth" (Job 29:14-17).

In order for a man to be a good shepherd of God's people, he must be like Job, who was clothed in righteousness. He must walk in moral uprightness. Only then will he be qualified to fairly and honestly arbitrate the affairs of God's people without partiality.

*Devout.* A man with a firm disposition who is committed to faithfully observing his religious obligations and practices is considered "devout." A devout man lives the life God requires and is an example of godly character and conduct. He is pious, loyal, and holy. Trench focuses our attention on the superb example of

Joseph, the devout man, through the story of Joseph and Potiphar's wife, "Joseph, when tempted to sin by his Egyptian mistress (Genesis 39:7-12), approved himself *hosios* [devout], in reverencing those everlasting sanctities of the marriage bond, which God had founded, and which he could not violate without sinning against Him . . ."¹⁵ (Brackets mine). This is the kind of man God wants to lead His people. One of the terrible facts of Israel's history is that many of its leaders were not "just" and "devout," so the people were led astray from God and His blessing. An elder must not lead people astray, but must model godly character and conduct.

*Self-controlled.* To qualify as an overseer, a man must be characterized by self-discipline, self-restraint, and self-control in every aspect of life—particularly over physical desires (Acts 24:25; 1 Corinthians 7:9; 9:25). Solomon warns against an undisciplined man's vulnerability in Proverbs 25:28: "Like a city that is broken into and without walls Is a man who has no control over his spirit." During Solomon's time, walls were a strategic part of a city's defense system. A strong and secure city fortified its walls (Isaiah 26:1). A man's stability can be likened to such fortifications. Without stability and self-control, a person is exposed to attack and becomes easy prey for an enemy.

An undisciplined man has little resistance to sexual lust, provocation, anger, slothfulness, a critical spirit, or other desires that seek to control him. He is easy prey to sinful desires and the devil. Self-control is an essential part of the Christian life. Leaders who lack discipline frustrate their fellow leaders as well as those they lead. Not only are they poor examples, but they cannot accomplish what needs to be done. Consequently, the flocks they shepherd are poorly managed and cared for.

In his book, *The Four Loves,* C. S. Lewis makes the following comment about the body and its desires, "It is a useful, sturdy, lazy, obstinate, patient, loveable and infuriating beast; deserving now the stick and now a carrot; both pathetically and absurdly beautiful."¹⁶ The elder in particular must be able to contend with this loveable and infuriating beast and its incessant demands. How can an elder exhort someone under his care to gain self-control when he himself has not gained it?

*A man committed to the faithful Word.* Finally, an elder must be solidly committed to the truth of God's Word, as indicated by the strength of the term *antecho*, which is used in the phrase, "holding fast the faithful word." In other words, an elder must cling firmly to, be devoted to, and adhere wholeheartedly to God's Word (cf. Matthew 6:24). This implies strong conviction and commitment to the Word. Newport White says that this requirement suggests "the notion of withstanding opposition."[17] Alford takes it to mean, "constantly keeping to, and not letting go" of God's Word.[18] Elders who are uncertain or half-heartedly committed to Scripture can never protect the flock from wolves or guide it to better pastures.

As often seen in church history, weak, vacillating, doubting shepherds will be devoured along with the flock. Weak shepherds are no match for the deceitful spirits and doctrines of demons (1 Timothy 4:1). The priests, kings, and leaders of the Old Testament who professed the law of God but did not hold firmly to God's Word, were destroyed by idolatrous religion. So, too, unqualified elders who were (and are) uncertain and uncommitted to the Word have done incalculable damage to the church of Jesus Christ. Because they did not guard themselves or the flock, many churches that once stood for sound, orthodox doctrine now reject nearly every major tenet of the faith.

Refuting opponents of God's truth—an excruciatingly difficult task—demands courage, much effort, spiritual maturity, and knowledge of the truth. But it must be done. The church must be protected from those who speak against the Word, and the elders, as leaders of the church, are called to do that job (Acts 20:28-31).

An elder must adhere wholeheartedly to the Word because it is a "faithful," trustworthy, sure, and reliable message. In direct contrast to the lies and deceptions of Satan's false messages (Titus 1:10 ff.), the Word is a "faithful word." Furthermore, Paul indicates that the only word an elder ought to consider faithful is the message that measures up to and is "in accordance with the teaching" they received from him as the apostle and teacher sent to the Gentiles. There is only one apostolic doctrine (Acts 2:42; Ephesians 4:5), one standard, and one teaching. Anything else is false (Titus 1:10 ff; Galatians 1:8,9).

Today, the apostles' teaching is recorded in Holy Scripture. Therefore, church elders must cling tenaciously to Scripture with their whole heart and mind rather than clinging to their own thoughts and inventions, or the vain philosophies and traditions of men. An elder must adhere firmly to God's trustworthy Word so he is able "to exhort" the saints "in sound doctrine" and "refute" false teachers. This is similar to the "able to teach" qualification in 1 Timothy 3:2.

*A man who can exhort in sound doctrine.* Because of man's basic dullness in divine matters (Romans 6:19), the Lord's people need constant exhortation or encouragement in doctrine. Exhortation is closely associated with teaching (1 Timothy 4:13), but while teaching primarily relates to the understanding, exhortation (based on teaching) chiefly influences the conscience, heart, will, and action of men. Exhortation is a broad term covering a wide range of meanings—from comfort and encouragement to urgent demand. An elder, then, must be able to motivate men and women through sound doctrine.

Specifically, elders are "to exhort" or encourage the saints "in sound doctrine." Paul uses an interesting term here: the word, "sound," literally means healthy or physically whole (Luke 5:31; 3 John 2). Because this word is used metaphorically to describe "doctrine," it ought to be understood to mean wholesome, sound, correct, or true doctrine. "Sound doctrine" is in direct contrast to false doctrine, which is diseased, corrupt, defiled, and abominable. Diseased doctrine ruins the lives of its adherents (1 Timothy 6:3-5), while sound teaching produces godly, clean, wholesome, healthy lives (Titus 1:13; 2:1). The congregation's health and well-being depends upon elders who continually "exhort in sound doctrine." No individual qualifies for eldership unless he is able to use God's Word in such a manner.

*A man who can refute opponents.* Not only must overseers be able to exhort the saints, they must also be able "to refute those who contradict" wholesome doctrine. As in Acts 20:28-31, the overseers' duty is to protect the people from false teachers—those who speak against "the faithful word." Paul conveys an air of intensity and urgent necessity about this last qualification in the following verses: "For there are many rebellious men, empty talkers and deceivers, especially those of the circumcision, who must be silenced because they are upsetting whole families, teaching things they should not teach, for the sake of sordid gain" (Titus 1:10,11).

The situation in Crete was alarming. There were "many rebellious men, empty talkers and deceivers." In such a situation, the church must be cared for and protected. That is why elders must have a good knowledge and firm allegiance to the "faithful word." In the face of fierce opposition, only those who hold fast to the

Word will not let go or abandon its truth. Such men will die for the Word because they are convinced it is the faithful Word of God.

The local elders, then, must know and believe their Bibles. They must be strong and skilled in the use of the sword of the Word against all opponents of truth. For if the spiritual leaders of the church do not cling firmly to the Word, what fate awaits the flock? The church can grow and be protected from corruption only by the Word. Ignorance of God's Word and lack of trust in its authority among Christian leaders is the principal reason so many false teachers freely invade God's churches. As "God's stewards," the elders must take the lead in holding fast God's "faithful word."

Paul ends his instruction concerning elders to his emissary Titus on this solemn warning. By means of this letter, Paul seeks to reinforce the directive he had previously given concerning elders' qualifications. Particularly noteworthy is the last qualification, for the consequences of appointing elders who are not firmly committed to the Word or are unable to use it for the believers' encouragement and protection could be ruinous to the churches. As Paul says, there are "many" false teachers who seek to upset God's family (Titus 1:10,11).

Titus greatly needed this apostolic authorization in order to fulfill his commission to appoint qualified elders in all the churches on Crete. Without Titus' work, these churches were destined to remain weak and disorderly. But with Titus' effort to appoint qualified elders, there was every reason to believe that the churches would flourish despite the surrounding dangers.

### *Disqualification of Elders*

Qualification for eldership implies the possibility of disqualification. This is an unpleasant matter, but necessary for the welfare of the church. In order to protect the church from troublesome men, God has graciously provided objective requirements for church leaders. Since many deluded, domineering, and prideful men seek leadership positions for their own purposes, the objective qualifications for elders give the congregation the means—and right— to refuse or remove all such men from eldership. Thus, scriptural requirements for eldership are a rich blessing to the Lord's people.

God requires that all potential elders and deacons be examined as to whether they meet His requirements for office (1 Timothy

3:10; 5:22-25). If a man meets the standards God has set, then he may serve as an elder or deacon. If not, he cannot serve. Furthermore, a man must not only meet the requirements for induction into the office, but must maintain those qualifications while serving in his position. If a man does not maintain the qualifications for eldership, he is disqualified.

The disqualification or discipline of erring elders is a serious matter. In 1 Timothy 5:19,20, Paul gives guidelines for handling the problem: "Do not receive an accusation against an elder except on the basis of two or three witnesses. Those who continue in sin, rebuke in the presence of all, so that the rest also may be fearful of sinning." Therefore, if an accusation of sin against an elder is found to be true, the elder is to be publicly rebuked, which will most likely result in the elder's dismissal from office. Despite such serious consequences, an elder's sin must not be hidden, as so often occurs. Instead, a church leader's sin should be treated more severely because it has far more serious consequences for the family of God. Allowing an elder's sin to go unjudged undermines the whole moral and spiritual character of the church.

But who has the courage to discipline a leader of the church? Aware of this weakness and the reality of life, Paul directly and emphatically charges Timothy, and the congregation with its elders, to carry out his instruction for the protection and discipline of an elder: "I solemnly charge you in the presence of God and of Christ Jesus and His chosen angels, to maintain these principles without bias, doing nothing in a spirit of partiality" (1 Timothy 5:21).

Of course, God also provides for the protection of elders from false rumors and accusations. Scripture says, "Do not receive an accusation against an elder except on the basis of two or three witnesses" (1 Timothy 5:19). An active elder who conscientiously involves himself in the problems of others runs a high risk of being falsely accused or questioned. Standing up against sin or injustice in the church can easily make an elder unpopular. Thus, unless there are witnesses to actual sin, most accusations are best ignored or silenced. Furthermore, it is absolutely essential to maintain the principle that an elder can only be disqualified for biblical reasons—not merely because of majority vote. He cannot be removed from his position because of prejudice, resentment, or sinful, irrational group action. In some cases, a godly man may have to stand up against the entire church if he feels the majority is wrong.

Not only will failure to meet biblical qualifications disqualify a man from serving as an elder, but failure to perform the task of shepherding the flock also disqualifies him. To hold the position of church elder but not to perform the duties of the office is a contradiction. The eldership is an arduous, shepherding work. Without the work, the office means nothing. Yet nonfunctioning elders who want the position, but cannot do the work, are a common problem. Neil Summerton is correct when he says that having the time available to do the work is in a real sense a qualification to eldership:

> There is however a more mundane qualification which is essential if a man is to be called to be an elder. It is the willingness and *opportunity* to devote time and energy to the task. It requires great personal commitment, and a readiness to make eldership a priority in Christian service. The demands of personal and group prayer, of meeting in oversight, of preparation for teaching, of pastoral visitation, and of giving necessary leadership and guidance to congregational activities are inevitably very great. A man may have the character and gifts, and even the inclination, to be an elder, but he may not have the time.[19]

Therefore, all the saints have the obligation to see that those who are elders are properly examined and that hasty appointments of elders are never made: "And let these also [like elders] first be tested; then let them serve as deacons if they are beyond reproach" (1 Timothy 3:10); "Do not lay hands upon any one too hastily . . ." (1 Timothy 5:22). When an elder is found to be unqualified, it is the elders, as leaders of the congregation, who are primarily responsible to see that such an elder is removed from church oversight. This, of course, can be very difficult, but is an essential part of any leadership role. To refuse to remove an unqualified, nonfunctioning, or sinful elder weakens and discredits the entire leadership body. In summary, in order to have a biblical eldership, we must insist upon the scriptural qualifications for all who join the pastoral oversight of the church. Those who aspire to this office must be men of maturity in moral character, in their ability to manage their families, and in their knowledge and use of God's Word. An individual must meet these requirements for induction into office, and continue to reflect these qualities in order to remain in his position. Biblical eldership can only exist in the presence of biblically qualified leadership.

## NOTES

1. "A Biblical Style of Leadership?," *Leadership* 2 (Fall, 1981): 119-129.
2. *Ibid.*, page 119.
3. Bruce Stabbert, *The Team Concept* (Tacoma: Hegg Bros. Printing, 1982), page 130.
4. Roland Allen, *The Ministry of the Spirit*, ed. David M. Paton (London: World Dominion Press, 1960), page 152.
5. Francis A. Schaeffer, *The Church at the End of the 20th Century* (Downers Grove: InterVarsity Press, 1970), page 65.
6. *The New International Dictionary of New Testament Theology*, s.v., "Determine, Appoint, Present," by Siegfried Wibbing, 1 (1975): 471.
7. Frederick F. Bruce, *The Letters of Paul* (Grand Rapids: Wm. B. Eerdmans Publishing Co., 1965), page 291.
8. Nigel Turner, *Christian Words* (Nashville: Thomas Nelson Pub., 1982), page 103.
9. William Hendriksen, *Exposition of the Pastoral Epistles*, New Testament Commentary (Grand Rapids: Baker Book House, 1957), page 346.
10. John C. Pollock, *Hudson Taylor and Maria* (Grand Rapids: Zondervan Publishing House, 1962), page 33.
11. J. B. Lightfoot and J. R. Harmer, eds., *The Apostolic Fathers* (1891; reprint ed., Grand Rapids: Baker Book House, 1984), pages 180, 181.
12. *Biblico-Theological Lexicon of New Testament Greek*, 4th ed., s.v. **φιλαγαθος**.
13. Hendriksen, *Pastoral Epistles*, page 348.
14. *Theological Dictionary of the New Testament*, s.v. **φιλαγαθος** by Walter Grundmann, 1 (1964): 18.
15. Richard Chenevix Trench, *Synonyms of the New Testament*, 9th ed. (1880; reprint ed., Grand Rapids: Wm B. Eerdmans Publishing Co., 1969), pages 333, 334.
16. C. S. Lewis, *The Four Loves* (San Diego: Harcourt Brace Jovanovich, Publishers, 1960), page 143.
17. Newport J. D. White, "The First and Second Epistles to Timothy and the Epistle to Titus," in *The Expositor's Greek Testament*, ed. W. Robertson Nicoll. 5 vols. (reprint ed., Grand Rapids: Wm. B. Eerdmans Publishing Co., 1976), 4:188.
18. Henry Alford, *Alford's Greek Testament*, 5th ed., vol. 3: *Galatians—Philemon* (1871; reprint ed., Grand Rapids: Guardian Press, 1976), page 411.
19. Neil Summerton, *A Noble Task* (Exeter: The Paternoster Press, 1987), page 25.

## Chapter 14

# *A Noble Work Demands Noble Men: More Qualifications*

*It is a trustworthy statement; if any man aspires to the office of overseer, it is a fine work he desires to do. An overseer, then, must be above reproach, the husband of one wife, temperate, prudent, respectable, hospitable, able to teach, not addicted to wine or pugnacious, but gentle, uncontentious, free from the love of money. He must be one who manages his own household well, keeping his children under control with all dignity (but if a man does not know how to manage his own household, how will he take care of the church of God?); and not a new convert, lest he become conceited and fall into the condemnation incurred by the devil. And he must have a good reputation with those outside the church, so that he may not fall into reproach and the snare of the devil.*

1 Timothy 3:1-7

\* \* \*

In relation to our topic, 1 Timothy is the most important epistle in the New Testament. It contains more instruction concerning eldership and deaconship than any other New Testament letter. It also comprises the most highly developed teaching on eldership and church order found anywhere in the New Testament. John Calvin, in the dedication of his commentary on 1 and 2 Timothy writes, "In short, in these two epistles we are shown a living picture of the true government of the Church. . . . For everything in these letters is highly relevant to our own times, and there is hardly anything needful for the building up of the Church that cannot be drawn from them."[1] The instruction found in 1 Timothy is essential to forming a complete picture of biblical eldership and church structure. Thus the next six chapters of this book center around 1 Timothy.

The reason for 1 Timothy's significance is found in the book's purpose. 1 Timothy was written so Christians would know how they ought to conduct themselves in God's household: "I am writing these things to you, hoping to come to you before long; but in case I am delayed, I write so that you may know how one ought to conduct himself in the household of God, which is the church of the living God, the pillar and support of the truth" (1 Timothy 3:14,15). From this explanation, it is clear that a proper understanding of eldership, deaconship, and women's role are essential to the proper ordering of God's church.

Paul begins his instruction about the qualifications for church leaders with a fascinating quote from the Christians themselves: "It is a trustworthy statement: if any man aspires to the office of overseer, it is a fine work he desires to do." This is one of five trustworthy sayings in Paul's letters to Timothy and Titus. The others are found in 1 Timothy 1:15; 4:9; 2 Timothy 2:11; and Titus 3:8. Each saying is marked for special attention by the formula, "a trustworthy statement [faithful is the saying, or reliable is the statement]." This expression both emphasizes and makes a positive judgment, or commendation, of the statement it is associated with. In effect, it says that what is stated is indeed true and reliable—a tried and time-proven truth that can be counted on and is fully endorsed by all believers and Paul the apostle through the Holy Spirit.

The saying, "if any man aspires to the office of overseer, it is a fine work he desires to do," then, is absolutely and uncontestably true, totally reliable, and completely trustworthy. It is a truth that God's Spirit has sovereignly placed in Holy Scripture for everyone's profit. It is a truth that deserves constant repeating among the Lord's people. These five sayings were popular maxims that the first Christians developed and perpetuated to express truths dear to their hearts. Paul is quoting, with complete approval, a Christian saying; he is not making a statement of his own. George Knight's conclusion regarding the trustworthy statement formula and the saying itself bears repeating:

> The conclusion reached is that the phrase is a citation-emphasis formula which serves to draw one's attention to the fact that a saying is cited and which serves at the same time to emphasize and commend that saying. Thus, even at this stage of the study the conclusion is dawning that that which the logos refers is indeed a "saying," not merely a statement written by the author in the course of his writing of the letter.[2]

The early Christian maxims provide invaluable insight into what was foremost in the first Christians' thoughts. The fact that the early Christians were prompted to create a special saying about church oversight reveals that they keenly understood the great value of overseers, the difficulties and sacrifices facing the overseers, and their own need for such leaders. George Knight goes on to point out:

> The fact that in the early church there has developed a saying about the *episkope* indicates how very important this office was considered to be for the life and well-being of the church. . . . And this high view of those who rule over the church is seen throughout the N.T. (Acts 15; Acts 20:17 ff., esp. 28; Philippians 1:1; 1 Thessalonians 5:12,13; Hebrews 13:7,17). This evaluation is enhanced even more by Paul's citing this saying with the strong citation-emphasis formula, faithful is the saying. . . . And no doubt he cites the saying at the beginning of the third chapter because it is an excellent summary and introductory statement to the qualifications for the *Episkopos*.[3]

Oh, that Christians today might truly realize the significance of the eldership and say with the same earnestness as the first Christians: "If any man aspires to the office of overseer, it is a fine work he desires to do."

### A Noble Task

From 1 Timothy 3:1, ". . . if any man aspires to the office of overseer, it is a fine work he desires to do," we see that the desire for church oversight is a good thing. Such ambition is not wrong. Jesus taught, ". . . If any one wants to be first, he shall be last of all, and servant of all" (Mark 9:35). Thank God there will always be men with the desire to care for and lead God's people. Christ's teaching doesn't depreciate the desire for human leadership. Rather, it transforms the desire from a worldly leadership style to a humble, servant style, which is the path to true greatness in God's eyes. A Christian who desires to be such a leader does not necessarily do so out of pride or worldliness.

God Himself gifts men to be leaders (Romans 12:8; 1 Corinthians 12:28; Ephesians 4:11). From the human perspective (1 Timothy 3:1) one personally desires the work of oversight, but from the divine perspective (Acts 20:28) the Holy Spirit places men in the church as overseers. The desire to be an elder, then, is ultimately the result of the Spirit's work in the human heart (Acts 20:28). However, the sad truth is that because of selfishness and irresponsibility few men really desire the work of oversight (Philippians 2:21). This is a matter of grave concern, for many able men dedicate their lives to other endeavors and have no time or energy to serve Jesus Christ. Our churches desperately need more dedicated elders, so we should pray earnestly that many more would desire to shepherd God's people.

The phrase, "the office of overseer," represents one word in Greek, *episkope* (literally, overseership), which is the duty or position of the overseer mentioned in 1 Timothy 3:2. The *New American Standard Bible*, by its translation of *episkope* as, "the office of overseer," stresses the position or office of an overseer. However, the word could also be rendered simply as *oversight*, stressing its duty or function. The latter rendering is perhaps preferable because of the absence of the definite article, the term's basically functional meaning, and its description in the context as a fine work. Either rendering presents no real problem, however, since neither sense can be completely eliminated from the word; it is both an office and a function (Numbers 4:16; Acts 1:20).

The reason for commending those who aspire to church oversight is because "it is a fine work" they desire to do. The word "fine" means noble, excellent, or praiseworthy. "Work" is used in the sense of task or occupation (the singular, work, not plural, *works*.) Since church oversight is not something everyone can do, or is qualified to do, "the office of overseer" is considered a noble task or praiseworthy occupation. Acts 20:28 shows why church oversight is a noble task. Overseers shepherd God's church that

He purchased with His own blood. The Church is the most precious thing on earth to God.

Overseeing God's people in God's way is extremely demanding and at times very trying. In the face of problems and labors, the greatest encouragement and incentive an elder can have is to know that he performs an exceedingly honorable and praiseworthy task— one that is worthy of the total sacrifice of one's life.

It is equally important that congregations today realize the noble character of the elders' task. They need to realize its significance so they will support and encourage elders in their work on behalf of the church. In brief, this early Christian saying declares the great value of the work of oversight while boldly encouraging those who desire this work.

After wisely introducing this new section (1 Timothy 3:1-13) with a quote from the Christian community, Paul proceeds immediately to his main point: "An overseer, then, must be above reproach . . ." (1 Timothy 3:2). The Spirit's great concern is that overseers of God's family be of irreproachable character. Paul emphasizes this point because the believers may not have properly understood it, even though they valued the overseers' work. Some men desire oversight simply for recognition, to satisfy their ego. Others are deceived about their own ability and character. Also, because there is always a deep need for leaders, it is tempting to allow unqualified men to take on this leadership responsibility. But, a rightly qualified overseer is an essential part of the proper order of God's church (1 Timothy 3:14,15). So Scripture provides *objective qualifications* to test the *subjective desire* of all who seek the elders' work. Desire alone is not enough. It must be matched by proper character.

Since church oversight is "a fine work," it follows that "an overseer" must be a man of the highest Christian character. A noble work demands a noble person. The verb "must be" stresses that it is required, necessary, and an apostolic imperative for the overseer/elder to be above reproach.

It's noteworthy that two previous uses of the word *overseer* have been plural, Acts 20:28; Philippians 1:1. Here, however, the word, as in Titus 1:7, is singular. The reason for the singular usage here is that it is a generic singular representing an entire class or type. Thus, the "overseer" stands for *all* overseers—*all* elders. J. N. D. Kelly writes, "In spite of its use in the singular both here and in Titus 1:7, it is extremely likely that the overseer is to be understood generically, and that a plurality of such officials is presupposed."[4] This is not an unusual way for Paul to express himself. For example, in 1 Timothy 5:3,5,19, and 2 Timothy 2:24, Paul freely uses the generic singular in reference to widows, elders, and the Lord's servants.

As we saw in our discussion of Philippians 1:1, the terms *elder* and *overseer* are used interchangeably for the same body of men. The reference to the "overseer" here, then, would likewise be a reference to the *elder* who elsewhere is primarily referred to in the plural. The presence of the elders (plural, in 1 Timothy 5) who teach and lead in the church is particularly relevant. The conclusion that the elders of chapter 5 are different from the leaders spoken about in chapter 3 is unwarranted. If there is a difference, what qualifications must the elders of chapter 5 have to teach and lead? Where are their qualifications?

With this in mind, no convincing argument can be made for the second century practice of elevating one man—the overseer/bishop—over the entire eldership and congregation, based on the singular use of overseer. The church order of 1 Timothy and Titus is pre-Ignatian and still follows the simple, brotherly, elder system of oversight that is recorded in Acts. E. K. Simpson remarks on the primitive church order apparent in these letters:

It is not our province to touch on denominational "differences of administration" concerning which we might not see eye to eye. But we cannot fail to perceive the unpretentious type of church rule that is here sketched, a sodalitas [a united fellowship] incapable in fact of coming into collision with civic authority without wanton aggression on the part of the latter. Does not this picture reflect primal conditions in contrast with later developments? (Brackets mine.)[5]

At the heart of Paul's concern for church order stand the moral qualifications of those responsible for the care of the church.

### The Overseer's Qualifications

*Above reproach.* Heading the list of qualifications stands the fundamental requirement that an overseer "be above reproach" (1 Timothy 3:2) or unassailable, uncensured, irreproachable, or without reproach. A man who is "above reproach" has a good moral and spiritual reputation. He is a man with an irreproachable life in the sight of others. He is free from any offensive or disgraceful blight of character or conduct. Hence, critics cannot discredit his profession or prove him unfit as a community leader. Since all God's saints are to live holy and blameless lives (Philippians 2:15; 1 Thessalonians 5:23), since the world casts a critical eye at the Christian community (1 Peter 3:15,16), and since Christian leaders lead primarily by their example (1 Peter 5:3), a blameless life is indispensable to the Christian elder.

Ecclesiastes 10:1 tells us, "dead flies make a perfumer's oil stink, so a little foolishness is weightier than wisdom and honor." In her book, *How to Fail Successfully*, Jill Briscoe points out how the seemingly small and insignificant flies of flirting and cheating (and I might add hypocrisy, lack of discipline, or lack of integrity) can have a devastating effect upon one's reputation.[6] Even a little folly can bring heavy reproach upon a wise and honorable reputation. First and foremost, a man's life "must be above reproach" to qualify for oversight. This is the overarching qualification. If an elder brings disgrace upon himself and the church because of sinful behavior, that man is disqualified from church oversight. He is no longer "above reproach."

*The husband of one wife.* This is a painfully controversial phrase. A wrong interpretation would restrict needed, qualified men from eldership, or permit unqualified men to have a place of leadership that God forbids. The phrase, "husband of one wife," is literally a one wife's husband, or a one-woman man, with the word *one* in the emphatic position. Such an absolute, unqualified statement (and the Bible contains a number of these difficult phrases) must not be given precedence over Scripture's general, clear teaching, nor must it be allowed to create contradiction. The Bible's general teaching regarding marriage is clear. One incidental, highly debatable, brief phrase cannot be allowed to cast a cloud of confusion over that which is plain.

The interpretation held by many ancient and modern expositors that disqualifies overseers and deacons who are remarried widowers must then be rejected. Although the interpretation that an elder can be married only once in a lifetime has the literalism of the phrase in its favor, and so must be taken seriously, it is in disharmony with the overall biblical teaching regarding marriage.[7]

Perhaps the best solution is to interpret the ambiguous Greek phrase, *miar gynaikos andra*, as a one-woman kind of man (rendering *gynaikos* as woman and as a genitive of quality, and *andra* as man). In other words, the elder must be characterized as a one-woman man who is not flirtatious, promiscuous, or involved in a questionable relationship with another woman. Viewed this way, Paul is not referring exclusively to the marital status of the prospective elder, but to a character trait—just as he does with most of the other qualifications for elders.[8] Thus, if a man remarries after his wife's death and is loyal to his second wife (as he was with the first), he would be characterized as a one-woman man.

The phrase therefore implies loyalty and faithfulness. Stated as it is in a positive form, it means that the overseer must have an exclusive relationship with one woman. It is a beautiful, striking, and positive way of expressing exemplary, irreproachable conduct in marriage. A one-woman man is a man above reproach in the marital relationship as well as in all other male-female relationships. The phrase also implies that the overseer cannot have several wives (polygamy). When God instituted marriage, He authorized only monogamous marriage (Genesis 2:20-25). Polygamy, as the Bible abundantly demonstrates, causes endless problems, gross unfairness, and terrible suffering.

Because the Bible emphasizes the holy status of marriage, a Christian—especially a leader of God's people—must be a faithful spouse. In marriage, the Bible says a man and a woman become "one flesh" (Genesis 2:24). Jesus Christ says, "Consequently they are no longer two, but one flesh. What therefore God has joined together, let no man separate" (Matthew 19:6). In this crucial matter, then, the enemy must have no ground for accusation or censure among God's people. Marriage is the most probing test of a man's character and beliefs. Therefore, a Christian marriage is one of the most powerful testimonies to the gospel's life-changing power. Conversely, ruined marriages among Christians have the greatest potential for bringing disgrace upon the Christian message and community. Thus, we do well to heed Scripture's logic: "but if a man does not know how to manage his own household, how will he take care of the church of God?" (1 Timothy 3:5).

Another question that immediately arises is whether or not a divorced man is a one-woman man who can serve as an elder. There is honest disagreement over divorce among godly Christians. These differing opinions obviously lead to diverse conclusions. (How we need extra wisdom and grace from God for questions like this! How sin confuses life and divides God's people!) Those who believe Scripture prohibits divorce and remarriage (Mark 10:2-12: Romans 7:1-3) are inclined to disqualify all divorced and remarried men from church eldership. On the other hand, Christians who believe that Scripture permits divorce and remarriage in certain cases (Matthew 19:9; 1 Corinthians 7:15) might allow certain divorced or divorced and remarried men to serve as elders. From their perspective, a biblical divorce—like death—dissolves the marriage bond and frees the individuals to remarry.

Throughout Christianity's history, reputable bible scholars have affirmed both viewpoints, and an analysis of these two views is beyond the scope of this study. But whether or not divorce and remarriage brings a prospective elder under reproach is a prime consideration in Paul's list of qualifications for eldership. So each local assembly must inevitably reach a conclusion on the matter of reproach.

We also must determine whether or not a man who divorced and remarried prior to his conversion is under reproach. Would, for instance, a man who has lived in faithful union with his Christian wife since his conversion qualify to be an elder? Ed Glasscock, I believe, rightly argues against holding pre-conversion sins against a new man in Christ who desires to shepherd the Lord's people:

> Certainly one cannot attempt to make the qualifications of 1 Timothy 3 apply to a man's life before he is saved. If God has forgiven him and made him a part of His church, why do Christians hold his past against him? . . .
>
> . . . It does not seem possible that by Paul's phrase in 1 Timothy 3:2 he intends to hold a man's pre-conversion sins against him. . . .
>
> . . . To judge a man's spiritual qualities on the basis of a sin committed before he was saved, before he was capable of understanding God's will or Word, and before he has the power of Christ's life within him is to create a false standard that detracts from God's wonderful grace and which also fails to deal with the real issue of 1 Timothy 3.[9]

It must be stated, however, that unlike other pre-conversion sins, a divorced and remarried man might be in a vulnerable condition which could lead to embarrassing circumstances or subtle reproach. Each local assembly, with its elders, will have to judge for itself whether a prospective elder or deacon is actually under reproach because of divorce and/or remarriage in his unconverted days. Yet the issue of reproach can be unjustly used by sinister (or even well-meaning) people. That is why it is equally important that the saints judge such situations in the full light of the New Testament's glorious doctrines of forgiveness, grace, and new life in Christ.

Regardless of one's view on divorce and remarriage, an acting elder who divorces while in office is under reproach and must be disqualified. The issue is not whether God forgives divorced people (of course He does) or whether a divorced person can serve God (of course he can). The real issue in this instance is the leader's public reproach on God's glory and the testimony of the assembly of saints. Furthermore, there is the supremely important issue of example, which is often forgotten in our day of professional ministry. The elder, by definition, is a community leader who is honored for his example and service. According to Peter, the elder's power to lead is dependent on his godly example (1 Peter 5:3). Since the elder's living example has an enormous influence over the congregation, the people will gradually follow that example. The Bible says people are like sheep, so the leaders' example will eventually influence the flock's thinking and direction (Ezra 9:1-4).

We must remember, too, that divorce often (but not always) reveals hidden character traits that would disqualify a man from church leadership. A divorced man may have been self-willed, quick-tempered, pugnacious, harsh, or not gentle toward his wife even though he may not have initiated the divorce.

There will be diverse opinions about critical questions such as these, but this in no way diminishes the elders' and congregation's responsibility to squarely face the issues and make wise, prayerful decisions. In all sad and grievous situations, the honor of Jesus' name, faithfulness to His Word, and prayer are the paramount guides. Finally, Paul does not imply that only married men qualify for church oversight. He does not say, "a husband of *a* wife," but, "the husband of *one* wife." Nowhere is a single man restricted from church oversight, nor should he be if he qualifies in every other way.

*Temperate: a stable man.* Literally, the Greek word for "temperate" means wineless, or sobriety in the use of wine. A few interpreters think the word should be understood in its literal sense, but that is unlikely. The word seems to be used metaphorically, referring to mental, behavioral, and spiritual sobriety. Sober or temperate are good translations of the Greek and imply self-control, clear-mindedness, and freedom from all excesses. As the verb form shows, temperance is a much-needed quality if one is to stand firm against the devil's subtle attacks (1 Peter 5:8), false teaching (2 Timothy 4:3-5), and moral and spiritual darkness (1 Thessalonians 5:6-8). A Christian must be sober, circumspect, steady, self-controlled, and alert. It is absolutely essential that a Christian leader who faces many serious problems, pressures, and decisions be a spiritually stable man.

*Prudent: a balanced, sensible man.* "Prudent" is a very difficult word to translate. In fact, no English word fully conveys its meaning. Literally, it means soundness of mind or sober-minded. Prudent means to be balanced, discreet, and controlled because of sound judgment, sensible thinking, and reasonableness. Paul exhorts the Romans to think soundly about themselves: "For through the grace given to me I say to every man among you not to think more highly of himself than he ought to think; but to think so as to have sound judgment, as God has allotted to each a measure of faith" (Romans 12:3). All excesses and imbalanced thinking that result in disconcerting behavior are restrained by sober-mindedness. Sober-mindedness greatly tempers pride, authoritarianism, and indiscretion. Prudence is an essential quality of mind for a humble, servant-leader who must handle problems and guide others in the Lord's ways. Diotrephes, the church tyrant, was not prudent (3 John 9,10). His prideful, high-minded thinking caused him to elevate himself over the congregation. As a result, innocent people were refused Christian fellowship.

*Respectable: an orderly, disciplined, and honorable man.* In the original language, "respectable" is the word *orderly*. It is used to describe orderliness in outward demeanor and dress (1 Timothy 2:9), but here undoubtedly means orderliness in the whole person and life style. At Thessalonica, Christians were living disorderly lives (1 Thessalonians 5:14; 2 Thessalonians 3:6-14). They had ceased to work for a living. They became loafers, meddlers, a burden to others, disobedient to the apostolic example, and a dishonor to the gospel. But Paul had worked to supply his own physical needs while living among them. He had displayed a well-ordered and disciplined life in every area. In 1 Thessalonians 4:11,12, Paul implores the Thessalonians to live orderly lives: "and to make it your ambition to lead a quiet life and attend to your own business and work with your hands, just as we commanded you; so that you may behave properly toward outsiders and not be in any need." An orderly life is most important for a manager of God's flock. An elder who leads a disorderly life is unable to properly and successfully care for God's flock. Under such a man's leadership, the sheep will soon show the pathetic signs of neglect and mismanagement.

*Hospitable.* Job, the exemplary Old Testament elder, was a model of hospitality: "'The alien has not lodged outside, For I have opened my doors to the traveler'" (Job 31:32). In the New Testament, John the apostle commends Gaius for his loving, faithful hospitality: "Beloved, you are acting faithfully in whatever you accomplish for the brethren, and especially when they are strangers; and they bear witness to your love before the church; and you will do well to send them on their way in a manner worthy of God. For they went out for the sake of the Name, accepting nothing from the Gentiles. Therefore we ought to support such men, that we may be fellow workers with the truth" (3 John 5-8).

Paul exhorts the Christians at Rome to pursue hospitality (Romans 12:13). Peter writes, "Be hospitable to one another without complaint" (1 Peter 4:9). The author of Hebrews bids his readers: "Do not neglect to show hospitality to strangers, for by this some have entertained angels without knowing it" (Hebrews 13:2). These New Testament passages on hospitality are found within the larger context of Christian love. Hospitality practically displays the Christian family's generosity, closeness, and love. Therefore, Scripture requires that church elders, as examples and leaders, practice hospitality. A man who closes his door to God's family cannot be an elder. Indeed, such action is symptomatic of more serious problems. Lack of hospitality among the Lord's people is a sure sign of selfish, lifeless, loveless Christianity.

*Able to teach.* Like Israel, the Christian community is built on Holy Scripture, and those who oversee the community must be able to guide and protect its members by instruction from Scripture. Therefore all elders must be "able to teach," which entails three basic elements: a knowledge of Scripture, the readiness to teach, and the capability to communicate. Elders must be able to open their Bibles and instruct others. This requirement has nothing to do with the "gift" of teaching (Romans 12:7; 1 Corinthians 12:28; Ephesians 4:11), nor does it have anything to do with preaching. (Some, but not all, elders will have the "gift" of teaching as is emphasized in 1 Timothy 5:17,18.)

It doesn't matter how successful a man may be at his business, or how eloquently he may speak, or how much education he may have. If a man cannot instruct people in the Word or protect the church from false doctrine, he does not qualify to be an elder. P. T. Forsyth's comment on the power of the Word in the hearts of men needs to be foremost in our minds: "The real strength of the Church is not the amount of its work but the quality of its faith. One man who truly knows his Bible is worth more to the Church's real strength than a crowd of workers who do not."[10] Only by the Word can the church grow and be protected from corruption. The failure of church leaders to know and teach the Bible is one of the chief reasons why biblical error floods our churches and drowns the power and life of the church. Therefore, the elders must be able to teach God's Word.

Author and church elder, Neil Summerton, emphatically states the importance of this qualification and shares some wise counsel:

Hence to both Timothy and Titus, Paul is crystal clear that the indispensable quality, which incidentally distinguishes the elder from the deacon, is the ability to master Christian doctrine, to evaluate it in others, to teach it, and to debate it with those who teach falsehood. (*1 Timothy* 3:2; *Titus* 1:9-16).

There may well be those who are inclined to rebel against this emphasis and to argue that elders need more practical gifts in order to ensure that their administration is smooth and efficient. In answer, it may be said, first, that this mistakes the emphasis which both Old and New Testaments place on the need for the flock of God to be led by shepherds who will ensure that it is fed spiritually. For this purpose soundness of character needs to be brought together with the reception and transmission of the word of the Lord as the means of feeding, protecting and restoring individual members of the flock. This ministry does not necessarily have to be exercised from the platform and the centre of gravity of the gifts of one elder may be towards teaching while that of another may be towards pastoring. But all need a sound grasp of the Faith and the ability to teach and instruct in small groups and one-to-one in the pastoral situation.

Secondly, if elders lack practical skill in such administration as is necessary in the flock, let them appoint a person or persons (perhaps as deacons if they have the high spiritual qualities also demanded for that office) to assist them. Moreover, in an eldership of any size one or more of the body may be able to discharge these tasks so long as they do not prevent them from giving priority to the overseeing tasks. But at all costs the error of appointing men who lack either the character and spiritual qualities, or eldership gifts, or both, should be avoided.[11]

*Not addicted to wine.* An elder must be above reproach in the use of wine. Paul uses a strong word here that literally means not beside wine, or not addicted, preoccupied, or overindulgent with wine. The term also has a secondary meaning, that of being violent or a brawler because of wine. The *Revised Standard Version* translates the original as *no brawler,* but in view of the similar traits mentioned in this passage (pugnacious, uncontentious), it is best to render the original term as, "not addicted to wine." Plainly, this is not a prohibition against drinking wine, but against the abuse of wine or any other chemical that would be destructive to a man's testimony.

*Not pugnacious.* A pugnacious person is a fighter—a quick-tempered, quarrelsome individual who is prone to physical assault on others. The Greek word is derived from the verb, to strike, and can be understood as a violent person, a striker, or a brawler. Wives and children especially feel the blows of a pugnacious man, and anyone who seriously frustrates a pugnacious man is a potential target for physical abuse. Because a pugnacious man will strike the sheep rather than gently leading them, he cannot be one of Christ's undershepherds. God only allows those He knows will be gentle to lead His sheep through the stresses of congregational life.

*Gentle: a forbearing, gracious, and conciliatory man.* The man who possesses the positive quality of gentleness stands in vivid contrast to the pugnacious man. The problem with the term "gentle," is that no English word adequately conveys the fullness of its beauty and richness. Forbearance, gentleness, magnanimous, equitable, peaceable, and gracious all help capture the full range of meaning of gentleness. A gentle man exhibits a willingness to yield and patiently makes allowances for the weakness and ignorance of the fallen human condition. He is gracious, reasonable, and considerate. One who is gentle refuses to retaliate in kind for wrong done by others, and does not insist upon the letter of the law or personal rights. He possesses God's pure, peaceable, gentle, reasonable, and merciful wisdom (James 3:17).

Gentleness is a characteristic of God: "For Thou, Lord, art good, and ready to forgive [the same Greek word in the LXX meaning forbearing or gentle], And abundant in lovingkindness to all who call upon Thee" (Psalms 86:5). Furthermore, gentleness radiates the life of Jesus upon earth: "Now I Paul myself urge you by the meekness and gentleness of Christ . . ." (2 Corinthians 10:1). Forbearance is of God and is a chief source of peace and healing among His people. So in his letter to the Philippian Christians, who were experiencing internal and external conflict, Paul says, "Let your forbearing spirit be known to all men . . ." (Philippians 4:5).

Gentleness is one of the elders' most important and attractive qualities. God fully expects His undershepherds to shepherd His people the same way He does. He will not let His people be driven, beaten, condemned, or divided. The shepherd must be patient, gracious, and understanding with the erring—and at times exasperating—sheep. So many wrongs, disagreements, faults, hurts, and injustices exist in this sinful world that one would be forced to live in perpetual division, anger, and conflict if it were not for forbearance. So elders must be "gentle" and forbearing, like Christ.

*Uncontentious: a peaceable man.* Since the day Cain killed Abel, his brother, men have been fighting and killing one another (Genesis 4:5-8). This is one of the horrible consequences of man's sinful nature. Christians, however, are commanded to be different, "to malign no one, to be uncontentious, gentle, showing every consideration for all men" (Titus 3:2). God hates division and fighting among His people. Yet fighting paralyzes, weakens, and kills many local churches. It may be the single most distressing problem Christian leaders face. Therefore, a Christian elder is required to be "uncontentious," which literally means, not fighting. That is, he is not quarrelsome. Positively stated, he is a peaceable man: "And the Lord's bond-servant must not be quarrelsome, but be kind to all, able to teach, patient when wronged, with gentleness correcting those who are in opposition, if perhaps God may grant them repentance leading to the knowledge of the truth" (2 Timothy 2:24,25).

There are occasions when the elders must confront false

teachers and sinful behavior (Acts 15:1,2; Titus 1:9 ff.). Indeed, at times it seems like a leader does nothing but confront others. But even these struggles must be dealt with in a Christian manner (2 Timothy 2:24,25). Scripture condemns a sinful disposition that is inclined toward fighting, contention, or quarrelsomeness: "Keeping away from strife is an honor for a man, But any fool will quarrel" (Proverbs 20:3). "There are six things which the Lord hates, . . . A false witness who utters lies, And one who spreads strife among brothers" (Proverbs 6:16-19).

*Free from the love of money.* Scripture likewise warns all Christians against "the love of money:" "Let your character be free from the love of money, being content with what you have . . ." (Hebrews 13:5). "For the love of money is a root of all sorts of evil, and some by longing for it have wandered away from the faith, and pierced themselves with many a pang" (1 Timothy 6:10).

Lust for money characterized the religious leaders of Jesus' day. The Pharisees, for example, were lovers of money (Luke 16:14) who devoured widow's houses (Mark 12:40) and were condemned for their greed. Like a powerful drug, "the love of money" can delude the judgment of even the best men. Because the elders handle money (Acts 11:30), and some receive wages (1 Timothy 5:17,18), those who love silver and gold can easily be tempted to lust after it. So, both Paul and Peter warn the elders against greed (Acts 20:33 ff; 1 Timothy 3:3; Titus 1:7; 1 Peter 5:2), and showed through their lives a character that coveted no one's possessions. Money-loving, materialistic elders set the wrong example and will inevitably fall into unethical financial dealings that disgrace the Lord's name. So elders must continually guard themselves against "the love of money," especially if that money is gained in the Lord's service.

*A man who manages his household well.* Concerning this qualification, Donald Guthrie remarks, "A most important principle, which has not always had the prominence it deserves," is that, "any man unable to govern his children graciously and gravely by maintaining good discipline, is no man for government in the Church."[12] The elder's control of his children is especially relevant. A biblical elder is best tested by how well he handles his children, not by how rich, successful, or well-known he may be. Scripture says an elder must keep "his children under control with all dignity." A Christian elder must have obedient and submissive children (age not indicated), but not be a spirit-crushing tyrant who gains submission by harsh punishment or unjust oppression. He must control his children in an honorable, respectful, and dignified way. The Bible implores fathers not to provoke or exasperate their children (Ephesians 6:4; Colossians 3:21).

The necessity and importance of this requirement is immediately supported by the question: "But if a man does not know how to manage his own household, how will he take care of the church of God?" Elders have the solemn responsibility to "take care" of God's church. As overseers, they give the thought, time, and energy to see that church needs are met—much as a father meets the needs of his household. Since it takes a great deal of ability and knowledge to care for God's church, it follows that, "if a man does not know how to manage [Greek, *prohistemi*; see 1 Thessalonians 5:12; 1 Timothy 5:17] his own household," he will not be able to manage the more difficult and demanding task of caring for God's church.

The importance of an elder's family life is clearly communicated in the list of qualifications for elders. God requires that an elder be a loyal and faithful husband, that he be an able manager of his home, that he be able to control his children while maintaining their respect, and that he practice hospitality. This emphasis upon the elder's domestic life illustrates a key aspect of the nature of the church—the family of God—and reveals something of the elder's position and role in the assembly of believers.

Caring for the local church is more like managing a family than managing a business or state. Therefore, a man's ability to manage God's church is directly related to his ability to manage his own household. A man may be a successful businessman, a capable public official, a brilliant office manager, or a top military leader, but a terrible church elder. In the family of God, a man's ability to lead his family is the test that qualifies or disqualifies a man to be an elder. An elder's relationship with his children will manifest itself in his relationship with the congregation. If he is too harsh with his children—rigid, impatient, insensitive, permissive, inconsistent, or passive—that is how he will respond to the congregation. If one wants to know what an elder will be like, observe how he manages his children.

*Not a new convert.* "A new convert" is a beginner in the faith, a baby Christian, a recent convert. No matter how spiritual, zealous, knowledgeable, or talented a new convert may be, he is not spiritually mature. Maturity requires time and experience for which there is no substitute, so "a new convert" is simply not ready for eldership. There is nothing wrong with being "a new convert." All Christians begin life in Christ as babies and grow to maturity (1 Corinthians 3:1,2). An elder, however, must be mature and know his own heart. A new Christian does not know his own heart or the craftiness of the enemy, so he is vulnerable to pride—the most subtle of all temptations and most destructive of all sins. The position of elder (especially in a large, well-established church like Ephesus where Timothy was residing) carries considerable honor, authority, and recognition. For a recent convert, the temptation of pride would be too great. Pride would destroy the man and hurt the assembly. So Paul warns against appointing a new convert as an elder, "lest he become conceited and fall into the condemnation incurred by the devil."

The Bible is right: "Pride goes before destruction, And a haughty spirit before stumbling" (Proverbs 16:18). "When pride comes, then comes dishonor, But with the humble is wisdom" (Proverbs 11:2; cf. 18:1; 29:23). Even the most mature and godly believers must continually battle pride's subtleties. Pride has destroyed the greatest of men (2 Chronicles 26:16; 32:25). Pride is a serious matter, for ruinous consequences await the inexperienced, prideful elder. Pride caused the devil's ruin (Ezekiel 28:11-19) and, like the devil, the prideful elder will inevitably fall. He will experience personal disgrace, loss, and exposure; divine chastisement; and possibly wreck his faith.

Since there is great danger when new converts serve as elders, one naturally questions Paul's practice of appointing elders in new churches (Acts 14:23). All members of the new churches were new converts, so wouldn't his appointment of elders in those churches violate this qualification? The answer is no, because special conditions existed in those early churches. The synagogue prepared the way for the rapid spread of the gospel and provided a ready-made congregation. Some of the new converts were well versed in Old Testament Scripture and godly living. Some may have already been community leaders. Unlike many missionary situations where there may be little or no exposure to spiritual truth, able men were available in some congregations right from the start because of the synagogue. First Timothy 3:6, however, speaks to an essential requirement for churches today. A congregation can only grow to the extent that its leadership is mature. So, for the health of each local assembly, an elder must not be a new convert.

*A man with a good reputation outside the Christian community.* Finally, and of particular importance, an overseer "must have a good reputation with those outside the church." All Christians are to bear a good testimony before the world (1 Thessalonians 4:11,12; Titus 2:5,8; 1 Peter 2:12,15; 3:16), especially Christian leaders. God hates hypocrisy. A man's image before his Christian brethren must not be different than his image at work, in the family, or in the neighborhood. People judge the community by its leaders. The real test of a man's character, then, is from Monday through Saturday, not on Sunday morning. The unsaved watch and are very astute. They observe what a Christian is like at work and in the community, and will be the first to see if there is a dichotomy between profession and practice. Their opinion of a Christian leader's character cannot be dismissed, for it affects the entire church's witness. An overseer, then, "must have a good reputation with those outside the church."

A Christian leader with an unfavorable testimony in the local community will "fall into reproach" in a far more destructive way than those he leads. Cynically, people will say, "He acts that way, and he's a Christian leader." They will ridicule and mock him. He will be discredited as a Christian leader and suffer disgrace and insults. His influence for good will be ruined. But that is not all. Fully aware of the devil's ways (2 Corinthians 2:11), Paul adds that the defamed elder will also fall into "the snare of the devil." The devil is a cunning hunter (1 Peter 5:8). Using public criticism and the elder's own inconsistencies, the devil will entrap the man into greater and more serious sin—uncontrolled bitterness, angry retaliation, lying, further hypocrisy, and even turning from the faith. What may begin as a small offense can become something far more self-destructive and evil (2 Corinthians 2:5-11). In order to avoid great problems, a potential overseer's reputation in the world must be examined.

All the qualifications mentioned in Timothy indicate that an individual must be mature in order to qualify as an overseer. He must be mature spiritually and morally as well as mature in his ability to teach the Word and manage his own home. Men such as these are the ones God has chosen to shepherd His flock.

## NOTES

1. John Calvin, *The Second Epistle of Paul the Apostle to the Corinthians and the Epistles to Timothy, Titus, and Philemon*, trans. T. A. Smail, Calvin's Commentaries (reprint ed., Grand Rapids: Wm. B. Eerdmans Publishing Co., 1976), page 182.
2. George W. Knight, III, *The Faithful Sayings in the Pastoral Letters* (Nutley, New Jersey: Presbyterian and Reformed Publishing Co., no date), page 1.
3. *Ibid.*, page 61.
4. John Norman Davis Kelly, *The Pastoral Epistles* (1963; reprint ed., London: A. & C. Black Limited, 1972), page 74.
5. E. K. Simpson, *The Pastoral Epistles* (Grand Rapids: Wm. B. Eerdmans Publishing Co., 1954), pages 10, 11.
6. Jill Briscoe, *How to Fail Successfully* (Old Tappan, New Jersey: Fleming H. Revell Co., 1982), page 47.
7. The following points demonstrate why such an interpretation is unacceptable:

(1) The Bible plainly teaches that death dissolves the marriage bond and frees the living spouse to remarry without sinning (1 Corinthians 7:39; Romans 7:2,3).

(2) Remarriage after the death of a spouse is not reproachful. Those who hold the married-only-once-in-life view cannot identify the shame or defect in remarriage that disqualifies a man from eldership or deaconship. It is difficult to understand the reproach deacons would face if remarried after the death of a spouse (1 Timothy 3:12). In fact, those who try to show the reproach of a second marriage only raise serious questions about the first marriage as well.

(3) This interpretation smacks of false asceticism. It questions the sacredness of marriage, the very thing Paul condemns in 1 Timothy 4:3.

(4) This interpretation creates two standards for two grades of saints. For some bewildering reason, elders, deacons, and certain widows cannot remarry following the death of a spouse, but other saints can. Such division is incongruous with the rest of the New Testament.

(5) In the context of marriage and remarriage, Paul says, "And this I say for your own benefit; not to put a restraint upon you . . ." (1 Corinthians 7:35). This interpretation, however, restrains an innocent man, penalizing him for not having the gift of singleness (1 Corinthians 7:7,9).

(6) First Timothy 5:9 uses a similar construction for certain qualified widows, "the wife of one man." Again, these words can be rendered as a character trait, a one-man type of woman. Moreover, 1 Timothy 5:14, which urges younger widows to marry, would result in confusing counsel if the phrase means one husband in a lifetime. What if a widow's second husband were to die? Would she then no longer be eligible for the widows' list because she followed

the apostle's advice? This would be confusing counsel indeed. First Timothy 5:9 is not the key to interpreting 1 Timothy 3:2. See Ed Glasscock, "'The Husband of One Wife' Requirement in 1 Timothy 3:2," *Bibliotheca Sacra* 140 (July-September, 1983): 256.

(7) It is unthinkable that Paul, who is so sensitive to marital issues (1 Corinthians 7:2-5,7,8,15,32-36,39), would use an ambiguous three-word phrase to teach something so vital to widows and widowers that is in apparent disharmony with the rest of Scripture. Therefore the phrase must mean something other than married-only-once-in-a-lifetime.

(8) Ed Glasscock comments, "If, on the other hand, one understands the phrase to mean that he possesses only one wife (though this does not seem best grammatically), then other qualifications must be made. First, it must be decided if this means only one wife in a lifetime or one wife at a time. Since neither the grammar of the phrase nor any reference in the context implies that Paul was discussing a once-in-a-lifetime situation, then that idea must not be forced into the text" (page 251).

8. An excellent defense of this view has been done by Ed Glasscock, "'The Husband of One Wife' Requirement in 1 Timothy 3:2," *Bibliotheca Sacra* 140 (July-September, 1983): 244-258.
9. *Ibid.*, pages 253-255.
10. P. T. Forsyth, *The Church and the Sacraments* (1917; reprint ed., London: Independent Press LTD., 1955), page 9.
11. Neil Summerton, *A Noble Task* (Exeter: The Paternoster Press, 1987), pages 24, 25.
12. Donald Guthrie, *The Pastoral Epistles*, The Tyndale New Testament Commentaries (Grand Rapids: Wm. B. Eerdmans Publishing Co., 1957), page 81.

# Chapter 15

# *Male Leadership*

*Likewise, I want women to adorn themselves with proper clothing, modestly and discreetly, not with braided hair and gold or pearls or costly garments; but rather by means of good works, as befits women making a claim to godliness. Let a woman quietly receive instruction with entire submissiveness. But I do not allow a woman to teach or exercise authority over a man, but to remain quiet. For it was Adam who was first created, and then Eve. And it was not Adam who was deceived, but the woman being quite deceived, fell into transgression. But women shall be preserved through the bearing of children if they continue in faith and love and sanctity with self-restraint.*

*1 Timothy 2:9-15*

\* \* \*

A full-scale revolution is taking place in denominations and churches throughout Western society. As part of the larger social upheaval created by the feminist movement, this revolution involves the dissolution of traditional male-female roles in the home and church. The revolution has succeeded in toppling male-dominated leadership in thousands of churches. It has created a flood of new literature and generated fierce debate. It has even spawned preliminary work on a new, de-sexed version of the Bible.

As a result, traditional Christian teaching regarding man's headship and woman's submission is under the heaviest siege since

Christianity began two thousand years ago. A. Duane Litfin puts
the significance of this revolution into perspective:

> The recent phase of the feminist movement, which is usually
> dated from the emergence of Betty Friedan's *The Feminine
> Mystique* in 1964, is but the current wave of a tide that has
> been encroaching on male dominion for over two centuries.
> Yet that current wave is broader and more powerful than any
> of its precursors, and it seems to be part of a worldwide
> trend that may now be inexorable. It will no doubt ebb and
> flow with political currents, but the overall result seems
> assured in the decades to come: the dismantling of distinctions
> between male and female that are as old as the race. So the
> dilemma for modern Christians may be deeper and more
> difficult than ever before.[1]

Thus, no study of church eldership can be considered complete
unless it grapples with the critical question of women elders.
1 Timothy emphatically states—within the context of church order,
eldership, and deaconship—that women are "not . . . to teach or
exercise authority over a man." The qualifications for eldership
rest upon this limiting statement about women in 1 Timothy 2:9-15.
The qualifications assume a male subject—a one-woman kind of
man and one who manages his household well. So a major feature
of biblical eldership as presented in Scripture is that it is strictly
a male leadership body. Although elderships consisting of both
men and women are rapidly becoming a reality in many churches,
this practice is not found in either the Old or New Testaments.
In fact, as we will see, the placement of women as elders violates
one of the Bible's most fundamental principles—male headship
in the home and religious community.

The problem some evangelicals who hold to biblical inerrancy
have with the principle of male headship, however, is its apparent
conflict with other verses that emphasize women's equality. One
such verse is Galatians 3:28, which says, "There is neither Jew
nor Greek, there is neither slave nor free man, there is neither
male nor female; for you are all one in Christ Jesus." Many have
thus concluded that no hierarchical order of male-female role
relationships exists in the New Testament. Ward Gasque aptly terms
this position the egalitarian view:

> The Egalitarian View argues that there is no scriptural reason
> for women not to share in leadership in the church, or to

participate in a marriage relationship that is based on the principle of mutual submission and interdependent love. The accent in the Egalitarian View is on mutual submission—not the submission of one party to the other, but each party to one another—both in the church and in the home.[2] The traditional view of male-female role relationships, on the other hand, maintains that there are strong, compelling, scriptural reasons for affirming male headship and female subordination within the church and home. Unlike the egalitarian view, the traditional view does not set passages on women's equality and submission at odds.

The traditionalist seeks instead to give equal weight to both truths, as explained by the well-known Old Testament scholar, Bruce Waltke: "These truths regarding the equality and inequality of the sexes must be held in dialectical tension, by allowing them the same weight at the same time, and by not allowing one to vitiate the other by subordinating one to the other.[3] In the following pages, we will discuss women's equality and submission defending the traditional viewpoint that women's submission is a sound, biblical truth. Since our focus is the issue of women elders, we will not deal with other questions surrounding women's ministry.

### *The Principle of Women's Equality*

In many societies women are dehumanized. They are crushed, enslaved, and exploited by men. This is one of the world's worst social evils and is in no way supported by Scripture. Even so, some Christian men have ignored the scriptural evidence for women's equality and grotesquely distorted the biblical doctrine of male headship so that they might justify sins against women. For such sins against women, men must repent and seek to understand the equality of men and women and strive to exemplify true, Christ-like headship (Ephesians 5:25,28-33).

In creation, both men and women are equal in their being (Genesis 2:18,21-23). Men and women bear the image of God (Genesis 1:27) and share God's commission to be fruitful and take dominion of the earth (Genesis 1:28). In redemption, men and women are equal in their approach and standing before God (Galatians 3:28). Both are children of God, priests to God, Spirit-gifted servants of God, and members of the body of Christ. First Peter 3:7, for instance, reminds husbands that their wives are fellow heirs of the grace of life. Therefore, in the body of Christ, men and women should care for one another equally (1 Corinthians 12).

In radical contrast to the ancient Jewish and pagan perspectives of his day, Paul counterbalances any false division between men and women by emphasizing their unity and interdependence: "However, in the Lord, neither is woman independent of man, nor is man independent of woman. For as the woman originates from the man, so also the man has his birth through the woman; and all things originate from God" (1 Corinthians 11:11,12). "Let the husband fulfill his duty to his wife, and likewise also the wife to her husband. The wife does not have authority over her own body, but the husband does; and likewise also the husband does not have authority over his own body, but the wife does" (1 Corinthians 7:3,4). "For this cause a man shall leave his father and mother, and shall cleave to his wife; and the two shall become one flesh" (Ephesians 5:31).

Plainly, Scripture indicates that women are not second-class human beings. The Lord Jesus never treated women unjustly or with contempt. He highly esteemed them. Hence, women followed Him and ministered to Him. Both men and women are God's special and unique creations—the ones for whom Christ died. Thus, Christian men should take the lead in affirming all that God says about women and seeking to remove the just criticisms of male cruelty, unfairness, and irresponsibility against women. Although the Bible teaches that women are to be submissive to their husbands and the elders, it in no way implies that women have less worth or fewer abilities than men. Women are of equal worth and value and, in fact, may be superior in spiritual devotion, abilities, and intelligence (see Proverbs 31). Nevertheless, God provides for headship and subordination among equals.

### *The Principle of Women's Submission in the Family*

For a better understanding of God's design for order within the family, let us review key New Testament texts. Our study will focus on the New Testament, but please understand that the whole Bible affirms the role distinctions between men and women. From the beginning, God created man to function as the head—to govern, protect, and provide for the family. He made woman to care for, support, and nurture the family. God perfectly designed men and women to biologically, psychologically, and socially fulfill these distinct roles, and whenever people alter God's order, society suffers.

*Ephesians 5.* "Wives be subject to your own husbands, as to the Lord, For the husband is the head of the wife, as Christ also is the head of the church, He Himself being the Savior of the body. But as the church is subject to Christ, so also the wives ought to be to their husbands in everything. . . . and let the wife see to it that she respect her husband" (Ephesians 5:22-24,33). What could be more certain? God says, in the plainest of terms, that the husband is the head of the wife. In this context of proper order within the marriage relationship (Ephesians 5:21), the husband is described as the head, which—just as Christ is the head of the church—connotes governance, authority, and leadership.

Some scholars wish to diminish the strength of the headship concept in this passage by redefining head (kephale) to mean source or origin, which implies some sort of creation order rather than the notion of rule or authority. But as James Hurley has demonstrated in his masterful work, Man and Woman in Biblical Perspective, "Only with violence to the text can it be asserted that the idea of authority is absent from the language of headship and submission in Ephesians 5:22,23."[4] Even if the idea of source or origin were correct, it would not rule out an underlying concept of submission, since most relationships of origin imply some sort of subordination (such as the parent-child relationship). As Stephen Clark says, "it is difficult to see how such a possible interpretation can cancel the idea of governance in the 'head'."[5] In short, Ephesians 5 teaches that the woman is to be submissive in marriage. The husband and wife relationship should mirror the relationship between Christ and His church. Christ is the Head, and the church is subject to Him. Likewise, the husband is the head of the couple and the wife submits herself to him in everything.

*Colossians 3:18,19.* In explicit language, Colossians 3:18,19 says that a Christian wife should be submissive towards her husband: "Wives, be subject to your husbands, as is fitting in the Lord. Husbands, love your wives, and do not be embittered against them." This imperative command for a woman's submission is reinforced by the phrase, "as is fitting in the Lord." Thus, a woman's subjection to her husband is the only proper behavior in a family where Jesus is Lord.

*Titus 2:4,5.* "That they may encourage the young women to

love their husbands, to love their children, to be sensible, pure,
workers at home, kind, being subject to their own husbands, that
the word of God may not be dishonored." The gospel does not dis-
solve traditional role differences in marriage. Rather, it supports,
corrects, clarifies, and improves these ancient social roles. As the
only true guide to the roles each partner must play within marriage,
Scripture instructs young women to be devoted to their husbands
and children, and specifically to be submissive to their husbands.

1 Peter 3:1-7. Peter, like Paul, holds to and reinforces the Old
Testament teaching on a wife's submission to her husband:

> In the same way, you wives, be submissive to your own
> husbands . . . as they observe your chaste and respectful
> behavior. And let not your adornment be merely external . . .
> but let it be the hidden person of the heart, with the imperishable
> quality of a gentle and quiet spirit, which is precious in the
> sight of God. For in this way in former times the holy women
> also, who hoped in God, used to adorn themselves, being
> submissive to their own husbands. Thus Sarah obeyed
> Abraham, calling him lord, and you have become her children
> if you do what is right without being frightened by any fear
> (1 Peter 3:1-6).

Clearly, a woman with a gentle and quiet spirit who is submissive
to her husband is precious in God's sight. The great women of old
who were submissive to their husbands are ideal models for Christian
women. Like Paul, Peter exhorts Christian husbands to understand
and honor their wives, saying, "You husbands likewise, live with your
wives in an understanding way, as with a weaker vessel, since she
is a woman; and grant her honor as a fellow heir of the grace of life,
so that your prayers may not be hindered" (1 Peter 3:7). It's
interesting to note that Peter refers to a woman as a "weaker vessel."
By this he means that a man is physically more powerful than a
woman and is also in a position of authority and headship over her.
Thus, as often happens in this corrupt world, a man can more easily
exploit a woman. However, Christian men must honor their wives,
never forgetting that they are equal heirs of God's gift of life.

### The Principle of Women's Submission in the Church

There are obvious and important parallels between the family
and the local church (an extended family of brothers and sisters).
The Bible unequivocally teaches that the husband functions as

head of the family and the wife subordinates herself in the marriage union. The roles of husband and wife—so carefully revealed in Scripture—must never be reversed in the church family. Likewise, the practices of the local church must never undermine the order of the individual family, for the church must support the family and build upon it. Stephen B. Clark expresses this point emphatically:

> There is a further consideration which points toward the desirability of having the men be the elders of the Christian community . . . the structure of leadership has to be set up in a way that supports the entire social structure of the community. If the men are supposed to be the heads of the family, they must also be the heads of the community. The community must be structured in a way that supports the pattern of the family, and the family must be structured in a way that supports the pattern of the community. It is in the family that they learn their community roles as well. Conversely, what they see in the community reinforces what they learn in the family. Thus, to adopt different principles on the community level weakens the family, and vice versa.[6]

First century Christian women played an active part in the Lord's work. Some of Paul's closest co-laborers, for example, were women (Romans 16:1-15; Philippians 4:2,3). Many passages give evidence of women working diligently in the Lord's service. However, their active role in advancing the gospel and caring for the Lord's people did not negate their subordination in church meetings. The New Testament insists that the sisters be submissive in the church, just as in the home. This is directly stated in 1 Timothy 2:11,12 and 1 Corinthians 14:33-35. Let us carefully consider these two passages in order to discern the proper role of women in the church.

*1 Timothy 2:9-15.* The inspired letter of 1 Timothy is concerned with proper behavior and order in the Christian community. Paul explains to Timothy, his co-worker at Ephesus: "I am writing these things to you, hoping to come to you before long; but in case I am delayed, I write so that you may know how one ought to conduct himself in the household of God, which is the church of the living God, the pillar and support of the truth" (1 Timothy 3:14,15). In this passage, the word *conduct* means to behave, act, or live. Paul is saying there is a Christian way to behave in the family of God; there are principles that govern relationships among believers, and there is a proper order for members of God's family. Deliberately, as part of his message on conduct, Paul instructs the women of the congregation about proper behavior in the household of God:

*Modest dress.* "Likewise, I want women to adorn themselves with proper clothing, modestly and discreetly, not with braided hair and gold or pearls or costly garments; but rather by means of good works, as befits women making a claim to godliness" (1 Timothy 2:9,10).

*Quietness in the church.* "Let a woman quietly receive instruction with entire submissiveness. But I do not allow a woman to teach or exercise authority over a man, but to remain quiet" (1 Timothy 2:11,12).

This text of Scripture, written through the power of the Holy Spirit, should alone settle the question of women elders. Paul unequivocally prohibits women from doing two things: (1) teaching, and (2) having authority over men in the family of God. Women cannot, and must not, be elders in the household of God. This is evident in the positive statement, "Let a woman quietly receive instruction with entire submissiveness," as well as the negative statement, "But I do not allow a woman to teach or exercise authority over a man, but to remain quiet." Even the positive statement, "Let a woman quietly receive instruction," is qualified by the strong condition, "with entire submissiveness."

Since church elders shepherd the entire congregation, they lead and teach the people, which implies authority over the church. A Christian woman then is automatically disqualified from serving as an elder, because Scripture says she must not "exercise authority over a man."[7] In this chaotic and rebellious world, God desires that His people know how to act properly in His church. So, Paul's instruction in these verses is not a concession to a unique local problem, but an abiding, timeless, universal, biblical requirement for all God's people: "For it was Adam who was first created, and then Eve. And it was not Adam who was deceived, but the woman being quite deceived, fell into transgression. But women shall be preserved through the bearing of children if they continue in faith and love and sanctity with self-restraint" (1 Timothy 2:13-15). By saying that Adam was created first, Paul implies Adam's authority and headship over his family. It is significant that God did not create Adam and Eve at the same time. Woman was made from man, for man, brought to man, and named by man (Genesis 2:20-23; cf. 1 Corinthians 11:8,9). In biblical thought, because Adam was Eve's source of origin, she must honor and subordinate herself to him. Like the doctrine of the first-born son (Deuteronomy 21:15-17; Colossians 1:15-18) Adam's position as head of the family is due to his prior formation.

Adam, as the first human formed, was the responsible and accountable religious leader. God did not appoint Eve to be the religious head of the family. He appointed Adam. Thus Eve was not equipped—apart from Adam—to discern the subtleties of Satan, the master liar. Satan circumvented Adam—the one God appointed to be head of the family—and went directly to Eve, whom he rightly perceived to be the one he could deceive (2 Corinthians 11:3). Eve was truly deceived by Satan. Adam, according to Scripture, was not deceived. He knowingly disobeyed God.

Because of the differences between man and woman that God established at creation, a woman must not exercise authority over a man in the church, which is what being an elder entails. Such action is a violation of divine order in creation, a conclusion carefully stated by James Hurley: "In the light of our consideration of 1 Timothy 2 and 3, I conclude that Paul taught that the office of elder/bishop/presbyter was restricted to men. He felt that the creational pattern of male headship in both home and church required that women should not exercise spiritual oversight of the flock. They could not be in positions of authoritative teaching or exercising discipline over men."[8]

*1 Corinthians 14:27-35.* First Corinthians 14:33-35 is similar to the 1 Timothy text, but directed to an entirely different congregation: ". . . as in all the churches of the saints. Let the women keep silent in the churches; for they are not permitted to speak, but let them subject themselves, just as the Law also says. And if they desire to learn anything, let them ask their own husbands at home; for it is improper for a woman to speak in church." Here, the Spirit of God emphatically prohibits women from speaking in public church meetings. The rationale behind this regulation is the fundamental precept of women's subordination. In 1 Corinthians 14:27-35, Paul lays down restrictions for certain utterance gifts exercised in public church meetings and concludes with the emphatic restriction, "Let the women keep silent in the churches." Women are not permitted to speak in Christian churches because they must "subject themselves" as the Law says. The Law is the Old Testament, and it teaches that the woman's role in the congregation and family is one of submission (see 1 Corinthians 11:7-10; 1 Timothy 2:13,14; and 1 Peter 3:5,6). Therefore, prophetic utterances, speaking in tongues, and teaching in the church meetings are all inappropriate activities for women.

Some will point out, however, that women prophesied during the New Testament era (Acts 21:9; 1 Corinthians 11:5) and may wonder if this practice contradicts Paul's teaching on women's subordination. Such is not the case. Paul directly forbids women from prophesying in the actual church meeting (1 Corinthians 14:34). Even when it is appropriate for women to prophesy, he adds that they must cover their heads (1 Corinthians 11:5).[9] Thus, there is no doubt that Paul taught subordination.

We can be sure that when women in the New Testament prophesied, taught, and evangelized, they did so in a way that harmonized and supported the divine order of male headship. This is true of all great New Testament women: Mary, Priscilla, Phoebe, Euodia, Syntyche, Lydia, and many more. We can be absolutely certain that Paul held to and taught role differences between men and women that involved subordination and headship.

*Conclusion.* These two explicit, didactic passages regarding the role of women in the church take precedence over incidental passages about women's activities in the general service of the Lord (Acts 12:13; 18:26; Romans 16:1-15; Philippians 4:2,3; Colossians 4:15; 1 Timothy 5:9,10). The 1 Timothy and 1 Corinthians passages are the key Scripture portions that govern the practice of women in church meetings. Therefore, since women cannot teach or exercise authority over men because they are called to submit themselves, there is no possible way that a woman can be an elder without disobeying God's divine plan for the family and the local church. Although the Bible never directly says a woman cannot be an elder, such a notion contradicts the entire biblical record and therefore would not be considered by the inspired authors.

### *Theological and Biblical Support for Women's Submission*

Some people plead special circumstances and consider the 1 Timothy 2 and 1 Corinthians 14 passages to be irrelevant for churches today. Paul, they say, was dealing with unique problems in specific churches: women were causing a disturbance by chattering noisily in church meetings at Corinth; women were uneducated at Ephesus; or Paul was concerned that the new freedom Christian women enjoyed would offend certain groups of people, thus hindering the gospel's effectiveness. Such special circumstances, however, are not indicated in these passages, but are imaginary circumstances created by scholars who cannot accept Scripture's explicit teaching. Furthermore, isolated local circumstances in no way justify the conclusion that these passages are no longer normative. Douglas Moo explains the significance of these isolated circumstances well:

> . . . sound hermeneutical procedure would require that there be very good evidence for any local situation which is held up as a factor limiting the application of a biblical command. Otherwise, one could limit the applicability of virtually any biblical text simply by suggesting possible local circumstances behind it.
>
> . . . The effort expended in detecting local circumstances behind certain NT texts appears often to have as its motivation the assumption that the demonstration of such factors constitutes evidence that the text in question cannot be applied universally. . . .
>
> The point then is this: the isolation of local circumstances as the occasion for a particular teaching does not, by itself, indicate anything about the normative nature of that teaching. . . .
> While Paul's advice to Timothy is undoubtedly occasioned by specific circumstances in the first century Ephesians church, and is directed primarily to those circumstances, the *"situation"* in which Paul's advice is applicable extends far beyond that *occasion,* embracing every Christian worship service in which men and women descended from Adam and Eve participate.[10]
> [Italics mine]

Paul solidly supports his instruction on women's subordination by (1) the universal, normative practice of all churches; (2) his own apostolic authority; (3) the Old Testament Scripture that reveals God's design for men and women; (4) a direct command from Jesus recorded in 1 Corinthians 14:34-38; and (5) theological principles.

First Corinthians 11:2-16 is the best example of how Paul bases his arguments of man's headship and woman's submission firmly in theological and biblical fact, not special circumstances: "Now I praise you because you remember me in everything, and hold firmly to the traditions, just as I delivered them to you. But I want you to understand that Christ is the head of every man, and the man is the head of a woman, and God is the head of Christ" (1 Corinthians 11:2,3). Even Christ, as the last Adam (1 Corinthians 15:45), was subject to God's headship—authority and rule—to provide salvation for the lost sons of Adam. Christ, as head of the new humanity, is subordinate to God (1 Corinthians 15:23-28). Thus, woman's subordination to man is part of a series of subordination and headship relationships: God is head, Christ is head, and man is head. Only woman is not referred to as head. These relationships have nothing to do with temporal and local circumstances, but follow a divinely constituted hierarchical order.

Further proof for the male-female order of authority is furnished by the Old Testament creation order, which Paul reviews in 1 Corinthians 11:7-9: "For a man ought not to have his head covered, since he is the image and glory of God; but the woman is the glory of man. For man does not originate from woman, but woman from man; for indeed man was not created for the woman's sake, but woman for the man's sake." This reference to submission and headship is similar to Ephesians 5:23,24, where Paul indicates that the husband reflects Christ's headship over the church and the wife reflects the church's subordination to Christ. Paul shows that man is the image and glory of God, which means he manifests God's headship when he acts in his proper role as head. Since woman is the glory of man, she manifests man's headship when she acts in her proper role as subordinate.

### *Two Common Errors*

The Bible explicitly, repeatedly, and clearly teaches the headship of man and the subordination of woman in the home and religious community. There is absolutely no conflict between biblical teaching on the equality and unity of men and women, and the subordination of women. Scripture plainly teaches both truths, and God's plan is accurately represented when both truths are understood together.

The chief error, then, lies when one pits a group of verses on subordination against another group of verses on equality, thus fabricating a conflict or inconsistency in the divine record. This is true of the way many interpreters pit Galatians 3:28 against numerous other verses. "Many contemporary interpreters," says Clark, "approach Galatians 3:28 as the great breakthrough that should abolish all role differences between men and women."[11] Indeed, the way this verse is used makes Paul appear inconsistent, vacillating, and contradictory. The problem, however, is not with Paul, but with his interpreters who are ill-disposed to women's subordination.

Paul's point in this verse is that all believers—regardless of race, social status, or sex—are sons of God through faith in Christ Jesus. So this verse primarily applies to one's standing with God. There is a comparison in the passage between the condition under the law which equally condemns all mankind (cf. v. 22) and the condition in Christ which equally justifies all men. Paul is not saying there are no sex role differentiations in life, marriage, or the church. The denial of such differentiations throws the entire New Testament teaching on men's and women's roles into utter confusion.

As a result of imbalanced, egalitarian interpretations, numerous verses that plainly discuss subordination are cleverly explained away. Straightforward and explicit texts are deemed obscure, difficult, problematic, and isolated, when in truth they are not. Incredible explanations are constructed to show that those passages do not mean what they obviously say, or to show that they could not possibly apply to today's churches. Even scholars who do not adhere to biblical inerrancy and women's submission find such interpretations of Paul and Peter to be unacceptable.[12] Even they recognize that the New Testament unquestionably teaches subordination and headship. It would be far more honest, then, to say that one does not agree with the Bible's teaching on women's subordination than to craftily explain away Scripture's obvious meaning. Such treatment of Scripture robs the Bible of its integrity and authority. Absolute fidelity to Scripture will not allow us to treat God's Word this way.

Another error concerning male headship and female subordination that we face today is due to people's perception of the word *subordination*. For many twentieth century people, the word *subordination* (or submission) has become a repulsive term that connotes inferiority, weakness, inequality, slavery, or oppression. This is unfortunate because subordination is actually a wonderful term. It primarily describes the way a relationship is ordered or conducted. As such, subordination can take on different forms of structure and style. Certainly subordination can be oppressive or unjust. But it can also be voluntary—for the betterment, protection, and care of the subordinate, or as the means by which a community or couple achieves higher goals and greater unity. In his book, *Man and Woman in Christ*, Stephen B. Clark clarifies this point:

> Neither "inferiority" nor "equality" have any conceptually necessary link to "subordination" unless the terms are defined with such a link. The head and subordinate can both be of equal worth and value. In fact, they can be equal in many other ways, and still be in a relationship involving subordination. The subordinate can even be of greater rank and dignity, as Jesus was in relationship to his parents. To equate subordination with inferiority or inequality is either a confusion, or an attempt to win an argument by defining the terms in a way that is advantageous to one's own side.[13]

***Conclusion***

In light of the woman's place of subordination in the family and church, which is plainly expressed by Paul's direct statement that she must not exercise authority over a man, it is simply not possible for a woman to be an elder because such a position involves authority and teaching in the church. God has clearly commissioned men to do that job, not women. Thus, the appointment of women elders is in direct disobedience to God's Word and will generate further male irresponsibility, which is already a monstrous problem in the family and Christian community.

The church elders must protect the church from all false feminist teaching that is destructive to the family, church, and society. At the same time, elders must consciously guard themselves from overreacting to women's liberation, thereby hurting women in the church who have legitimate complaints and frustrations because of male prejudice and insensitivity. God's Word is perfectly balanced, and only by teaching and obeying it will elders be able to guide the saints in these vital matters.

---

**NOTES**

1. A. Duane Litfin, "Theological Issues in Contemporary Feminism," *Walvoord: a Tribute*, ed. Donald K. Campbell (Chicago: Moody Press, 1982), page 333.

2. W. Ward Gasque, "The Role of Women in the Church, in Society, and in the Home," *Crux* 19 (September, 1983): 3, 4.
3. Bruce Waltke, "The Relationship of the Sexes in the Bible," *Crux* 19 (September, 1983): 14.
4. James B. Hurley, *Man and Woman in Biblical Perspective* (Grand Rapids: Zondervan Publishing House, 1981), page 147.
5. From *Man and Woman in Christ*, copyright 1980 by Stephen B. Clark Published by Servant Publications, Box 8617, Ann Arbor, Michigan 48107. Used with permission.
6. *Ibid*, page 630.
7. An excellent defense of this translation can be found in an article by George W. Knight III, "Authenteo in Reference to Women in 1 Timothy 2:12," *New Testament Studies* 30 (January, 1984): 143-157.
8. Hurley, *Man and Woman*, page 233.
9. First Corinthians 11:2-16 does not refer specifically to a church meeting. It refers generally to wherever it would be proper for women and men to pray and prophesy. Verse 17 begins the context of the church gathered. There is absolutely no conflict between chapters 11 and 14.
10. Douglas J. Moo, "The Interpretation of 1 Timothy 2:11-15; A Rejoinder," *Trinity Journal* 2NS (Fall, 1981): 218, 219.
11. Clark, *Man and Woman*, page 150.
12. Paul K. Jewett, *The Ordination of Women* (Grand Rapids: Wm. B. Eerdmans Publishing Co., 1980), page 67.
13. Clark, *Man and Woman*, page 44.
    Clark expands this definition of subordination throughout his book (see pages 23, 24, 92):
    The English word "subordination" means literally "ordered under," and its Greek counterpart means almost the same. The word does not carry with it a notion of inferior value. A subordinate could be more valuable in many ways than the person over him or her. Nor does the word carry with it a notion of oppression or the use of force for domination. The word can be used to describe an oppressive relationship, but its normal use is for relationships in which the subordination involved is either neutral or good.
    "Subordination" simply refers to the order of a relationship in which one person, the subordinate, depends upon another person for direction. The purpose of this order is to allow those in the relationship to function together in unity. Subordination is a broader concept than obedience and command. As will be seen, subordination usually implies a form of obedience. A person can give some commands to a subordinate and expect obedience, but to place the emphasis on obedience is to narrow the meaning of "subordination." A person could be subordinate without ever having to obey a command. People can subordinate their lives or actions to another in many ways: by serving another, by observing and cooperating

with the other's purposes and desires, by dedicating their lives to the cause the other is upholding, or by following the other's teaching. The more that love and personal commitment are part of subordination, the more these other elements will be present along with whatever obedience is asked. . . .

Although "subordination" primarily describes a way of relating to another person, it also involves a character trait, a disposition to respond in a certain way. Subordination extends beyond obedience to commands to also include respectfulness and receptiveness to direction. "Submissiveness" is probably the best English term in such contexts. "Submissiveness," in this sense, is an overall character trait related to humility which all Christians should possess. The Christian character is portrayed in scripture as respectful of authority, not rebellious. Men as well as women should be submissive in their subordinate relationships.

# Chapter 16

# The Laying on of Hands and Ordination

*Do not neglect the spiritual gift within you, which was bestowed upon you through prophetic utterance with the laying on of hands by the presbytery.*

1 Timothy 4:14

\* \* \*

In her book, *Ordination*, which is one of the few books on the subject, Marjorie Warkentin writes,

All kinds of suppositions about ordination abound. . . . that it confers on the recipient a special "character" that remains with him or her for life, that it protects the church from heresy, that only the ordained should administer the ordinances, that it transmits "grace" for office, that it does not transmit "grace" for office, that it conveys authority, that it conveys nothing whatsoever, and so on. The Scriptures of the New Testament are called upon to substantiate many of the assumptions, but contradictory doctrines continue to coexist.[1]

To a Roman Catholic, ordination means one thing—the Sacrament of Holy Orders, part of the "seven holy sacraments." Administered only by the bishop, this sacrament entitles the recipient to the Holy Spirit's endowment and the endowment of an indelible sacramental character that remains with the individual for life.

Among Protestants, however, a great diversity of opinion exists

[223]

regarding ordination's significance and practice. Generally speaking, most Protestants believe ordination is a ceremonial rite that formally authorizes or acknowledges a person's call or gift to a special ministerial function. For most Protestants, the difference between ordained and unordained is primarily a difference of function, rather than a difference in character as is the case in the Roman Catholic, Orthodox, and (to a lesser extent) Anglican churches.

Other Protestants, like myself, believe that ordination in the modern ecclesiastical sense doesn't exist in the New Testament. If by *ordination* one means to place a person in a specific office or appoint a person to a special task, everyone would agree that ordination is a New Testament concept and practice. But if the word is used in the modern sense, meaning to invest with priestly character or grant exclusive ministerial rights to administer the sacraments and the Word, we stand opposed to the belief that this is a New Testament practice. Indeed, we believe ordination in the latter sense is contrary to God's Word. It is a false human tradition without basis in the New Testament.

### The Texts of Scripture

The passage before us, 1 Timothy 4:14, is commonly quoted as a prime example of ordination. So let us begin by expounding 1 Timothy 4:14. Then we will survey all the relevant New Testament texts to see if the prevalent ideas of ordination are of apostolic origin.

*Elders laying hands on Timothy.* Timothy was converted during Paul's first missionary journey. Thus, he was Paul's true child in the faith. At the beginning of the second missionary journey, Luke says that Paul wanted Timothy to go with him (Acts 16:3). Three significant things happened to Timothy on this second visit: first, Timothy and Paul learned, by a series of supernatural, prophetic utterances, that God's Spirit had revealed Timothy's unique commission in the gospel to all the saints: "This command I entrust to you, Timothy, my son, in accordance with the prophecies previously made concerning you, that by them you may fight the good fight" (1 Timothy 1:18). Timothy had been singled out by explicit prophetic predictions for a very specific task, just as Paul and Barnabas had (Acts 13:1-3).

Second, in complete accord with the prophets' words, Paul placed his hands on Timothy in order to convey a gift—that is, a charisma—a special endowment for service: "And for this reason I remind you to kindle afresh the gift of God which is in you through the laying on of my hands" (2 Timothy 1:6). This is a unique New Testament experience. There is no other record of anyone receiving a spiritual gift by the laying on of hands. Unlike the believers in Acts 8 and 19, Timothy already had the Holy Spirit, so the gift he received by Paul's hands was a gift for service. This was not a standard ordination practice. By the laying on of Paul's hands, Timothy became subordinate to Paul and was to share in Paul's commission in the gospel. The New Testament scholar, F.J.A. Hort, draws the following conclusion from these events:

> All the circumstances . . . explain themselves naturally if the passages in the two Epistles to Timothy refer to a single absolutely exceptional solemn act by which the one man Timothy received a commission to go forth as St. Paul's chosen colleague, because a prophetic oracle had singled him out for this unique function.[2]

It's important to understand that Paul did not ordain Timothy to a church office. *Charisma* does not mean office, but "spiritual gift," a divine empowerment to perform a function. Timothy was not the minister, pastor, or bishop of a church or body of churches. Instead, Timothy was a specially gifted servant who acted as Paul's delegate. He was Paul's assistant (Acts 19:22), traveling constantly on his behalf. Most likely, Timothy was an unmarried man, totally devoted to spreading and guarding the gospel, but always as Paul's assistant. He was an evangelist (2 Timothy 4:5), a co-worker, and partner with Paul in the gospel's work.

Third, and closely associated with the prophecies and the laying on of Paul's hands, was "the laying on of hands by the presbytery." The elders' action had different significance than Paul's action. Paul and the prophecy spoken were the people, "through" (Greek, *dia*), whom God conferred the "spiritual gift." The laying on of the elders' hands, Scripture shows, was done *in association with* (Greek, *meta*) Paul and the prophecy. What the laying on of the elders' hands signified, however, is not stated. Perhaps (as in Acts 13:1-3) the church elders released Timothy to the work the Holy Spirit had called him to. By "the laying on of hands," the elders, representing the church, set Timothy apart for this special task. By so doing, they identified themselves as partners with him. In accord with the "prophetic utterance," the elders, as witnesses to that word, placed their hands upon him. Timothy was to remember this act and not allow men to despise his labor or youth.

The word "presbytery" is a transliteration of the Greek word *presbyterion*, the collective noun for elders (Greek, *presbyteroi*). It would have been better if the *New American Standard Bible* had translated *presbyterion* as eldership, elderhood, council of elders, or body of elders, since it renders the other two occurrences of *presbyterion* as *the council of elders* (Luke 22:66; Acts 22:5). By using the collective noun *eldership*, Paul stresses the elders' official role and the significance of their act. The official body of church elders, not merely some of his friends, laid hands upon Timothy. Hence, the local church shared in Timothy's labor for the gospel, a fact he was never to forget.

The eldership referred to in this account was the eldership Paul and Barnabas appointed on their first missionary journey. Again, not one elder, but the entire body of elders laid hands on Timothy. As community leaders, their function was to represent the church in the communication of its fellowship, concurrence with God's appointment, and love by laying their hands on one of their own members.

*Jesus appoints the twelve*: "And He appointed twelve, that they might be with Him, and that He might send them out to preach" (Mark 3:14). The *King James Version's* translation of *poieo* in this verse as *ordained* has resulted in confusion in the modern English reader's mind. The Greek verb (*poieo*), from which the word *ordained* is taken, literally means *made* or *created*. So there is no reason to suppose that any sacred rite of ordination is intended by its use here. The *New American Standard Bible's* rendering, *appointed*, is more accurate.

Unfortunately, most people today think of a rite of ordination when they read in the *King James Version* that Jesus *ordained* the Twelve. Awareness of this potential misunderstanding caused J. A. Alexander to comment: "Ordained is in Greek not a technical expression, but a very common verb, meaning made, i.e., out of the whole number present, or, as some think, out of the selected number whom he called to him, he constituted or created twelve to be a body by themselves; for what purpose, and with what official functions, is expressed in the remainder of the verse. That they might be with him, as constant personal attendants, and as learners, to be trained for their subsequent work."[3] The passage does not say that Jesus laid hands on the Twelve or that He established a special ceremony for ordination. Jesus' appointment of the Twelve was, as far as the record shows, a personal, non-ceremonial act.

*Jesus commissions his disciples*: "And when He had said this, He breathed on them, and said to them, 'Receive the Holy Spirit. If you forgive the sins of any, their sins have been forgiven them; if you retain the sins of any, they have been retained'" (John 20:22,23). This is John's account of the Great Commission. Clearly, Jesus was speaking to a larger crowd of disciples than just the apostles (John 20:19; Luke 24:33-49). This is certainly not an ordination service or special ceremony. Instead, the act of breathing the Holy Spirit upon them was done to enable them to understand, endure, and receive all that Jesus would teach during his post-resurrection ministry. Thus, the Gospels give no record of Jesus establishing a normative ordination rite or special ceremony for placing men in sacred ministry.

*Laying hands on the seven*: "'But select from among you, brethren, seven men of good reputation, full of the Spirit and of wisdom, whom we may put in charge of this task'. . . . And these they brought before the apostles; and after praying, they laid their hands on them" (Acts 6:3,6). One example of how this account has been improperly handled is found in Richard Rackham's classic commentary on Acts, in the *Westminster Commentary* series. He writes:

S. Luke evidently means us to take this first instance as a typical picture of apostolic ordination, and we should compare the briefer notices in 13:3; 14:23. . . . Still there remains a part peculiar to the apostles, viz what we now call the ordination, the ceremony by which is conferred the necessary spiritual authority or "character." . . . The whole church, then appoints: the multitude elect and present: The gift of the Spirit required for office in the church is conferred by the apostles, who themselves had received the gift from above.[4]

Because the Acts 6 account has been so misused, we must first state what it does not mean.

- Here, the laying on of hands did not convey the Holy Spirit or any special power or grace. The seven were already well-recognized, gifted leaders who were full of the Spirit and wisdom.
- The seven were not ordained to a higher office, the teaching

ministry, or the pastorate. On the contrary, they were selected specifically to serve the poor and were to share their responsibility as a team of servants.

• This is not an example of congregationalism in which each member has an equal vote and where ultimate authority rests in the members themselves. The apostles—the body of overseers—presented a specific plan, set the qualifications for the seven, and officially appointed those selected by the congregation. The selection of the seven men was made under the apostles' supervision and counsel.

Acts 6:6 is the first example of the laying on of hands in the Christian community. The imposition of hands is used for various purposes in the Bible, but as James Orr says, "The primary idea seems to be that of conveyance or transference (cf. Leviticus 16:21) but, conjoined with this, in certain instances are the ideas of identification and of devotion to God."[5] Orr's observation is in keeping with examples of the laying on of hands in both the Old and New Testaments. For example, in the Old Testament the laying on of hands was used:

• to convey blessing (Genesis 48:14)
• to identify with a sacrifice to God (Leviticus 1:4)
• to transfer sin (Leviticus 16:21)
• to transfer defilement (Leviticus 24:14)
• to identify man's actions with God's (2 Kings 13:16)
• to set people apart: to convey a special commission, responsibility, or authority (Numbers 8:10,14; 27:15-23; Deuteronomy 34:9)

In the New Testament the laying on of hands was used:

• to convey blessing (Matthew 19:15; Mark 10:16)
• to convey the Holy Spirit's healing power (Mark 6:5; 8:23,25; 16:18; Luke 4:40; 13:13; Acts 9:12; 19:11; 28:8)
• to convey the Holy Spirit to certain believers through the apostles' hands (Acts 8:17-19; 19:6)
• to convey healing and the Spirit to Paul through Ananias' hands (Acts 9:17)
• to convey a spiritual gift to Timothy through Paul's hands (2 Timothy 1:6)
• to set apart or place in office (Acts 6:6; 13:3; 1 Timothy 4:14; 5:22)

In some instances, the precise significance of the laying on of hands is difficult to understand. This is particularly true of the accounts in Acts 13:3 and 1 Timothy 4:14; 5:22, in which Luke and Paul do not explain its significance. It is certain, however, that the New Testament gives no normative regulations for the laying on of hands. The act is not restricted to a particular person or group in the church (Acts 9:12; 13:3), and it is not an ordinance like baptism or the Lord's Supper.

It seems reasonable to conclude that the imposition of hands in Acts 6 visually expressed the apostles' setting apart or appointment of the seven. In verse three, the apostles instructed the congregation to select seven men who they would place in charge or appoint (Greek, *kathistemi*) to care for the church funds and widows. So, when the congregation set the seven before the apostles, the apostles publicly and officially placed them in charge of their highly responsible task by prayer and the imposition of hands. As in Numbers 27:22,23, the laying on of hands in this instance appears to be associated with conveying a special commission or task, or setting a person apart for a specific function.

Because of the seven's highly responsible task of handling large sums of money (Acts 4:34-37), and the growing tensions between the Helenistic Jews and Hebrews, the apostles knew that the situation demanded an official, public appointment. (Grammatically, it is possible that the entire congregation laid hands on the seven, but the account as a whole favors laying on of hands by the apostles only.) We must not overlook the fact that the laying on of hands in this account did not install priests or ministers to higher ministerial positions, but simply set apart a team of men to care for widows and finances.

*Laying hands on Paul*: "'. . . and he has seen in a vision a man named Ananias come in and lay his hands on him, so that he might regain his sight.' . . . And Ananias departed and entered the house, and after laying his hands on him said, 'Brother Saul, the Lord Jesus, who appeared to you on the road by which you were coming, has sent me so that you may regain your sight, and be filled with the Holy Spirit'" (Acts 9:12,17). The details of this account make it plain that Ananias did not ordain Paul:

• Paul was a new convert.
• Ananias was not a higher ecclesiastical official but "a certain disciple" (Acts 9:10).
• This was not a formal church ceremony. In fact, Ananias was hesitant to even meet Paul (Acts 9:13). Instead, the event

shows Christ's supernatural dealing with His "chosen instrument" either directly (Acts 9:5), or through one of His servants (Acts 9:10). In this case, the Lord appeared to Ananias in a vision, and Ananias was the channel through whom Paul received his sight and possibly the Holy Spirit (Acts 9:12,17,18).

The entire account rubs against the grain of later ecclesiastical practice. If Paul received the Holy Spirit through Ananias' hands (and this is not certain since Acts 22:16 indicates that Paul may have received the Spirit after he received his sight), he wasn't set apart by any lofty person. Peter, John, the council of elders, or a congregation did not lay hands on Paul. Only a lowly disciple—a nobody who immediately disappears from the pages of Scripture—laid hands on Paul. In this encounter, God stripped away all potential pride and human boasting from both Ananias and Paul.

*Paul and Barnabas appoint elders*: "And when they had appointed elders for them in every church, having prayed with fasting, they commended them to the Lord in whom they had believed" (Acts 14:23). As the exposition of Acts 14:23 shows, all Scripture says is that Paul and Barnabas appointed a body of elders for each local church (Greek, *cheirotoneo*). Scripture does not reveal their procedure in appointing elders, nor does it mention the laying on of hands.

*Laying hands on Paul and Barnabas*: "Then, when they had fasted and prayed and laid their hands on them, they sent them away" (Acts 13:3). Despite what leading commentators say, this passage has nothing to do with ordination in the modern sense. It is another example of how tradition blinds the eyes of even the best expositors. J. B. Lightfoot, for instance, wrongly refers to this account as Paul's ordination to apostleship: "It does not follow that the actual call to the apostleship should come from an outward personal communication with our Lord, . . . But the actual investiture, the completion of his call, as may be gathered from St. Luke's narrative, took place some years later at Antioch (Acts 13:2)."[6] This passage cannot refer to ordination as we know it for the following reasons:

• Barnabas and Paul were already eminently gifted men in the church (Acts 13:1). The Jerusalem church had sent Barnabas to investigate and encourage the new work at Antioch (Acts 11:22-26). Both Paul and Barnabas were the leading teachers in the church and were veteran laborers for Christ. Paul was already an apostle—

appointed directly by Jesus Christ. No man or group could claim to have ordained him as an apostle (Acts 26:16-19; Galatians 1:1). Thus, this act was not ordination to the ministry, for Paul and Barnabas were already in the ministry. Instead, the Spirit selected Paul and Barnabas for a special task in spreading the gospel, not for higher office or gift.

• According to the record, Paul and Barnabas did not receive the Holy Spirit, spiritual gifts, or any other power for service on this occasion. They already possessed the Holy Spirit and His gifts (Acts 13:1).

• Higher officials did not lay hands on Paul and Barnabas. It appears that the church and its leaders placed their hands on their two brethren (Acts 14:26; 15:40) who were leaving the church to minister, not coming to the church to minister.

What, then, is the significance of the imposition of hands in this situation? The context indicates that the church, by prayer and the laying on of hands, set Paul and Barnabas apart to a special mission in the gospel. Jesus had said, ". . . 'The harvest is plentiful, but the laborers are few; therefore beseech the Lord of the harvest to send out laborers into His harvest'" (Luke 10:2). So, led by the prophets and teachers, the church was fasting (Acts 13:2) and offering special prayer concerning laborers for the harvest in obedience to Jesus' instruction. Thus, this is the first organized church missionary outreach recorded in Acts. It is a critical turning point in Christian church history. Until this time, missionary expansion was due to persecution or individual desire. But here, for the first time, a local assembly sought to be involved in praying for laborers for the harvest while ministering to the Lord and fasting.

Both the divine and human involvement in sending out Paul and Barnabas are beautifully woven together in these few verses. The Holy Spirit responded by means of a prophetic utterance: ". . . 'Set apart for Me Barnabas and Saul for the work to which I have called them'" (Acts 13:2). So, the Holy Spirit called and sent out the two men—the divine initiative. By ministering to the Lord and fasting, the local Christians became an active and intimate part of Paul's and Barnabas' sending out by the Holy Spirit—the human initiative.

In obedience to the Holy Spirit's command to set Paul and Barnabas apart, the church prayed, fasted, and laid hands on them. They then released them to the new work of evangelizing the

Gentiles (Acts 14:27; 15:3,12). The text suggests that the prophets and teachers (Simeon, Lucius, and Manaen), took the lead throughout this event. But from Acts 14:26, where it says, ". . . they sailed to Antioch from which they had been commended. . . .", it is evident that the whole church commended Paul and Barnabas to God for the work. Later, Paul and Barnabas reported their success to the whole church: "And when they had arrived and gathered the church together, they began to report all things that God had done with them . . ." (Acts 14:27). The farewell ceremony for the two departing messengers of the gospel (cf. Acts 14:23) involved fasting, praying, and laying on of hands. Some Christians today have overreacted to elaborate religious ceremony by eliminating all ceremony. But it is noteworthy that the first Christians were not averse to public ceremony.

Luke does not explain the significance of the laying on of hands in this instance. But as in Acts 6:1-6, the context involves setting apart select men in the church for a special task (in verse two, the Greek word *aphorizo* is used, meaning to set apart). First Timothy 5:22 also indicates that the laying on of hands signifies appointment or setting apart. So, by the laying on of hands (probably the hands of the other prophets and teachers) the church set Paul and Barnabas apart for the special work that the Holy Spirit called them to in response to their prayers. Commenting on the ceremony, R. C. H. Lenski writes: "This, of course, was not ordination for Barnabas and for Saul, who were already 'prophets and teachers.' Yet it was the ceremony the church deemed proper formally to carry out the will of the Spirit in order to separate these two for their special work."[7] According to 1 Timothy 5:22, the laying on of hands in appointment establishes a partnership or bond between two parties. There is a sense in which the one (or ones) who appoints shares in the failure or success of the one appointed. Also, the one set apart has some accountability toward those who placed their hands on him. Thus, the laying on of hands creates a deeper sense of responsibility, accountability, and fellowship between the parties involved.

*Appointing elders*: "For this reason I left you in Crete, that you might set in order what remains, and appoint elders in every city as I directed you" (Titus 1:5). As Paul's personal delegate in Crete, Titus was to appoint elders. (The Greek word for *appoint* is *kathistemi*.) As in Acts 14:23, this passage says nothing about the laying on of hands or manner of appointment.

*No hasty appointments*: "Do not lay hands upon anyone too hastily and thus share responsibility for the sins of others . . ." (1 Timothy 5:22). Timothy, as Paul's representative in Ephesus, was to appoint local elders. It was a solemn duty. So Paul, in order to avoid the problems created by the appointment of unworthy men to a responsible position, said not to appoint anyone too quickly. The context here obviously indicates that the laying on of hands is used to appoint to an office.

This is the only New Testament instruction concerning the imposition of hands. In addition to Paul's instruction not to lay hands on a person too soon, the passage reveals that there is mutual accountability in the laying on of hands. Those who place their hands on others share in their success or failure. Therefore, the laying on of hands should not be done lightly or thoughtlessly.

The passage seems to indicate (appearing as it does in the context of elders) that Timothy laid hands on elders. But it is possible that the laying on of hands is used as a figure of speech meaning appointment. The New Testament does not clearly reveal whether or not Paul's custom was to lay hands on newly appointed elders. Possibly Paul did lay hands on the elders, and Timothy (who represented him at Ephesus) did the same. Whatever Paul's practice was, there is certainly no great emphasis on the imposition of hands in the appointment of new elders, nor are there explicit instructions to do so.

### Appointment, not Ordination

The conclusion we must come to, then, is that while the New Testament speaks of appointment to specific tasks or positions, the original Greek words (*poieo, tithemi, kathistemi, cheirotoneo*) do not express or imply a modern ordination rite or special ceremony. In fact, as difficult as it may be to accept, there is simply no way to use the word *ordination* without inferring ideas that are contrary to the New Testament teaching and language.

The word *ordination* is another example of misleading terminology that needs reform. Just as there is no way to use the words *clergy* or *bishop* without misleading God's people, there is no proper way to use the word *ordination* without creating misconceptions. Although *ordination* is accepted ecclesiastical terminology, it needs to be questioned because it creates false concepts in the listeners' minds. Until such unscriptural terminology is removed, it will be difficult—if not impossible—to adopt genuine, apostolic Christianity.

Even well-known Bible scholars who support clerical ordination say the New Testament's vocabulary speaks only of general appointment—never of a special ordination rite. For example, Leon Morris says: "Considering the role played by the ministry throughout the history of the church, references to ordination are surprisingly few in the N.T. Indeed, the word 'ordination' does not occur, and the verb "to ordain" in the technical sense does not occur either. A number of verbs are translated 'ordain' in AV, but these all have meanings like 'appoint'."[8] In similar fashion, Alfred Plummer makes the following remarkable comments on the Greek verb *appoint* in Titus 1:5:

> In the A.V. the phrase runs "ordain elders in every city. . . ." In these passages three different Greek words (*poieo, tithemi, kathistemi*) are used in the original; but not one of them has the special ecclesiastical meaning which we so frequently associate with the word "ordain"; not one of them implies, as "ordain" in such context almost of necessity implies, a rite of ordination, a special ceremonial, such as the laying on of hands. When in English we say, "He ordained twelve," . . . the mind almost inevitably thinks of ordination in the common sense of the word; and this is foisting upon the language of the New Testament a meaning which the words there used do not rightly bear. . . . The Greek words used in the passages quoted might equally well be used of the appointment of a magistrate or a steward. And as we should avoid speaking of ordaining a magistrate or a steward, we ought to avoid using "ordain" to translate words which would be thoroughly in place in such a connexion. The Greek words for "ordain" and "ordination," in the sense of imposition of hands in order to admit to an ecclesiastical office (*cheipotheti, cheipothesia*), do not occur in the New Testament at all.[9]

So, to translate the New Testament words *poieo, tithemi, kathistemi,* or *cheirotoneo* as *ordained* imposes erroneous meanings that create unscriptural priestly or clerical connotations. The New Testament employs no special words to convey the concept of ordination, even though its authors could have used such words if they so intended. Furthermore, to equate the laying on of hands with ordination is an error that only confuses the issue even more.

The laying on of hands in the New Testament has no real connection with later ecclesiastical notions of ordination or succession. Surprisingly, not only is ordination not found in the New Testament, it is not found in the writings of the early second century church writers. One can be sure that *Ignatius would have used the rite of ordination to bolster his arguments for the bishop's supremacy over the local congregation if he found any basis for it!* But no such practice existed in the first century. Warkentin makes the following observation about the postapostolic period: "Installation into office in the early postapostolic period apparently involved little in the way of ceremony or protocol. . . . we see the simple vocabulary of the New Testament still being used for appointment to office."[10] Later she states, "The earliest postapostolic evidence for the imposition of hands in induction to church office comes from late second—or early third—century writings."[11]

Ever since the fourth century, however, the vast majority of churchmen have not questioned ordination as the assumed requirement for all clergy. Indeed, ordination has become the very lifeblood of clerical authority, power, and position. The principal problem with the modern concept of ordination is that it falsely divides the Lord's people into secular and sacred categories. In his book, *A Theology of the Laity*, Hendrick Kraemer refers to ordination as the line of demarcation between clergy and laity:

> Particularly has the West, under the leadership of Rome, been very diligent in elaborating this fundamental pattern expressed in the simple but weighty words: *"duo sunt genera Christianorum"* the clergy including those who chose the monastic life, and the laity, sharply demarcated from each other. The line of demarcation was formed by "ordination." The *"duo genera"* (two bodies or classes) with increasing emphasis meant a superior and inferior class.[12]

Even Roman Catholic theologian Hans Kung decries the sacralization of the church minister and the seeming elevation of ordination over baptism:

> It has likewise become clear that there is neither a sociological nor even a theological basis for . . . sacralization of the Church's ministry (which accompanied the formation of a social class) which sets its holder as a sacred person apart from the rest of men and raises him above ordinary Christians to be a

mediator with God—thus making ordination appear more important than baptism.[13]

In the New Testament, no exclusive class of men are admitted into ministerial office by the rite of ordination. No one needs to be ordained to preach Christ or administer the ordinances. All such concepts are foreign to the New Testament apostolic churches. Marjorie Warkentin is right in her observation that some Protestants are dangerously close to the sacramental idea of ordination: "The insistence among some that only the ordained may administer baptism and conduct the Lord's Supper demonstrates the persistence of the sacramental view of ordination."[14]

Ordination also clashes with Jesus Christ's teaching on humility and servanthood. The risen Christ gives gifts to all His members. Therefore all must minister to one another so the body of Christ—the church—will grow. Thus, the entire church of Jesus Christ is a ministerial body anointed by God (2 Corinthians 1:21). Ordination, however, was created to legalize and reinforce the authority, control, power, and position of the clergy, which is totally incompatible with Jesus Christ's teaching and Paul's example of humble servanthood.

In Acts 6, certain brethren were set apart and hands were laid on them so they might serve the poor—not as an act of ordination to authorize them to preach and administer the sacraments. How contrary God's Word is to man's vain traditions! In Acts 13, the church laid hands on the leading ministers to set them apart for their task of spreading the gospel in new lands (Acts 13:3; cf. 14:27; 15:4). In a similar way, the elders laid hands on Timothy before he left to serve with Paul (1 Timothy 4:14). Timothy did not become a priest or a clergyman. He remained brother Timothy, his only distinction being that he labored as Paul's personal delegate.

Possibly the missionary-founders or their delegates (like Timothy) laid hands on aspiring elders at their appointment. But remember, the Christian elders form a nonclerical body. Therefore, brethren can appoint their fellowbrethren to specific tasks or positions, or single out certain men for their labor in the gospel in a special way, without creating a clerical structure with its sacred people, anointed men, or ordained professionals.

*Appropriate use of the laying on of hands.* Because of the confusion and superstition surrounding the laying on of hands, many churches avoid its use entirely. This is tragic because the laying on of hands can be a meaningful, precious expression. The imposition of hands is a custom which, like fasting, is not commanded in the New Testament but was practiced by the first Christians because it was a blessing to all. Christians are free, then, to use the laying on of hands if they desire, or to refrain from practicing it if it creates misunderstanding or division.

## NOTES
1. Marjorie Warkentin, *Ordination* (Grand Rapids: Wm. B. Eerdmans Publishing Co., 1982), page 1.
2. Fenton John Anthony Hort, *The Christian Ecclessia* (1897; reprint ed., London: Macmillan and Co., Limited, 1914), page 188.
3. Joseph Addison Alexander, *Commentary on the Gospel of Mark,* Classic Commentary Library (1864; reprint ed., Grand Rapids: Zondervan Publishing House, no date), page 65.
4. Richard Belward Rockham, *The Acts of the Apostles,* 5th ed., Westminster Commentaries (London: Methuen & Co. Ltd., 1910), page 84.
5. *The International Standard Bible Encyclopaedia,* 1955 ed., s.v. "Hands, Imposition of," by James Orr, 2:1335.
6. J. B. Lightfoot, *Saint Paul's Epistle to the Galatians* (1865; reprint ed., London: Macmillan and Co., 1892), page 98.
7. R. C. H. Lenski, *The Acts of the Apostles* (1934; reprint ed., Minneapolis: Augsburg Publishing House, 1961), page 496.
8. New Bible Dictionary, 2nd ed., s.v. "Ordination," by Leon Morris.
9. Alfred Plummer, "The Pastoral Epistles" in *The Expositor's Bible,* ed. W. Robertson Nicoll, 25 vols. (New York: A. C. Armstrong & Son, 1903), 23:219-221.
10. Warkentin, *Ordination*, page 33.
11. *Ibid.*, page 104.
12. Hendrick Kraemer, *A Theology of the Laity* (Philadelphia: The Westminster Press, 1958), pages 53, 54.
13. Hans Kung, *Why Priests?*, trans. Robert C. Collins (Garden City, New York: Doubleday & Company, Inc., 1972), pages 77, 78.
14. Warkentin, *Ordination*, page 100.

# Chapter 17

# *Elders Who Labor at Teaching: Worthy of Double Honor*

> *Let the elders who rule well be considered worthy of double honor, especially those who work hard at preaching and teaching. For the Scripture says, "You shall not muzzle the ox while he is threshing." and "The laborer is worthy of his wages."*
>
> *1 Timothy 5:17,18*

\*   \*   \*

It is no exaggeration to say that this passage contains the New Testament's most significant and advanced teaching on elders. This is understandable since the church at Ephesus was mature and well-ordered. Paul spent more time at Ephesus than at any other church, and when he departed he left the church oversight in the care of a well-developed eldership. Furthermore, this passage runs counter to almost every theory of church polity. It is such a perplexing and uncomfortable passage that most books on pastoral care or church organization simply ignore it. But it is impossible to fully understand biblical eldership without grasping this highly informative passage: 1 Timothy 5:17-25.

The context surrounding 1 Timothy 5:17-25, where the honor of elders is discussed, addresses the proper treatment of various

classes of people: older men (5:1),[1] younger men (5:1), older
women (5:2), younger women (5:2), widows (5:3-16), non-Christian
employers (6:1), and Christian employers (6:2). In these verses,
Paul instructs the congregation how to properly treat church elders.
That is, he gives further instruction on how Christians must act
in God's household (1 Timothy 3:14,15), particularly towards
the church elders.

***All Elders Rule***
Paul begins the section on church elders by writing, "Let
the elders who rule well be considered worthy of double honor. . . ."
The word, "rule," translates a common Greek term for leading,
caring for, managing, guiding, or protecting (Greek, *prohistemi*).
E. K. Simpson refers to this term as "expressive of superintendence."[2]
Kelly renders it as "elders who exercise leadership well,"[3] and
F. F. Bruce translates it as "elders who direct the affairs of the
church well."[4] The same word is used in 1 Thessalonians 5:12,
but there is translated as, "have charge over." The *New American
Standard Bible's* translation of *prohistemi* as, "rule," is a bit strong,
and the translation "care for," which a number of scholars prefer,
is too weak unless one clearly understands that the care involved
is that of leading the people. Therefore, it is best to translate
*prohistemi* as those who take the lead, direct, or guide, keeping
in mind that this leading has a distinct, Christian meaning. (Christ's
teaching on humility and servanthood governs how we are to lead
in God's household.)
The emphasis in this passsage is on the adverb, "well,"
meaning excellently, commendably, or notably. Some elders do a
more commendable job than others. Such elders have a greater
Spirit-given interest in the work, give more time and energy to the
work, gladly make greater personal sacrifices, and bear a deeper
sense of responsibility for the flock. This doesn't discredit other
elders, but merely states a fact. Employment, family, and life's
many routine chores consume most elders' time and energy—just
like everyone else's. But some elders, moved by the Spirit, give
themselves to the flock in a fuller, more sacrificial way. Also,
some elders have greater personal ability and gift and are simply
more skilled at their task.
Such differences in commitment and ability must not be
allowed to create jealousy or division among the elders. By stating

God's approval of more gifted and dedicated elders and their right to double honor, all contention should be removed. These elders ought to be viewed by the congregation and other elders as a source of blessing, joy, and profit. So this verse refers only to "elders who rule well," particularly "those who work hard at preaching and teaching." These elders are "worthy of double honor."

### Elders Deserving of Double Honor
What God says concerning "double honor" is particularly directed to elders who labor "at preaching and teaching." "Especially" is a superlative adverb meaning most of all, chiefly, above all, or particularly. An elder who leads notably well deserves "double honor," but according to this passage those who teach are particularly deserving. All elders lead, some lead well, and some also labor "at preaching and teaching." So the double honor statement applies above all to elders who teach. Observe, too, that Paul refers to "those [plural] who work hard." In a large church like Ephesus, numbers of elders would be needed, some of whom would "work hard at preaching and teaching."

Certain elders were known for their strenuous labor in teaching the Word, something few elders are willing or able to do. Such labor involved more than the expected reading, studying, and sharing of God's Word in which all Christians should engage (Hebrews 5:12; Colossians 3:16). The labor Paul refers to is an intense, Spirit-imparted devotion to Scripture, a Spirit-imparted gift to teach (Ephesians 4:11,12), and a love and desire to fully work at teaching.

Paul uses the same term for "work" here that he uses in 1 Thessalonians 5:12, denoting strenuous labor that results in weariness and fatigue. Good teachers "work hard" at long hours of study, preparation, and demanding teaching situations. Teaching is strenuous, mental, time-consuming work, yet it is exceptionally rewarding. Tragically, in many churches today, no one strenuously works at teaching and preaching. Thus, many of God's people are ignorant and spiritually immature. As God said of Israel, so He could say today, "My people are destroyed for lack of knowledge . . ." (Hosea 4:6).

Some elders work hard at "preaching," or in the original text, work hard *in word* (Greek, *logos*). The context, which is the primary consideration for translating a term with such a broad range of meaning, demands the rendering "preaching" in a general sense such as in exhorting, admonishing, gospeling, and comforting.

FIRST TIMOTHY 5:17,18

Throughout the New Testament, considerable emphasis is placed on the centrality of teaching God's truth. Jesus taught, and commissioned others to teach all that he had commanded (Matthew 28:20). The apostles were teachers, and the early Christians steadfastly devoted themselves to their teaching (Acts 2:42). Barnabas sought Paul to come to Antioch to help teach (Acts 11:25,26). Paul exhorted Timothy to give attention to the public reading of Scripture, exhortation, and teaching (1 Timothy 4:13.) In the order of gifts in 1 Corinthians 12:28, the teaching gift is listed third after apostle and prophet. So, teaching is one of the greater gifts a congregation should desire (1 Corinthians 12:31). Teaching should be taken seriously by those who desire it (James 3:1). According to Paul, teaching should be taken seriously enough by those who benefit from it that they provide support for their teachers (Galatians 6:6).

The Christian community comes into existence by the Spirit's use of God's Word (1 Peter 1:23). The community matures, grows, and is protected by further teaching and preaching of the Word. Therefore, those with the spiritual gift of teaching God's Word are especially vital to the congregation's growth and protection. Scripture teaches that Christ gives gifted teachers to His church to equip His people for better service on behalf of the body: "And He gave some as apostles, and some as prophets, and some as evangelists, and some as pastors and teachers, for the equipping of the saints for the work of service, to the building up of the body of Christ" (Ephesians 4:11,12). For a brother, then, to be both an elder and a gifted teacher who desires to work very hard at teaching and preaching is a great benefit and blessing to the assembly. Sound teaching is the best bulwark against false teachers.

It might be good to focus our attention on the passage just cited (Ephesians 4:11,12), since it is a significant passage in the doctrine of biblical eldership. According to the Greek sentence structure, shepherds and teachers are closely linked together. It appears that shepherds are included in the category of teachers. The passage does not seem to indicate, however, that shepherding and teaching are the same gift, or that all teachers are shepherds.[5]

Teachers are instructors who may function locally, or as itinerant. They may be elders or they may not, depending on the needs of the local situation. A great deal of flexibility exists as to how teachers operate.

Shepherds, on the other hand, are more than teachers since they teach, govern, protect, and practically care for the flock. While shepherds may be itinerant, their gift can be most effectively used in caring for the needs of one local flock. Since the elders' task is to shepherd the whole flock (1 Peter 5:1-4), elders with the shepherding gift are highly effective. They are the kind of elders Paul speaks of in 1 Timothy 5:17, who are worthy of double honor.

One must clearly understand that not all elders are gifted shepherds, nor do they have to be. Elders may have other gifts. That is why it is not exactly correct to say that Ephesians 4:11 lists the gift of presbyter or overseer. Being an elder is never listed as a spiritual gift (*charisma*). Scripture is careful not to confuse the office of eldership or deaconship with a spiritual gift. Men are appointed as elders to a local office (Acts 14:23; 1 Timothy 5:22; Titus 1:5), but gifts are given to all believers by Christ and are to be exercised anywhere in His body (Timothy's case is a unique, historical situation). Elders must meet certain objective, moral qualifications before they can serve—no matter what their gifts are. In fact, no special spiritual gift is listed as a qualification or requirement for elders. This is important to remember so good men are not eliminated from eldership. F. J. A. Hort offers the following comment: "Teaching was doubtless the most important form in which guidance and superintendence were exercised. But to all appearance the Ephesian Ecclesia used freely the services of men who had no special gift of this kind, but who were well qualified to act as Elders in other respects."[6] From the New Testament perspective, it is assumed that every elder will have his own spiritual gift or gifts. Each elder will contribute his gift to the leadership body, whether it be shepherding (Ephesians 4:11), teaching (Ephesians 4:11), leading (Romans 12:8), administration (1 Corinthians 12:28), etc. So, then, "those who work hard at preaching and teaching" well deserve "double honor." To neglect to honor them is to restrict their labor and hinder the congregation's maturity and knowledge of the Word.

### What Is Double Honor?

What is the double honor that elders who lead in a notable manner and who labor at teaching and preaching deserve? If the word "double" is given the meaning of twofold, as it is elsewhere in Scripture (Genesis 43:15; Exodus 22:4; Deuteronomy 21:17; 2 Kings 2:9; Job 42:10; Isaiah 40:2; Zechariah 9:12; Matthew 23:15), then the expression indicates honor for excellent service in addition to the general honor all elders rightly receive. Thus, "double honor," ought to be honor received as an elder plus honor received as an elder who renders commendable service. By using the expression, "double honor," Paul avoids slighting other elders of their due honor and is able to call special attention to those who labor diligently, particularly those who teach.

What does honor entail? The word *honor* (Greek, *time*), usually means respect, consideration, or high regard, and in certain instances includes material assistance. This latter sense appears to be predominant in 1 Timothy 5. Both the verb and the noun used for honor have the prevailing sense of material provision, a point that needs further explanation:

(1) Although the word itself does not necessarily mean material assistance (2 Chronicles 32:33; Proverbs 26:1; Ephesians 6:2; 1 Timothy 6:1), the concept of honor is at times closely associated with material substance (Numbers 22:17,37; 24:11; Proverbs 3:9; 14:31; 27:18; Daniel 11:38; Matthew 15:3-6; Acts 28:10).

(2) First Timothy 5:3 states, "Honor widows who are widows indeed." The widow indeed is a truly destitute Christian widow. The instruction that follows (verses 4-16) shows that honor primarily involves financial assistance (verses 4,8,16).

(3) The biblical quotation in verse 18 (not muzzling the threshing ox) demonstrates that material provision is uppermost in Paul's thought. The immediate context, therefore, shows that "honor" means respect involving financial assistance.

(4) Using "honor" rather than a more definite term is harmonious with Paul's usual choice of expression for financial matters. Paul avoids words expressing mercenary or professional ideas. He favors terms that express the grace, liberality, love, and oneness of Christianity:

- Service (Romans 15:25,27; 2 Corinthians 8:4; 9:1,12,13)
- Fellowship (2 Corinthians 8:4; Galatians 6:6; Philippians 1:5)
- Grace (1 Corinthians 16:3; 2 Corinthians 8:6,7)
- Liberality (2 Corinthians 8-9)
- Bounty (2 Corinthians 8:20)
- Blessing (2 Corinthians 9:5)
- Good work (2 Corinthians 9:8)
- Good things (Galatians 6:6)
- A fragrant aroma, an acceptable sacrifice (Philippians 4:18)

- Seed (2 Corinthians 9:10)
- Harvest of your righteousness (2 Corinthians 9:10)
- Gift (Philippians 4:17)
- Honor (1 Timothy 5:3,17)

Thus, "honor" expresses financial assistance in a thoroughly Christian manner. Christianity displays itself in every detail of a believer's relationship with his fellow Christians, including the financial. Material provision for elders, then, is really honor due the elders. Such honor conveys the congregation's concern, esteem, closeness, thoughtfulness, and loving regard for the brethren who minister in this responsible position.

(5) The rights of some in the brotherhood to receive material provision is in full agreement with other passages of Scripture (Matthew 10:10; Luke 8:3; 10:7; 1 Corinthians 9:4-14; Galatians 6:6; Philippians 4:16; 1 Thessalonians 2:5,6; 2 Thessalonians 3:8,9; Titus 3:13; 3 John 6-8).

Just because all elders are honored, it does not follow that all elders should automatically receive financial consideration. Honor does not necessarily imply material help, but those who rule well deserve two-fold honor. Since the "double honor" is related to extra labor (particularly in the teaching ministry), the "double honor" has more relevant application to financial consideration than the general honor due all elders.

Finally, and most important, elders who work hard thoroughly deserve double honor. Paul says, "Let them be considered worthy." This main verb is an imperative form of a verbal root, meaning rightfully deserving or entitled to. Because of their highly responsible, sacrificial task and strenuous labor, the elders who work hard are rightfully entitled to double honor. What a rich blessing it is to have excellent elders to protect, guide, and teach the congregation! Indeed, they deserve double honor. Verse 18 supports the teaching about certain elders' worthiness of double honor by quoting two Scripture passages, one from each testament: "For the Scripture says, 'You shall not muzzle the ox while he is threshing,' and 'The laborer is worthy of his wages.'" Here Paul indicates the reason for certain elders' worthiness of double honor. Note that Paul begins the statement by saying, "For the Scripture says." For the believer, just the mention of the word "Scripture" signals the ultimate voice of authority—God's Word (John 10:35). This is the only direct biblical quotation in 1 Timothy, so it alerts the reader to something significant. By using this qualifying phrase, Paul is saying that complete unity exists between the Old and New Testaments—both Moses and Jesus say that a laboring man, including an elder, "is worthy of his wages."

The Old Testament quotation is from Deuteronomy 25:4, "You shall not muzzle the ox while he is threshing." The context of Deuteronomy concerns equity and justice in everyday life, even the right of an animal to enjoy the fruit of its labor while working for its owner. God's full intent in Deuteronomy 25:4 is explained in 1 Corinthians 9:6-14:

> Or do only Barnabas and I not have a right to refrain from working? Who at any time serves as a soldier at his own expense? Who plants a vineyard, and does not eat the fruit of it? Or who tends a flock and does not use the milk of the flock? I am not speaking these things according to human judgment, am I? Or does not the Law also say these things? For it is written in the Law of Moses, "You shall not muzzle the ox while he is threshing." God is not concerned about oxen, is He? Or is He speaking altogether for our sake? Yes, for our sake it was written, because the plowman ought to plow in hope, and the thresher to thresh in hope of sharing the crops. If we sowed spiritual things in you, is it too much if we should reap material things from you? If others share the right over you, do we not more? Nevertheless, we did not use this right, but we endure all things, that we may cause no hindrance to the gospel of Christ. Do you not know that those who perform sacred services eat the food of the temple, and those who attend regularly to the altar have their share with the altar? So also the Lord directed those who proclaim the gospel to get their living from the gospel.

Twice in the New Testament, Deuteronomy 25:4 is quoted to support the right of laboring teachers and workers to receive financial support (1 Corinthians 9:9; 1 Timothy 5:18). To refuse to support laboring elders is as unjust, heartless, and selfish as muzzling an animal while it is working. Yet that is precisely what some Christians do by their vain traditions and high-sounding rationalizations that deny financial help to worthy elders. The passage clearly implies adequate living support for the worker, not token financial gifts.

The New Testament quotation, "the laborer is worthy of his wages," is from Luke 10:7. Jesus originally spoke these words to the seventy before He sent them out to preach. Paul later applied His words to all who teach and preach the gospel (1 Corinthians 9:14). Then, in 1 Timothy 5:17,18, Paul applies the same words to elders who labor diligently at preaching and teaching, indicating that they are deserving of wages. This is God's law as taught by Jesus Christ and His apostle, Paul.

However, Scripture is silent about the practical administration of this double honor. As with similar church subjects, the implementation of the general principle is left to the discretion of the congregation and its leaders. What a congregation in London does, if faithfully seeking the Lord's guidance by the power of the Holy Spirit, will certainly be different from the action of a congregation in Communist Changsha or primitive Bomili, Zaire. Yet God's Word that encourages believers to render "double honor" to those who rule well remains unchanged.

It's important to note that Paul is addressing the entire congregation, not the elders. This truth must be faithfully taught to God's people. The congregation has the responsibility to support their elders. No matter how poor Christians may think they are, they must exercise faith and liberality before the Lord, giving to those who teach, preach, and lead on their behalf. In short, God's people must honor their elders.

### *False Conclusions*
This passage has been used to justify dividing the elders into two separate categories—ruling elders and teaching elders. Generally speaking, this viewpoint results in the establishment of a board of lay ruling elders and one ordained teaching elder. In such a system, the teaching elder must be specially educated, licensed, and ordained. He alone can preach the gospel and minister baptism and the Lord's Supper. He is the ordained minister, pastor, or reverend—a part of the professional clergy class. In a very real sense, he is the Protestant priest—the man who prays and administers holy things. Without him, the saints are unqualified and unfit to celebrate the Lord's Supper. The ruling elders are reduced to the status of lay elders—glorified deacons or board members—who fulfill legal requirements for the organization.

This practice, however, is utterly false, both in light of Scripture and the nature of the church. The real culprit behind this practice is the clergy-laity division. But there is no more justification in the New Testament for the ordained minister-clergyman than there is for the Pope. In fact, a more elaborate and impressive case has been made for the Pope than for the ordained clergyman espoused by the majority of Protestants.

In the New Testament, there are no separate classes of elders, nor are there three separate offices (teaching elders, ruling elders, and deacons). On the contrary, only two offices are referred to: the overseers (plural) and the deacons (Philippians 1:1; 1 Timothy 3:1-13). Paul appointed a body of elders (much like the Old Testament elder system) to oversee newly planted congregations, not a teaching elder plus a body of ruling elders (Acts 14:23). Both Paul and Peter charge the entire body of elders to pastor the flock (Acts 20:17,28; 1 Peter 5:1-4). Thus, the New Testament authorizes no arrangement of pastor or minister and elders.

*All elders are pastors.* In the list of qualifications, all elders are required to be able to teach (1 Timothy 3:2) and exhort in sound doctrine, and refute those who contradict (Titus 1:9). Thus, the idea of elders who only rule is pure human invention—a teaching that demeans the elders and robs them of their God-given mandate. All elders, then, must be armed with a knowledge of Scripture and be able to teach, judge, exhort, admonish, shepherd, and defend the flock against false teachers. Scripture teaches that the entire eldership pastors God's flock, not just the pastor.

First Timothy 5:17 does not speak of the teaching elder, but of a number of elders who labor at preaching and teaching and elders who are more capable of leading the flock. We often overlook the fact that Paul is also referring to elders without a special teaching gift who rule notably well. They, too, are "worthy of double honor." So, elders with a teaching gift and elders who rule capably deserve the congregation's financial support. By imposing the rigid concepts of contemporary church structure upon this text, one can easily make a wrong interpretation.

There is no reason to require that a local church be permanently limited to one teaching elder (cf. Acts 13:1; 15:35), nor do all gifted teachers need to be or qualify to be elders. All gifted teachers should be given the opportunity to teach in the local congregation. Also, a gifted teacher may need to help a number of churches that need better teaching. Although teaching is an exceedingly important task, teachers should not be unscripturally elevated above their fellow brethren. They must not be given special titles, special clothes, or special credentials. They are fellow brethren whose function is to build up the saints by teaching the Word. Jon Zens also decries the elevation of the teaching elder to an almost entirely different office:

> We would do well to consider all elders as equal in the one office, but as diverse in terms of personal gifts and particular ministries.
>
> It seems to me that confusion has arisen in a very practical way by assigning men who "labor in the Word" in a category *above* the other elders. The "especially" of 1 Timothy 5:17 certainly does not allow us to view men with eminent gifts (the "minister") to be elevated above the other elders. This text makes it clear that those who give themselves to the ministry of the Word are part of a body of equals, some of which may also be worthy of double honor. Yet in many churches where a plurality exists, equality of elders is denied by such statements as "the pastor is the *leading* officer of a congregation" (*Covenanter Witness*, August 30, 1972, p. 6.). There is no Biblical warrant for elevating the so-called "teaching-ruling" elder to an almost entirely different office.[7]

Furthermore, this passage has nothing to do with the modern notion of a senior pastor and his staff. Only Jesus Christ can be called Senior Pastor (1 Peter 5:4). Indeed, true biblical eldership has nothing in common with the organizational structure of a senior elder and his subordinate staff.

### First among Equals

While it is true that equal status exists among the elders, each elder has his own spiritual gift or gifts, so there will be distinct individual gifts, talents, education, and devotion among the eldership. The church eldership is not a faceless bureaucracy. The personality, gifts, and spirituality of its individual members make up the overall temperament and competency of the church eldership. In 1 Timothy 5:17,18, for example, individual elders who take the lead more diligently and effectively are prominent. Those who have the spiritual gift of teaching are perceived as first among their equals.

One common misconception people have concerning joint leadership is that it suppresses gifted or talented men. Shared leadership, however, actually protects and sharpens talented leaders.

Although the elders act jointly and share equal responsibility in overseeing the flock, all are not equal in their gifts, knowledge, leadership ability, or dedication. Thus, one or more of the elders will naturally stand out as the motivator or leader among the others. This is what the Romans referred to as *primus inter pares*— first among equals, or *primi inter pares*—first ones among equals. That type of leadership is found among the twelve apostles and New Testament elders.

Among the twelve apostles, Jesus singled out three for special attention—Peter, James, and John. The Gospels show that among the three, as well as among the Twelve, Peter stood out as the most prominent, or "first." In all four lists of disciples' names, Peter is always first (Matthew 10:2-4; Mark 3:16-19; Luke 6:14-16; Acts 1:13). In Luke 22:32, Jesus charged Peter to ". . . strengthen your brothers." Among the Twelve, who jointly shared the oversight of the early church (Acts 2:14,42; 4:33,35; 5:12,18,25,29,42; 6:2-6; 8:14; 9:27; 15:2-29), Peter was the spokesman and leading figure (Acts 1:15; 2:14; 3:1 ff; 4:8 ff; 5:3 ff; 5:15,29; 8:14-24; 9:32-11:18; 12:3 ff; 15:7-11; Galatians 2:7-14). Since Peter was the natural leader, the preacher, the man of action, he acted as a motivator for the other eleven. Without Peter, the Twelve would have been much weaker. Surrounded by the other eleven apostles, Peter was much richer and safer from his impetuosity and fear. In spite of his recognized leadership and speaking ability, Peter possessed no rank or title above the other eleven, nor were they subordinate to him. They were not his staff or his disciples. Peter was simply first among his equals.

This leadership relationship is also observed among the seven who were chosen to relieve the apostles in Acts 6. Philip, and particularly Stephen, stood out as prominent figures among the other brothers (Acts 6:8-7:60; 8:4-40; 21:8). Yet, they held no special rank or title within the body of the seven.

The same principle of *primus inter pares* operates within the body of elders. Inevitably there will be one or more leading figures within any council of elders. In a sense, all of the elders are first ones among equals in the congregation (Acts 15:22). Yet there will be first ones within the body of elders itself, particularly those elders with the spiritual gifts of shepherding or leading. According to our passage, those elders who do a more noble job at taking the lead (and above all, those who labor at teaching) are to receive double honor from the congregation. When a congregation makes material provision for certain gifted elders, those elders are enabled to give part or all of their time to the work of the eldership, which greatly strengthens both the eldership and the local body of believers. Just as the leading apostles bore no title or class distinction from the other apostles, so too, elders who receive double honor create no official class, special title, or appointment within the eldership.

Of course, there is a constant danger that other elders will relinquish their responsibilities and obligations to one or two exceptionally gifted men. This danger will always exist because of man's selfish and lazy tendency, particularly in spiritual matters, to let someone else do all the work. In the Christian family, for example, many fathers have relinquished the spiritual training of their children to the mother or Sunday school teacher. The rise of an overseer above the elders, which took place in the second century, was undoubtedly due to Christians who surrendered their obligations and privileges to one gifted man. Was not Israel quick to hand over her freedom, rights, and privileges to a king like her neighboring nations (1 Samuel 8)?

In the church, however, gifted teachers, pastors, and leaders must not monopolize the ministry or be raised to unscriptural status. As humble servants, gifted leaders are to build up their fellow brethren so that all can more fully serve the body of Christ (Ephesians 4:11,12). In no way does the principle of primus inter pares mean that one person is authorized to take final responsibility for all decisions. No one individual among the elders calls the shots. Instead, decisions are made in mutual dependence upon one another.

Although the elders share primary leadership responsibility within the church, every member of the congregation must also fulfill his or her responsibility and obligation to the Lord and to one another in service (1 Peter 4:10,11). As free men in Christ, the congregation cannot be passive. If it is, it may be responsible for creating a leader like Diotrephes, the church dictator, about whom John writes: "I wrote something to the church; but Diotrephes, who loves to be first among them, does not accept what we say. For this reason, if I come, I will call attention to his deeds which he does, unjustly accusing us with wicked words; and not satisfied with this, neither does he himself receive the brethren, and he

[250]

forbids those who desire to do so, and puts them out of the church" (3 John 9,10).

By the Holy Spirit's design, a plurality of elders shares the responsibility of church oversight. Even though there will be first ones, or leaders, among equals in the leadership body, the New Testament authorizes no individual elder to be above the other elders. Thus, the contemporary division between lay elders and ordained pastor is totally without God's authorization. There are no lay elders, only elders of the church placed in that responsibility by the Holy Spirit.

The New Testament eldership is not merely membership in a board of trustees, where members are selected to fulfill legal requirements. The eldership is not an organizational structure that gives everyone an opportunity to make decisions. The eldership is not a quota to be filled, or a means of roping rich, influential people into the church's organizational structure. Instead, the elders are a body of committed shepherds who have been placed in their position by the Holy Spirit of God (Acts 20:28). They are God's stewards (Titus 1:7). As such, a team of qualified, dedicated, Spirit-placed elders is not a passive, ineffective committee. Rather, biblical eldership is a fair and powerful form of leadership that avoids both the pitfalls of one-man rule and the confusion of every-man rule.

---

**NOTES**

1. Here in 1 Timothy 5:1,2, the Greek word *presbyteros* is translated correctly as older man. The context refers to age and sex, not office. Hence, the comparison is between older women and younger women. Paul is not referring to elders and elderesses in an official capacity. In verse 17 of this same chapter, however, *presbyteroi* must be translated as elders in the sense of official community leaders, not older men. The word *presbyteros* bears both meanings, with the context determining the exact meaning.

This same issue over *ho presbyteros* arises in two of John's letters. The second epistle of John begins with the words, "The elder to the chosen lady and her children. . . ." The third epistle also begins with the words, "The elder to the beloved Gaius." At the time John wrote these epistles, he was a very old man—probably the oldest living apostle. So he most likely expected his readers to understand *presbyteros* in its primary meaning of age. If this is the case, then John is simply referring to himself as the old man, aged one, or ancient one.

Paul used the corresponding term (Greek, *presbytes,* meaning old man) in Philemon 9 to strengthen his appeal to Philemon on behalf of Onesimus. In this passage John seems to be doing the same thing. As the "aged one," John was in a unique position; at the end of the first century, no one else equaled his status. No one else could better speak the truth to his friends than John, who had personally walked with the Truth and walked in the truth for many long years (John 14:6).

2. E. K. Simpson, *The Pastoral Epistles* (Grand Rapids: Wm. B. Eerdmans Publishing Co., 1954), page 77.

3. John Norman Davis Kelly, *The Pastoral Epistles* (1963; reprint ed., London: A.&C. Black Limited, 1972), page 124.

4. Frederick F. Bruce, *The Letters of Paul* (Grand Rapids: Wm. B. Eerdmans Publishing Co., 1965), page 307.

5. An exceptional exegetical work has been written in defense of this position by Daniel B. Wallace ("The Semantic Range of the Article-Noun-Kai-Noun Plural Construction in the New Testament," *Grace Theological Journal* 4 [Spring, 1983]: 59-84.) Wallace articulately argues against the commonly held notion that the two terms "pastor" and "teacher" refer to one group, "pastor-teacher" because of the Granville Sharp rule ramifications. He concludes that in no plural construction made up exclusively of "nouns" are the two terms ever regarded as identical. This does not mean that the two terms are totally distinct, but that the first term "pastor" is a subset of the second, "teacher" since similar formations are well attested in many other adjective and noun constructions.

6. Fenton John Anthony Hort, *The Christian Ecclesia* (1897; reprint ed., London: Macmillan and Co., Limited, 1914), page 197.

7. Jon Zens, "The Major Concepts of Eldership in the New Testament," *Baptist Reformation Review* 7 (Summer, 1978): 30, 31.

# Chapter 18

# *Nonclerical Leadership*

*But do not be called rabbi; for one is your teacher,
and you are all brothers.*

Matthew 23:8

\*   \*   \*

In contrast to the attitude prevalent throughout much of church
history, the subject of lay renewal has recently become a widely
discussed topic. "In the Twentieth Century," Kenneth Chafin observes, "the theologians rediscovered the doctrine of the laity."[1]
Commenting on how Ephesians 4:11,12 is applied today to laymen,
Chafin adds, "This emphasis upon the laymen represents the most
radical thing which has happened to the church in this century."[2]
Even the Roman Catholic Church, at Vatican Council II, avoided
the negative and passive concepts of laity that have historically
been one of its major theological features.[3]

And yet, despite Vatican II's glowing terms regarding the
laity, there is still an impassable gulf between clergy and laity,
priest and people. Unfortunately, this is true in many Protestant
churches as well. Even in churches that claim they do not support
the clergy-laity division, a conspicuous division often exists in
practice between the ordained minister and lay members. As Robert
Girard observes, our churches have a two-caste ministry system:

> There is thoroughly entrenched in our church life, an un-
> biblical two-caste system. In this two-caste system there is a
> clergy-caste which is trained, called, paid, and expected to do
> the ministering. And there is a laity-caste which normally

functions as the audience which appreciatively pays for the performance of the clergy—or bitterly criticizes the gaping holes in that performance (and there are always gaping holes). No one expects much of the lower or laity caste (except 'tendance, tithe, and testimony). And everyone expects too much of the upper or clergy caste (including the clergy themselves!).

The greatest problem in the whole business is the fact that the Bible's view of ministry totally contradicts this system. So we are found in the awful dilemma of trying to fulfill the ministry-ideals of Scripture with an unscriptural ministry system that is totally inadequate for the job! And, no matter how high we raise the requirements for the clergy, it will never be adequate to approach the kind of production and life envisioned in the Bible![4]

Furthermore, even scholars who address the unbiblical two-caste system merely reform that which needs to be totally eradicated from the family of God. John Stott, for example, rightly attempts to expose the errors of clericalism:

... it is only against the background of the equality and unity of the people of God that the real scandal of clericalism may be seen. What clericalism always does, by concentrating power and privilege in the hands of the clergy, is at least to obscure and at worst to annul the essential oneness of the people of God. ... I do not hesitate to say that to interpret the Church in terms of a privileged clerical caste or hierarchical structure is to destroy the New Testament doctrine of the Church.

... In other words, in revealing the nature and work of the Church, the overwhelming preoccupation of the New Testament is not with the status of the clergy, nor with clergy-laity relations, but with the whole people of God in their relations to him and to each other, the unique people who have been called by his grace to be his inheritance and his ambassador in the world.[5]

Unfortunately, Stott does not take his criticism far enough. Although critical of clericalism's obvious abuses, Stott still supports the clergy-laity division and uses what he admits is unbiblical terminology: "So the question before us now is: what is the relation between these two groups, between teachers and taught, shepherds and Flock, or in modern, unbiblical terminology between 'clergy' and 'laity'?"[6]

## NONCLERICAL LEADERSHIP

If the clergy-laity terminology is indeed unbiblical, why does a fine biblical expositor like John Stott continue to use such spurious terminology? We must not forget that the terms a society uses for its leaders reveal much about the society's character and beliefs. Knowing this, the New Testament writers chose the terminology for church leaders very carefully. The terms clergy and laity, as used by people today, distort both the New Testament language and the liberating reality of the Christian brotherhood.

Every teacher of the Word has the solemn responsibility to expose and correct any practice—including the use of terminology—that misrepresents Scripture's precious truth. Moreover, although Stott claims that the clergy are only servants of the laity, his practice betrays a lingering clericalism with its unbiblical division of God's family and establishment of the clergy as superior to the laity: "Of course we should largely restrict the administration of Word and Sacraments to the clergy. As Article XXIII puts it: 'It is not lawful for any man to take upon him the office of public preaching, or ministering the sacraments in the congregation, before he be lawfully called, and sent to execute the same.'"[7] These words do not represent the apostolic, brotherly, New Testament Christian community; they represent clericalism. Clericalism, in addition to wrongly dividing the holy brotherhood and suppressing the masses of God's people, has done more to diminish church eldership than almost any other doctrine. Furthermore, appealing to eldership passages like 1 Timothy 5:17,18 as justification for clericalism only further distorts Scripture and New Testament ecclesiology.

In order to fully restore the eldership to its proper place and role in the church, we must identify and entirely eliminate the clergy-laity dichotomy. In loyalty to the Word of God and Jesus Christ, we must completely avoid all clergy-laity terminology, because such terminology conveys concepts that are antagonistic to the New Testament church. Perhaps even more important, we must dismantle every practice that falsely divides the Lord's people into secular and sacred, ministerial and non-ministerial, ordained and non-ordained Christians. We must courageously insist on Jesus' teaching that we are all brothers—whether teachers or taught, pastors or flock, leaders or followers.

## All Believers Have the Privilege of Ministry

We must never forget that the church of Jesus Christ is a supernatural, Spirit-indwelt, Spirit-empowered, living community of Christ-like servants (1 Corinthians 12:7,25; 1 Peter 4:10). The same Spirit who links Christians together in one body also empowers and enables every Christian to serve and build up the body (Ephesians 4:1-16).

The indwelling Holy Spirit is the truly distinctive mark of the new community formed on the day of Pentecost. In contrast to the people of Israel who lived under the old covenant, the Holy Spirit indwells each and every believer, forming the body of Christ. Through the indwelling Holy Spirit, a glorious, new bond—a dynamic interdependence—is created within the community of believers that is unlike any other relationship in the world. Under the new covenant, ratified by the blood of Christ, all true Christians possess God's righteousness. All are equally saints. All are priests. All are washed clean by Christ's blood. All are indwelt by the Holy Spirit. All are members of Christ's body, gifted to minister to one another.

To illustrate the new and wondrous interrelationship of all believers under the new covenant, Paul uses the imagery of the body and its many parts. In Romans 12:5 we read, "so we, who are many, are one body in Christ, and individually members one of another." This shared life, or *fellowship*, is illustrated many times throughout the New Testament by the one-another commands. For example, believers are commanded to love one another, encourage one another, build up one another, teach one another, and admonish one another. Therefore, within the body of Christ, ministry is the sacred privilege and duty of every believer. There is no passive, inactive majority. All members are to perform a function— caring for one another, building one another up, and ministering to one another. When each and every member of the body functions as God intended, the community of believers will grow, and an amazing, living interplay of gifts and services will result. Referring to this unique, Spirit-indwelt body, Larry Richards writes,

> There is no notion here of any distinction in the body between "clergy" and "laity." The work of the Spirit is in all and through all. Every believer, as a member of the *laos* of God, is a minister. Leaders in the church, as servants of the servants of God, are to guide others into the exercise of their

gifts so that the whole body might grow. The "superstar" approach to ministry is clearly rejected, for each member's function is vital to the growth of the body, and thus indispensable. As there is cooperation between muscles, bones, joints, and ligaments in a human body, so in the body of Christ ministry is a coordinated or team effort.[8]

Since ministry is the duty of every believer, no one person or group of people is responsible to provide the total ministry for the rest of the local congregation. The concept that only certain professional, ordained men are qualified to perform "the ministry" totally contradicts the fact that the church is a ministerial body. The New Testament conveys no concept of "the laity" with all its passive, negative connotations. As God's people, we must stand in loyalty to what God says of us in His Word and reject all demeaning ideas such as the clergy-laity division.

However, the fact that the whole congregation of saints is to be a ministering body does not eliminate the need for supervision and leadership within the body of Christ. To better understand God's intention for leadership within His family, let's observe the leadership example set by the New Testament churches. As Alfred Kuen says, "The churches established by the apostles remain the valid models for churches of all times and places."[9]

### The Example of the New Testament Churches

*No clerical or priestly hierarchy*. It is a simple but profound fact that no clergy-laity dichotomy appears in the New Testament. Paul, the great church planter, taught that there is a wide diversity of gifts and services among the brethren, but no sacred clergy. In his many greetings to fellow workers and helpers, Paul never greets anyone as a clergyman or a layman. The more one comprehends Paul's teaching on the gospel and body of Christ, the more one realizes the falsehood of the clergy-laity division. In fact, the very concept of a small, professional, ministerial body that is vested with superior rights and privileges over the sacraments and the Word, and is alone qualified to "minister" would be unthinkable to the inspired writers of Scripture. Such a concept is foreign to the New Testament writers, who taught that the whole body of Christ is ministerial, saintly, and priestly.

New Testament evidence against an exclusive priestly or clerical body in the church is further confirmed by the way in which

Paul established new congregations. When he left a newly established church, Paul left behind only a body of elders to oversee each church (Acts 14:23). Obviously that was all he felt was needed. Since all believers were saints, priests, Spirit-empowered, and complete in Christ, none of the traditional religious structures such as sacred sites, sacred buildings, or sacred personnel (priests, clerics, or holy men) were needed—or could be tolerated. The only need was for community leadership, and Paul appointed a local council of elders to meet that need. As Alexander Hay notes, the elders are those who "preside over an assembly of priests of royal lineage. . . . They are not priests ministering to laity, but leaders of equals; not professors teaching a class that never graduates, but leaders of a team."[10]

It is interesting to observe that even the converted Jewish priests exercised no distinct priestly or clerical function in the early church. In Acts 6:7 we read, "And the word of God kept on spreading; . . . and a great many of the priests were becoming obedient to the faith." The cross of Jesus Christ brought earth-shattering changes to the old distinctions between people: clean and unclean, secular and sacred, priest and people, Jew and Gentile. Thus, none of the apostles established a new priestly body—a profoundly remarkable fact considering that all were devout Jews who had been raised under the Old Testament priesthood.

Furthermore, nowhere in the New Testament are the elders called priests. The *Douay-Rheims* version of the Bible, an official Roman Catholic translation, departs from the original Greek text of the Bible when it translates the Greek word, *presbyteroi* (literally, elders), as *priests.* New Testament writers never use the Greek word for priest, *hiereus,* to describe church officers. Changing the meaning of words and concepts as originally used in Scripture is one of Satan's most successful and subtle tactics. By changing the word "elder" to "priest," Roman Catholics have changed the New Testament concept of eldership to mean priestly ministry. In a similar fashion many Protestants have superimposed their ideas of the ordained clergyman, the professional minister, upon the texts of Scripture referring to elders. Both groups misrepresent the language and concepts of the apostolic writers pertaining to eldership.

*No official titles.* It is deeply significant that the early Christians did not give lordly, hierarchical, or clerical titles to their leaders.

Although both the Greeks and Jews had a wealth of titles for their political and religious leaders, the early Christians avoided borrowing such titles. Jesus Christ explicitly forbids His followers from assuming honorific titles that separate and elevate one brother over another (Matthew 23:6-10). Therefore, the early Christians used lowly, unofficial, common, and functional words to describe themselves—brother, beloved, fellow-workers, laborers, slave, servant, prisoner, fellow-soldiers, and steward. Even the leadership terms the New Testament writers used were generic terms that could easily be applied in the Christian context.

There were prophets, teachers, apostles, pastors, evangelists, leaders, elders, and deacons within the early church, but these terms were not used as formal titles. For example, all Christians are saints, but there is no "Saint John." All are priests, but there is no "Priest Philip." Some are elders, but there is no "Elder Paul." Some are pastors, but there is no "Pastor James." Some are deacons, but there is no "Deacon Peter." Some are apostles, but there is no "Apostle Andrew."

Rather than gaining honor through titles and position, New Testament believers received honor primarily for their service and work (Acts 15:26; Romans 16:1,2,4,12; 1 Corinthians 16:15,16,18; 2 Corinthians 8:18; Philippians 2:29,30; Colossians 1:7; 4:12,13; 1 Thessalonians 5:12; 1 Timothy 3:1). The early Christians referred to each other by personal names—Timothy, Paul, Titus, etc.—or referred to an individual's spiritual character or work: ". . . Stephen, a man full of faith and of the Holy Spirit . . ." (Acts 6:5); Barnabas, ". . . a good man, and full of the Holy Spirit and of faith . . ." (Acts 11:24); ". . . Philip the evangelist . . ." (Acts 21:8); "Greet Prisca and Aquila, my fellow-workers in Christ Jesus" (Romans 16:3); "Greet Mary, who has worked hard for you" (Romans 16:6); etc. The array of ecclesiastical titles accompanying the names of Christian leaders today is completely missing from the New Testament, and would have appalled the apostles and early believers.

*No mass of laity.* One beauty of true Christianity is that God's Spirit indwells ordinary, common people. Through those people the Spirit manifests Jesus' life. In fact, the greatest witness to the gospel's reality and power has been the changed lives of ordinary people. Everyone expects the clergy to act religiously, but ordinary men and women who are on fire for God—living holy lives, studying Scripture, sacrificing, serving, and even teaching

NONCLERICAL LEADERSHIP

and leading the religious community—are powerful testimonies to the transforming power of the gospel of Jesus Christ.

This has been true from the beginning of Christianity. Jesus Christ Himself was a poor, uneducated carpenter. Everything about the way He lived, spoke, and dressed was different from the elitist religious leaders of His day. His chief disciples were also ordinary men. The established religious leaders saw this, and despised Him and His disciples because of it. Yet even they had to acknowledge the zeal and power of such laymen: "Now as they observed the confidence of Peter and John, and understood that they were uneducated and untrained men, they were marveling, and began to recognize them as having been with Jesus. And seeing the man who had been healed standing with them, they had nothing to say in reply" (Acts 4:13,14). In true Christianity, sinners who are saved by grace and indwelt by the Spirit enjoy a new, holy, and priestly status before God. They share a privileged, lofty position as sons and daughters of God. Free in Christ, each individual can serve God and one another as the indwelling Spirit's power enables. The apostles demonstrated this marvelous new freedom and status by not placing restrictions on which community members could administer the Lord's Supper or baptize others. Unlike the clerical structure prevalent in today's churches, the early Christians—as brothers and sisters in Christ—celebrated the Lord's Supper together without the help of sacred personnel (1 Corinthians 11:33).

This new freedom and holy status was far too glorious for Satan to leave untouched. Shortly after the apostolic era, the cleavage between the "sacred clergy" and "profane laity" began to appear. As centuries passed, God's people became beggars and slaves to powerful bishops. Even salvation was dependent upon the bishops. No longer were believers viewed as saints, royal priests, free men, or gifted members of Christ's body. As "the laity," they became unqualified and unfit to do religious work. The grand privileges of all believers became the privileges of a select few, and the holy brotherhood of free men disintegrated. Just as Israel did not appreciate her glorious privileges and position as God's people, but desired to be like other nations and live in slavery to a king (1 Samuel 8), so, too, Christians relinquished the holy status and privileges that Christ had won for them.

The tragedy of the clergy-laity error is that it inevitably establishes a secular-sacred division between the Lord's people.

Two levels of people are created—an elite clerical order that performs the community's religious functions and a mass of unqualified laymen. Such a division fragments the body, destroying the lofty status, oneness, and simplicity of Christ's holy community.

Historically, the sacred-secular division has hindered Christians from fully participating in the community and limited the exercise of their spiritual gifts. The division has also hindered their growth in faith and prayer, and diminished their eagerness to witness and mature spiritually. In fact, the wider the gulf between the clergy and laity, the farther the people are from their God and the less significant their participation in community life. Robert Munger readily sees the danger of the clergy-laity division, and contrasts it with early Christianity:

Christianity in its beginnings was a lay movement . . . taking fishermen from their boats and nets. Jesus made them fishers of men. He dared to believe that ordinary people could become extraordinary servants of God. He would build his church upon believers like Peter. From among the common people he would call disciples who in turn he would send to disciple the nations. In our time it may well be that the greatest single bottleneck to the renewal and outreach of the church is the division of roles between clergy and laity that results in a hesitancy of the clergy to trust the laity with significant responsibility, and in turn to a reluctance on the part of the laity to trust themselves as authentic ministers of Christ, either in the church or outside the church.[11]

Each New Testament church was led by its body of elders, who were the qualified men of the local assembly who desired to lead God's flock. In contemporary terms, they would be a body of laymen. Historically, the New Testament elders were not separated from the rest of the congregation like priests or clerics, so no one has the right to give them a clerical or priestly designation. Yet that is precisely what Roman Catholics and many Protestants do. They interpret the Scriptures that refer to local church elders in light of their particular priestly or clerical ideas.[12] As a result, those who cling to the unscriptural clergy-laity division will inevitably totally eliminate biblical eldership or subordinate it to an ordained minister. Hence, biblical eldership is redefined according to traditional concepts rather than biblical truth.

Although this study asserts that the clergy-laity division is a false tradition, it in no way condemns or intends any hatred against clergymen. Such an intent would be contrary to the spirit of love. Many godly clergymen—servants of God's people—faithfully minister to the saints. My contention is that the clergy-laity division, as a system, is contrary to the apostolic church model and ultimately damages both the spiritual development of the Lord's people and biblical church eldership.

### Leadership without Clericalism

Just because no special priestly or clerical class exclusively performs the church ministry does not mean that the church is leaderless, or that all believers are equal in their gifts, abilities, influences, desires, or devotion to God. All Christians are priests, saints, and ministers, but not all are apostles, teachers, leaders, pastors, and elders. Not all have the same measure of maturity, wisdom, and love for God.

There is no false egalitarianism in the Bible. God chose only certain believers to hear and see His Son. To those He chose to reveal His truth (Romans 16:25; Galatians 1:12,15,16; Ephesians 2:20; 3:3,5; Hebrews 2:3,4; 2 Peter 3:2,15). Christians depend upon the teaching of these men, as recorded in Scripture, for truth and life (Acts 2:42). Some of the brethren were publicly set apart to perform special, delicate tasks involving money and widows (Acts 6). The Spirit placed others as overseers to shepherd the local church (Acts 20:28). Some individuals fully devoted themselves to teaching or spreading the gospel, and received material assistance from their brethren as the Lord instructed (1 Corinthians 9:3-14; Galatians 6:6; 1 Thessalonians 2:6; 1 Timothy 5:17,18; Titus 3:13; 3 John 5-8). Some sowed while others reaped (John 4:37). Some planted while others watered (1 Corinthians 3:6-8).

Because many Christians are weak and immature, and because false teachers and hostile forces abound, God in His loving grace provides human instruments who protect and build up His people. Therefore, teaching and shepherding are essential to the equipping of people for their ministries (Ephesians 4:11-16), and selected brethren must bear that great responsibility. However, such leadership in no way justifies the establishment of a separate clerical order over the household of God.

The fundamental error of the clerical system is that it violates Jesus' teaching on humility and servanthood, which in turn alters the very character of the Christian community. Clericalism falsely exalts and separates those with teaching and leadership gifts from the rest of the Christian brotherhood. It gives those select few lofty titles (e.g., Reverend) and exclusive privileges that have little to do with their spiritual gift. From its beginning, clericalism has been obsessed with power, position, control, and authority. Thus it is a continuation of the prideful, self-centered religious structures Jesus so vigorously denounced in His day (Matthew 23:1-12).

Jesus Christ, our great Teacher and Leader, did not seek lofty status or title for Himself. Instead, by His life, He exemplified the way of humility, lowliness, and servanthood. He set the example for all who follow Him—especially those who are teachers and leaders of His Kingdom—to be humble servants (John 13:16). Therefore, Christian teachers and leaders must never seek to elevate and separate themselves from their brethren through lofty, clerical status. Instead, by God's grace, they must be the chief examples of lowliness, servanthood, and sacrifice.

In keeping with Jesus' example, it is difficult even to define the difference between those in the New Testament church who evangelize, teach, and shepherd in a full-time capacity, and those who serve as the Bible charges all Christians to do (Romans 12:11; 1 Corinthians 15:58; 16:15,16; Colossians 3:23,24; 1 Peter 2:16; 4:10). Precisely defined divisions such as priest and people, clergy and laity, or official and unofficial—so much a part of most religious practice—are nonexistent in the New Testament Christian brotherhood. Paul was the chief enigma of all, for he supported himself by manual labor and at the same time evangelized and taught (Acts 18:3; 20:34; 1 Corinthians 4:12; 9:6), without diminishing his divine commission as the apostle to the Gentiles. The elders, then, who take on the vital task of teaching and overseeing the brotherhood, are not special priests or clergymen. In the words of Scripture, they are, ". . . leading men among the brethren" (Acts 15:22).

1. Kenneth Chafin, *Help, I'm a Layman* (Waco: Word Books, 1966), page 1.
2. *Ibid.*, page 9.
3. Bonaventure Kloppenburg, *The Ecclesiology of Vatican II*, trans. Matthew J. O'Connell (Chicago: Franciscan Herald Press, 1974), page 313 ff.

Kloppenburg states that the Vatican II doctrine "puts an end to the purely negative and passive conception of the layman, unequivocally rejects clericalism (the conception of the Church as domain of the clergy and the world as domain of the laity), gives the layman an active role in the Church, and makes him a sharer in the three powers (of sanctifying, teaching, and ruling) or total mission of the Church."

4. Robert C. Girard, *Brethren Hang Together* (Grand Rapids: Zondervan Publishing House, 1979), page 123.

5. John Stott, *One People* (Old Tappan, New Jersey: Fleming H. Revell Co., 1973), pages 25, 26.

6. *Ibid.*, page 34.

7. *Ibid.*, page 47.

8. Lawrence O. Richards and Gilbert Martin, *A Theology of Personal Ministry* (Grand Rapids: Zondervan Publishing House, 1981), page 122.

9. Alfred Kuen, *I Will Build My Church* (Chicago: Moody Press, 1971), page 253.

10. Alexander Rattray Hay, *The New Testament Order for Church and Missionary* (St. Louis: New Testament Missionary Union, 1947), page 291.

11. Robert B. Munger, *Training of the Laity for Ministry*, cited by Richards and Martin, page 13.

12. It is interesting to note that Stott uses verses referring to church elders (who in the New Testament were not ordained clergymen or priests) to defend his concept of the clergy.

    He argues, for example, that *prohistemi* (rule, direct, lead) and *hegeomai* (lead, guide) are two verbs used in the New Testament to designate clerical leadership (*One People*, pages 41, 42). However, these words were general leadership terms used to describe the elders' leadership within the early church (1 Timothy 5:17; Hebrews 13:17). They are totally free of clerical connotations. It is impossible to use the term *clergy* to describe first century leadership practices and structures without imposing religious connotations that did not occur until later.

    By appealing to verses that actually refer to elders to defend clericalism, Stott is doing exactly what the Roman Catholic Church has done for centuries to defend the priesthood. But in no way can the New Testament eldership be considered a clerical caste or priestly body.

# Chapter 19

# *Protecting, Disciplining, and Assessing an Elder*

> *Do not receive an accusation against an elder except on the basis of two or three witnesses. Those who continue in sin, rebuke in the presence of all, so that the rest also may be fearful of sinning. I solemnly charge you in the presence of God and of Christ Jesus and of His chosen angels, to maintain these principles without bias, doing nothing in a spirit of partiality. Do not lay hands upon anyone too hastily and thus share responsibility for the sins of others; keep yourself free from sin. No longer drink water exclusively, but use a little wine for the sake of your stomach and your frequent ailments. The sins of some men are quite evident, going before them to judgment; for others, their sins follow after. Likewise also, deeds that are good are quite evident, and those which are otherwise cannot be concealed.*
>
> 1 Timothy 5:19-25

\*    \*    \*

## Protecting your Elders

Honoring our spiritual leaders includes protecting them from damaging rumors, accusations, and false reports. Scripture warns, "Do not receive an accusation against an elder." So we must not be naive. People who are evil, mentally or emotionally unstable, bitter, hateful, envious, and misguided aim to ruin church leaders. In the Old Testament, people falsely accused godly men like Joseph, Moses, David, Jeremiah, Nehemiah, and others. David, for example, pleaded with King Saul not to listen to false reports about his intentions toward him: "And David said to Saul, 'Why do you listen to the words of men, saying, 'Behold, David seeks to harm you'" (1 Samuel 24:9; cf. Nehemiah 6:5-9)?

Discontent, unstable members of the China Inland Mission who made false reports and complaints about their saintly leader, Hudson Taylor, nearly destroyed the mission during its first year of service. Hudson's wife, Maria, indignantly wrote to one of her husband's accusors, reminding that person of 1 Timothy 5:19. She wrote:

I am aware that (your husband) has received . . . serious misrepresentations—to call them nothing worse. Would it not have been the right course, before allowing these to affect his *conduct,* to have endeavoured to ascertain the other side of the question? 'Against an elder'—and such my dear Husband surely is to the rest of our party—'receive not an accusation but before two or three witnesses.' I am more intimately acquainted than anyone else with the whole tenor of my beloved Husband's private and social walk, and . . . that walk is in all *meekness* and *forbearance,* in all *purity,* in all *sincerity of purpose,* and all *singleness of eye.*[1]

Unfortunately, Maria's excellent counsel from Scripture was not heeded until considerable pain and damage was done by well-meaning Christian people.

If an elder stands between a husband and wife in conflict or disciplines a prominent church member, accusations will fly. In fact, the more diligently and conscientiously an elder becomes involved in others' problems, the greater the risk of false accusation. I have seen elders verbally torn to pieces by sincere Christian people who had misinformation or unfounded ideas about that elder's action or character. Those making the accusations thought they had all the facts, but they didn't. When people become angry at their leaders, they think they have the right to strike out at them and say whatever they want.

Scripture, however, instructs us not to "receive an accusation against an elder." That is, do not inquire into every unsubstantiated charge made against an elder. Do not listen to such accusations. Most accusations are best ignored or silenced.

At heart, we all love to hear rumors and scandals. Proverbs 18:8 says, "The words of a whisperer are like dainty morsels, And they go down into the innermost parts of the body." But Christians are to be people of truth, love, and light. We should hate scandalous tales and rumors. We should silence them whenever we hear them. They are destructive and harmful to individual people and to the community of saints. Good people have been ruined by unfounded accusations. We should not allow this to happen in the Christian community. Love always tries to see others in the best possible light, not the worst (Proverbs 17:9). Also, our judgments are to be governed by facts and witnesses, not rumors. Thus we would be wise to live by the principle: "no judgment without the facts." Never believe any rumor until you have all the facts from all the people involved.

However, reasonable protection from, "accusation," does not imply immunity from "accusation." So Paul adds a condition to his instruction, "except on the basis of two or three witnesses." This means that an accusation brought by two or three people, who in a legal sense have witnessed the sin, must be investigated. The legal principle on which this directive is based is in the Old Testament: "'A single witness shall not rise up against a man on account of any iniquity or any sin which he has committed; on the evidence of two or three witnesses a matter shall be confirmed'" (Deuteronomy 19:15). An accusation of sin that is substantiated by witnesses must be heard and inquired into. It cannot be brushed aside. Remember, one of the qualifications for elders is that they be just. As unpleasant and time-consuming as a fair investigation into an accusation might be, it must be done. Sin must not be hidden, nor can an innocent man remain falsely accused.

### Disciplining an Elder

But how should an elder be treated if an accusation is found to be true? Verse 20 gives us this instruction: "Those who continue in sin, rebuke in the presence of all, so that the rest also may be fearful."[2] Some expositors think that verse 20 begins a new and broader subject regarding treatment of sinners in general, but this conclusion is incorrect for the following reasons: first, the break in thought would be too abrupt and unexpected. As the exposition which follows clearly demonstrates, verses 19-25 are one unit dealing with elders. Second, the severe treatment of public exposure is not for everyone, just leaders. If this passage refers to sinners in general, great destruction and confusion would result. Expositors who take this to mean sinners in general would not for a moment dare to practice such severe discipline on a broad level. There would be so much public rebuking that it would devastate the congregation. New, struggling converts would falter under the load.

A sinning elder[3] is to be rebuked in everyone's presence. The word, "rebuke," is difficult to translate. Here, the idea is to convict as in exposing, bringing to light, or proving guilt. This is to be done whether or not the individual admits to or repents of the wrong. In this instance, rebuking is not so much for public reprimand as for public exposure to the sin. The sinning elder is to be convicted in "the presence of all," meaning public exposure before the entire congregation, not just the council of elders. J. N. D. Kelly writes, "We do not . . . hear . . . of such private sessions, and public exposure before the church suits the atmosphere of apostolic Christianity much better."[4] An elder's sin cannot be hidden or swept under the carpet. A leader's sin must be treated more severely because it has more serious ramifications; it can lead more people astray and can cause the unbelieving world to mock God, the church, and the gospel.

God has His purpose in this difficult task: "so that the rest also may be fearful of sinning." "The rest" most likely refers to the other elders.[5] To see a fellow elder publicly exposed for sin will produce fear of sin and its shameful consequences in all elders. God uses such fear as a powerful deterrent to keep men from sinning.

*A call to courageous obedience.* First Timothy 5:20 expands the New Testament doctrine of church discipline by giving instruction regarding the discipline of an elder. Although it is not stated, "sin" that calls for witnesses and public action would undoubtedly result in disqualification from eldership. A man who has sinned in such a way would no longer be above reproach and thus would be unqualified (1 Timothy 3:1-7). Verse 20 does not indicate excommunication (Matthew 18:17; 1 Corinthians 5), although that could result if there were not proper repentance. Great wisdom and care needs to be prayerfully applied in such cases.

But who has the courage to discipline a church leader? At heart we are all cowards, afraid to take action, afraid to disturb the balance of church politics. Knowing our weakness, Paul directly and emphatically charges Timothy and the church to keep his instructions. Solemnly, Paul warns Timothy that he speaks, "in the presence of God and of Christ Jesus and of His chosen angels," and that Timothy also acts in their presence. By saying this, Paul reminds Timothy of the bigger picture of reality: it is before "God" Himself, the Mediator "Christ Jesus," and the elect "angels" of God (all who see and will someday judge) that he lives and speaks. No matter how difficult or unpleasant the duties may be, obedience to God must come first. The fear of God and His evaluation of our stewardship is to be our constant motivation and encouragement.

The instructions regarding an accusation against an elder and the public rebuke of an elder are to be conscientiously observed before God without prejudice or favoritism. "Without bias" literally means without pre-judgment or prejudice, and without judging someone guilty before the facts are known. It is possible to be prejudiced towards those who accuse an elder of sin, or towards certain elders, so we are to guard ourselves against such prejudices.

The second part of Paul's warning is against "partiality"— favoritism or preferential treatment—a grave danger whenever prominent leaders are involved. Whether listening to the accuser or convicting the accused, all proceedings must be done fairly, justly, and "without bias," knowing that God, Christ, and the angels see and will someday judge.

Despite its great importance, the exercise of church discipline is almost unheard of in evangelical churches. This serious failure ultimately demonstrates a lack of love for God and His truth. Love demands discipline. Yet under the guise of love, many Christians refuse to exercise church discipline. Unfortunately, such Christians misunderstand God's love. As Leon Morris points out, such behavior is actually inspired by sentiment, not love.

But the prophets see equally clearly that a God who really loves his people will discipline them from time to time. In modern times we often confuse love with sentimentality, and we do not always see as clearly as the prophets did that there is a stern side to real love. An easy sentimentality will decline to take stern action when the beloved does what is wrong. But this leaves the beloved secure in his wrongdoing, unfairly confirming the very action that makes him less of a person. Because sentimentality refuses to do what is distasteful, it ignores the long-term benefits of reproving the beloved because it sees that he will dislike the immediate unpleasantness. Sentimentality thus takes the easy way out.[6]

Christians today must realize that church discipline is as much a part of church life as partaking of the Lord's Supper. Since the local church is a close-knit family of brothers and sisters—a household, a community of God's children, a fellowship of believers—there should be a strong sense of mutuality and accountability among its members and between the elders and the community. The practice of discipline within the community protects and ensures the well-being of each individual and the entire company of saints. Many believers will never face their distorted doctrines, immoral behavior, bitterness, divisive conduct, or hatred unless they are called into account. A lack of accountability within the church family demonstrates a lack of love and dishonors the lordship of Jesus Christ by honoring man above God.

Furthermore, the nature of the Church of Jesus Christ demands the discipline of its impenitent members. The local church is not a religious social club. The Church is, as Peter says, "a spiritual house for a holy priesthood" (1 Peter 2:5). Paul refers to the local church as "a temple of God:" "Do you not know that you are a temple of God, and that the Spirit of God dwells in you" (1 Corinthians 3:16)? "Or what agreement has the temple of God with idols? For we are the temple of the living God; just as God said, 'I will dwell in them and walk among them; And will be their God, and they shall be My people. Therefore, come out from their midst and be separate,' says the Lord" (2 Corinthians 6:16-17). Christians are priests and saints. The Spirit of God inhabits their gatherings. Therefore, sinful, unrepentant members must be disciplined or the holiness and spiritual life of the assembly will be spoiled.

Never underestimate the leavening power of sin in your midst. Refusal to discipline our sinning members makes us hypocrites before the world. Thus, both Jesus Christ and His chosen apostle, Paul, gave explicit instruction on disciplining sinning, impenitent members—instruction that has been almost totally ignored by churches today (Matthew 18:15-20; 1 Corinthians 5). It is necessary for us to obey and act, even if obedience requires disciplining a church elder.

### Assessing an Elder

After dealing with the difficult matter of leadership failure, Paul advises Timothy how to avoid it. Prevention is still the best cure, so Paul discusses how to prevent unqualified leaders from attaining positions of authority: "Do not lay hands upon any one too hastily and thus share responsibility for the sins of others; keep yourself free from sin." One of the first ways to prevent unqualified men from becoming leaders is to avoid hasty appointments. The laying on of hands is a biblical expression for appointment to a specific task or position (Numbers 27:18-23; Acts 6:6). So in verse 22, Paul says not to appoint people too hastily, suddenly, or rashly. This admonition is similar to 1 Timothy 3:2,10, where an aspiring overseer must first qualify and be tested.

Because of the continual need for church leadership, there is always pressure to make hasty appointments that can create more serious, long-lasting problems. Donald Guthrie correctly observes that, "Undue haste in Christian appointments has not infrequently led to unworthy men bringing havoc to the cause of Christ."[7] Time and testing are still the best procedures to guide in leadership appointment.

Even though the advice to "not lay hands upon anyone too hastily" is expressed as a general principle of appointment, it applies to elders in this context. This, of course, would imply that elders were often appointed by laying hands on them. Although there is no specific example of this action in the New Testament, it was perhaps practiced at Ephesus. Some interpreters explain the laying on of hands here as the means of reconciling repentant sinners back to the church. But this is completely false. Such a view condemns itself in light of the New Testament doctrine of forgiveness. It is a Pharisaical interpretation (Luke 15:25-32) that distorts the New Testament teaching of forgiveness, reception, and love. What an insult to the Father's love for those for whom His Son died (Luke 15:2-22). All who return to Christ are welcomed with open arms, not the laying on of hands. Paul would never have said, "Do not receive a repentant sinner back in full fellowship too hastily," which is this interpretation's implication. I agree with E. K. Simpson's evaluation that, "The notion that the reference is to the restoration of penitents to membership seems exceedingly farfetched."[8]

No other religion can match Christianity for its teaching on forgiveness (Matthew 18:21-35; Luke 17:3,4; Galatians 6:1; 2 Corinthians 2:5-11). Jesus, for example, says, "'And if he sins against you seven times a day, and returns to you seven times, saying, "I repent," forgive him'" (Luke 17:4). Paul's advice to the Corinthians was to, ". . . forgive and comfort . . . reaffirm your love . . . in order that no advantage be taken of us by Satan. . . ." (2 Corinthians 2:7-11). Thus the obvious interpretation of the laying on of hands in this passage is that it refers to the appointment or setting apart for special service, not reconciling repentant sinners.

Paul's warning against hasty appointments continues with the statement: "and thus share responsibility for the sins of others." The laying on of hands creates a bond or partnership between two parties. The one, or ones, who appoint "share" in the failure or success of the one appointed. A rash appointment could result in publicly commending an unqualified, unworthy person to an important leadership position. So, if the appointed person creates division, teaches false doctrine, or falls into immoral behavior, those who placed their hands on him would also "share responsibility" for the failure because they appointed him.

The more one understands the solemn responsibilities of imposing hands, the more one exercises reservation, thoughtfulness, and carefulness in the laying on of hands. One good reason for the practice of laying on of hands is that it creates a deeper and truer sense of responsibility and fellowship between parties.

Finally, to those who make such appointments, Paul says, "keep yourself free from sin" (literally, pure, guiltless, or unstained). Dealing with the ambitions, sins, and faults of others can easily taint a leader. An unwise appointment could stain Timothy's character and reputation, so Paul cautions Timothy to guard himself, remaining above reproach with others, particularly other leaders.

Verse 23 is a short digression sparked by the last exhortation, "keep yourself free from sin," which requires clarification. Knowing the situation at Ephesus (1 Timothy 4:1-5), and Timothy's personal habits and frequent health problems, Paul encourages him to drink "a little wine for the sake of your stomach." "A little wine" will not defile, although using much wine would. Hence, Timothy could take some wine and remain pure before those he leads. Out of regard for Timothy's personal health, Paul encourages him to drink "a little wine."

Verses 24 and 25 resume the subject Paul began in verse 22.

Kelly states that, "The Apostle now returns to his theme of the importance of taking pains to assess the character of prospective elders."⁹ Paul's ominous instruction in verse 22 could frighten those who must assess others for responsible positions. How is it possible to rightly estimate a man's character and ensure that unqualified men are not placed in responsible positions? Paul calms the fears of those who must assess the character of others through two maxims (verses 24 and 25). He shows that decisions for appointment can be confidently made. Lenski emphasizes this same point: "As far as avoiding mistakes is concerned and thus possibly making the wrong man an elder, Timothy need not worry, for the difficulty as to judging is not great. This is said for Timothy's comfort."¹⁰ E. K. Simpson adds, "Timothy has been called on to diagnose character, and Paul supplies him with a clue for the task, and the verdicts he has to pass."¹¹

*Those obviously unfit for eldership.* Some men's sins are so obvious that no evaluation for appointment to leadership is necessary: "The sins of some men are quite evident, going before them to judgment." Their "sins" precede them, showing in advance that they are utterly unfit for the position to which they aspire. The "judgment" Paul speaks of is human assessment or decision making (Matthew 5:21; John 7:24), not God's judgment. God is not the subject here, since all sins are evident to Him (1 Corinthians 4:5), so Paul definitely refers to the human examination process. Some men's sins are so obvious that they don't even need to be examined.

*Those proven unfit for eldership upon examination.* The sins of some men are not easily seen, so action must be suspended until an examination is made: "For others, their sins follow after." Paul assures Timothy that their "sins" will "follow" them to the examination and will be exposed through careful evaluation. God is not the only one who can see their sin—men can too, if they look carefully.

A hasty appointment could result in sharing in the sins of others, so an inquiry into a man's life and qualifications is necessary. However, sin cannot be totally hidden and will be made clear at its proper time. Even if some sins happen to remain hidden during examination, there is no need for alarm as Lenski explains:

Timothy and the churches will need to consider only the question in regard to men whose sins are not so evident. Even in their case the difficulty disappears: the more hidden sins of these men follow close on the heels of these men when their cases come up for decision. Their sins march right into the meeting behind them and refuse to be left outside. Thus Timothy will easily be able to refuse these men. "In exceptional cases of deception and hypocrisy, which only one who is able to see the heart could detect, evidently no sin can be charged against the conscientious judge who has nevertheless been deceived." In such rare cases Timothy will not be fellowshipping the sins of such men; he will still be pure.[12]

If no examination or inquiry is made regarding a prospective elder, the worst of men may be appointed to the eldership. For example, I know of a man who was excommunicated from one church because of sexual immorality and moved to another church where he became an elder again in less than a year. If a true examination of the man had been made, he would never have been appointed as a church elder.

*Those obviously fit for eldership.* The good works of some men are obvious before any judgment is made: "Likewise also, deeds that are good are quite evident." These men are easily identified as men fit for the task of church oversight.

*Those proven fit for eldership upon examination.* Some men's good works are not obvious, but upon investigation their good deeds become apparent: "and those which are otherwise cannot be concealed." That is, their good works cannot be hidden and it will be made known that they are fit candidates for appointment to eldership. Thus, Timothy need not be distraught over his responsibility in appointing elders and deacons. Some men will obviously be unfit for leadership positions while others will be proven unfit upon examination. However, there will always be some men, who by God's Spirit, are obviously fit for managing God's household.

---

**NOTES**

1. A. J. Broomhall, *Hudson Taylor and China's Open Century*, 6 vols., vol. 4: *Survivors' Pact* (London: Hodder and Stoughton, 1984), page 289.
2. The clause, "Those who continue in sin," represents the present participle, *tous hamartanontas*, "the ones *sinning*." I believe that the *New American Standard Bible*'s translation, "continue in sin," lays too much stress on the present continuous tense. Some who

accept this rendering suggest that only elders who stubbornly persist in sin after a warning are subject to the discipline in question. But as J. N. D. Kelly states, "This introduces an entirely fresh idea" (*The Pastoral Epistles*, London: A.& C. Black Limited, 1972, page 127). The primary thought is simply that the accusation of sin (which was probably a repeated practice or fault) has been substantiated, and thus, it must be rebuked before all.

3. The plural participle, "those who continue in sin," that refers back to the singular "elder" is no problem. Such oscillation in number is found elsewhere, in 1 Timothy 2:9-15; 5:1,3-16. Note also that the word, "elder," in the official sense, is used generically in the singular. John P. Meier, "*Presbyteros* in the Pastoral Epistles," *The Catholic Biblical Quarterly* 35 (July, 1973): 330-332.
4. Kelly, *Pastoral Epistles*, page 127.
5. *Ibid.*
6. Leon Morris, *Testaments of Love* (Grand Rapids: Wm. B. Eerdmans Publishing Co., 1981), page 25.
7. Guthrie, *Pastoral Epistles* The Tyndale New Testament Commentaries (Grand Rapids: Wm. B. Eerdmans Publishing Co., 1957), page 107.
8. E. K. Simpson, *Pastoral Epistles* (Grand Rapids: Wm. B. Eerdmans Publishing Co., 1954), pages 79, 80.
9. Kelly, *Pastoral Epistles*, page 129.
10. R. C. H. Lenski, *The Interpretation of St. Paul's Epistles to the Colossians, to the Thessalonians, to Timothy, to Titus, and to Philemon,* (Minneapolis: Augsburg Publishing House, 1961), page 691.
11. Simpson, *Pastoral Epistles*, page 80.
12. Lenski, *Interpretation of St. Paul's Epistles*, pages 691, 692.

# Chapter 20

# *Deacons*

*Deacons likewise must be men of dignity, not double-tongued, or addicted to much wine or fond of sordid gain, but holding to the mystery of the faith with a clear conscience. And let these also first be tested; then let them serve as deacons if they are beyond reproach. Women must likewise be dignified, not malicious gossips, but temperate, faithful in all things. Let deacons be husbands of only one wife, and good managers of their children and their own households. For those who have served well as deacons obtain for themselves a high standing and great confidence in the faith that is in Christ Jesus.*

*1 Timothy 3:8-13*

\*   \*   \*

There is as much misunderstanding and error concerning the subject of deacons as there is concerning elders. For example, in his book *The Deacon and His Ministry*, Richard L. Dresselhaus portrays deacons as those who control the church's shepherding ministry. He writes: "One of the most awesome responsibilities of the deacon board is to provide continued pastoral ministry in the church. When a pastor resigns, it becomes their responsibility to present to the congregation a nominee or nominees to fill the office of pastor."[1]

In some churches, the deacons are mere figureheads, but in a great many churches, they function as a quasi body of elders.

Within these churches, the deacons are viewed as the board of directors, business administrators, or the official church board. The New Testament, however, clearly shows that the elders are the overseers, directors, and church leaders—not the deacons! Indeed, the deacons' very designation means servant, not overseers. The fact that churches insist on having deacons and not elders (when Scripture gives far greater support and recognition to elders) is a prime example of how human tradition blinds people from seeing Scripture's truth. I agree with Michael Green, who concludes: "The diaconate of the New Testament is awaiting rediscovery."² But there can be no true rediscovery of the diaconate without a correct view of eldership. In this chapter we can only briefly suvey the diaconate as it relates to elders.

### The Example of the Seven

In the first Christian community, the twelve apostles were the overseers. In a real sense they were the body of elders. As the community grew, so did their work. Not only did they lead and teach, they also administered the community's funds and distributed funds to the poor (Acts 4:34-5:11). This responsibility soon became too much of a burden, and a problem arose over the fair distribution of food to the widows: "Now at this time while the disciples were increasing in number, a complaint arose on the part of the Hellenistic Jews against the native Hebrews, because their widows were being overlooked in the daily serving of food" (Acts 6:1).

Wisely, the Twelve realized the urgent need for organizational change to relieve themselves from some of the heavy tasks they had assumed that were not part of their original commission in Christ. As a solution, they called the congregation together and explained the problem (Acts 6:2). Next, they proposed that the congregation select seven qualified men who were known to be full of the Holy Spirit and wisdom, who the apostles would place in charge of handling funds and caring for the material needs of the poor. The apostles would then be free to devote themselves wholly to the Word and prayer (Acts 6:4). The plan pleased the congregation, and the apostles prayed and laid hands on the seven who were chosen by the congregation (Acts 6:5,6). The laying on of hands, as we've seen, was simply the apostles' way of expressing formal appointment and delegating their work and the authority to do the work to the seven. The situation demanded official public appointment because of the task's highly responsible and sensitive nature.

Even though the seven are never called deacons, Luke's account of their appointment is indispensable to the study of deacons. When Luke later refers to Philip in Acts 21:8, he calls him "one of the seven," not one of the deacons. As always, Luke is accurate in his use of terminology. The seven were not called deacons. That does not mean, however, that there is no connection between the Acts 6 account and the later development of the deaconship. Although there is not an exact correlation, there is a connection; Acts 6 provides a dynamic, apostolic example that later leaders could follow and adapt to their own situations. So Luke does not refer to the seven as deacons because they were not called deacons in the sense of the later, specialized meaning of the word. The seven were a prototype of the later deaconship.

### The Servants' Role

The problems the twelve apostles confronted in Jerusalem would have occurred in other large cities, too. As congregations grew, so did the amount and diversity of the elders' work. As community leaders, the elders could look back at what the apostles had done in Jerusalem and do the same. Like the Twelve, elders today need relief, and modern congregations certainly need the loving care of a body of servants.

To relieve the elders' burden, some early churches chose a body of qualified men to serve on behalf of the whole assembly. In time, based on their work of serving the saints as a recognized, appointed body, these men acquired the humble designation, *diakonoi*, meaning *the servants* or *the helpers*. Hence, a special sense of the word developed that was applied only to the body of men who served the saints in this unique manner. Unfortunately, this special use of *diakonoi* is transliterated into English as *deacons* rather than *servants*.

But what a wonderful name the group we know as deacons have—servants! Jesus said, ". . . 'but whoever wishes to become great among you shall be your servant [*diakonos*]'" (Mark 10:43). It is a great privilege to be a deacon. A deacon who serves well gains good standing in the church and greater boldness in faith. This enables him to better serve God and His people, as Paul says in 1 Timothy 3:13: "For those who have served well as deacons obtain for themselves a high standing and great confidence in the faith that is in Christ Jesus."

The special use of *diakonoi* to describe a select group of men appears in only two portions of Scripture: Philippians 1:1 and 1 Timothy 3:8-12. These passages reveal the following facts about the deacons:

• In both places, deacons are closely related to overseers. As the terms and the order in which they are placed indicate, deacons are subordinate to overseers. Overseers perform certain functions that deacons as a corporate body do not, but the overseers can perform all the deacons' functions. Unlike deacons, however, elders are responsible for the overall leadership, supervision, and teaching of the congregation.

From the example of the seven in Acts 6, we learn that deacons provide a complementary service to the elders who bear the overall burdens of administration and teaching. Deacons bear some of the elders' load, freeing them to concentrate on the essential aspects of their ministry—prayer, teaching, and protecting. So, the deacons' work ought to be done in harmony with the elders and complement the elders' work.

• The word, *deacons*, is always plural. Like the elders, the deacons are a corporate body or team of servants.

• Deacons must meet specific qualifications that are similar to those required of overseers (1 Timothy 3:8-12). Like elders, a man's qualifications must be examined before he is permitted to serve as a deacon (1 Timothy 3:10). The reason for this examination is that the deacons handle highly responsible and sensitive tasks on behalf of the assembly. Not just anyone can do some of the deacons' duties such as dispensing money to the needy. Because of the way they serve the congregation, they must be men in whom the saints have confidence and trust. In order to do their work effectively, the deacons must be men of proper moral and spiritual character.

Not all the qualifications for deacons are the same as for elders, however. Deacons do not have to be able to teach. They are not responsible for the protection of the church from false teaching or feeding God's Word to the flock, although an individual deacon may well be a gifted teacher (Acts 6:8-7:60).

• The New Testament intentionally lists no fixed duties for deacons. As their name indicates, deacons are good servants who serve in whatever capacity they are needed. They adjust to meet the needs at hand. There is great latitude in their work.

The very existence of deacons is based on need. Some churches do not need deacons because the elders can handle the work. But as a church grows, the need for deacons becomes apparent (Acts 6:1). At that time, the overseers should ask for the establishment of deacons and define their areas of service. This obviously demands that the elders have a clear understanding of their own task and their importance to the church. Only then will the deacons be able to properly relieve the elders of some of their work and be useful to the congregation.

Scripture's picture of deacons is quite different than what is seen on many contemporary deacon boards. In Scripture, deacons are servants, not shepherds. They relieve the elders from burdensome tasks that are essential to the church's welfare. Thus, the elders are better able to shepherd the whole flock, and the church is better served. Even though they are not called to teach or lead the flock, deacons must still be of proper moral and spiritual character. There is great flexibility in their work, but all deacons must be servants-at-large—men who have a servant's heart.

## NOTES

1. Richard L. Dresselhaus, *The Deacon and His Ministry* (Springfield, Missouri: Gospel Publishing House, 1977), pages 43, 44.
2. Michael Green, *Called to Serve* (Philadelphia: The Westminster Press, 1964), pages 54, 55.

# Chapter 21

# *Making Biblical Eldership Work*

*If you know these things, you are blessed if you do them.*
*John 13:17*

\* \* \*

The purpose of this final chapter is to offer suggestions for implementing biblical church eldership without creating church division. God is not pleased when His redeemed people strive against one another or try to force new programs and changes on the church without regard for His timing or sensitivity to the feelings of brothers and sisters in the community. Love, humility, unity, and absolute fidelity to the Word are the marks of a Spirit-obedient church. The implementation of eldership—or any truth from God's Word—must be done in God's way (2 Timothy 2:24-26), not through fighting, hatred, and manipulation. Assuming that some readers will agree with the perspective on biblical eldership presented in this book, I have five general suggestions for those who might desire to establish biblical eldership in their own churches.

### Search God's Word
In Acts 17:11, Luke records a shining example of believers who searched God's Word: "Now these [the believers at Berea] were more noble-minded than those in Thessalonica, for they received the word with great eagerness, examining the Scriptures

daily, to see whether these things were so." Just as the believers at Berea diligently examined Paul's teaching, everything that has been written in this book must be scrutinized in light of God's Word. God's Word is unerring truth, but man's interpretation of it is subject to error.

The pastor and congregation together must thoroughly study the doctrine of eldership in an attitude of prayerful humility, honestly facing man's tendency to cling to tradition more than to God's truth. Perhaps a study committee could examine Scripture's truth concerning eldership and the clergy-laity division. Unless Scripture convinces men of the truth of eldership, there is little reason for them to change. Without a solid scriptural foundation, there is no way to answer opposing viewpoints or deal with the problems that will arise when implementing biblical eldership. Commitment to biblical church eldership will occur only if it is motivated by God's truth as found in Scripture.

### Patient Prayer

We are all like sheep and find it difficult to change our comfortable ways. Change is painful, disruptive, and often dangerous to a congregation. Some people simply cannot change. God must do the work of changing His people. It may take years or even decades of study, teaching, and prayer before a pastor and congregation can agree on the truth of biblical eldership. But we must never underestimate the power of persevering prayer and God's power to change His people. We must be patient, allowing God to teach us through long and trying situations. Anyone who shepherds sheep knows they move slowly, so we must be wise and skillful, not dividing the sheep by running into the flock and screaming for new direction.

If you are a pastor who seeks to adopt biblical eldership, you must teach the Word, pray, and personally train the leading men of the church for their future role (2 Timothy 4:2). If you are not the pastor, you must pray and lovingly entreat your pastor to study this subject with you. (But be patient; he has a lot more at stake than you do!) Above all, guard against pride, anger, or self-will. Do not tear others down because they do not yet understand this doctrine. You, too, have blind spots in your theology and life. Pride can even use Scripture's precious truth to divide the Lord's people. In the final analysis, it is God's job to enable people to see His truth and believe. So keep on praying that God's Spirit will make hearts receptive to His truths.

Remember, too, that biblical eldership is not a panacea. A church may have a body of elders who take the lead, but are spiritually lifeless. Do not be naive and think that eldership will solve every problem or make a church more spiritual. Jon Zens provides a superbly balanced viewpoint from which to approach this subject: "Before coming to the New Testament data, please consider with me three important introductory matters: (1) we must not idolize the subject of eldership; (2) we must not polarize over this subject; and (3) we must not minimize this subject."[1] Commenting on point one, Zens goes on to say,

> As men grow in the truth it is quite often the case that a newly-found Biblical concept can be magnified out of proportion. . . . It is possible to have the eldership doctrine straight, and somewhat implemented on the local level, and still be far from the overall New Testament pattern for church order. It is shameful if a church blessed with elders manifests a superior attitude and looks down their nose at other churches who are not "straight" in this area. . . .
>
> Having an eldership certainly will not cure all church problems. The realization of an eldership in a church may create some difficulties, and churches with an eldership have had to go through some of the thorniest problems imaginable. The real point before us is that if oversight by elders is Biblical, then it will indeed provide a Christ-ordained way of handling general order and special problems. But in no way must it be regarded as a panacea for all the problems churches face today.[2]

### Remove All Clerical Titles and Garb

If you are the ordained minister, step down from the unscriptural and elevated pedestal upon which you stand. It is not of God's making. Clericalism creates a false division in God's household. You are a fellow brother—perhaps a teacher or shepherd among your brethren, but not a sacred, ministerial person. The title reverend is an offense to Jesus Christ's teaching and your fellow brethren (Matthew 23:8). Jesus is Lord, so courageously follow His teaching, not man's.

If you do not remove the clerical titles and garments that

falsely divide you from your brethren, your church will never experience true biblical eldership. People will be programmed to let the ordained man—the one who is ministerial or priestly—do their religion for them. One major reason biblical eldership does not work for many churches is that men are spiritually lazy and indifferent. They are willing to let one person do all the work, particularly if that person is the only one "called" and "ordained" to the ministry. Thus, false theories of ministry hinder the eldership and every church member from developing fully. Men need to be challenged to their responsibility to provide leadership for the local church. It is hard enough to urge men to take their community responsibility seriously. If they are taught that they are laymen, and the professional clergyman is responsible for the church, they will never seriously oversee the community. So, they must be taught that they are responsible for the community to which they belong.

### *Train Men*

If you are a pastor or missionary-founder of a church, it is absolutely essential to realize that the elders and potential elders need training. Most newly founded elderships fail because those involved simply do not know enough, or are not skilled enough, to do the work. Without a conscious effort to train elders and share the pastoral oversight with them, biblical eldership will turn into another empty church theory. Training elders is a key part of the transition and implementation of biblical eldership. Bruce Stabbert speaks of discipleship as an essential ingredient in developing plurality:

One church may already have several men in it who are mature leaders, men who know the Scriptures, who meet the qualifications of an overseer given in 1 Timothy 3, Titus 1, and 1 Peter 5, and who would be willing to take a significant part in the leadership of the church. If this is the case, then a move into plurality would involve a minimal game plan. . . .

Most churches however, find the majority of their men sadly stunted spiritually and with little knowledge of the Bible. If this is the case, such men would probably be very reticent to view themselves as prospective pastors. This is where the plan becomes work.

We might imagine Peter being informed upon his first encounter with Christ that within three years he would be an apostle and preach to thousands of people at one time. He would probably have said, "Who me?" How did Jesus prepare Peter and the other apostles for church leadership? He discipled them. He spent time with them. He taught them. He prayed with them and for them.

And that is the primary way that true elders will be developed in a local church. Somebody is going to have to disciple some men. We may not have much more than a bunch of fishermen in our congregation, but they should be discipled. Someone must spend time with them. Someone must teach them. Someone must pray with them and for them. But they can be discipled![3]

Ask God for a training plan that will fit your particular situation. God wants us to depend on Him in prayer for the wisdom, guidance, and strength we need. We will face failures, disappointments, and trials, but God uses such difficulties to test our beliefs and help us grow in humility and grace. (I have prepared a practical study guide for training church elders. You can adapt the guide to your particular situation and purposes.)

Once training begins, it may take years for all elders or potential elders to function as genuine shepherds, and for the people to acknowledge the elders as their spiritual leaders. Whenever we try to faithfully honor God by obeying His Word, Satan and his evil hosts strive to destroy what is good. So we must be prepared for prolonged struggles and set backs.

In practical terms, the training of elders entails:

*Training in personal character.* According to biblical requirements, an elder must be a disciplined, orderly, and balanced man. He must also have his home in order and be forbearing, gentle, just, and devout. He cannot be quick-tempered or pugnacious, and must be free from the love of money.

Jesus taught that those who lead His kingdom must have a humble, servant-like character. Jesus' self-sacrificing love for others must be evident in every elder. Most modern educational institutions train only the mind. But in the Christian community, an elder must have the moral and spiritual qualifications God requires. So, discipleship has failed if it does not include evaluating, admonishing, and developing a man's moral character and life.

*Training in the Word.* Men must be urged to study Scripture and its doctrines on a consistent, orderly basis. There is no shortcut to faith or maturity in the Word. Listening to a sermon once a week will never equip a man to oppose false teachers or instruct others. Instead, one must devote considerable time to reading and studying Scripture. There are schools, home study courses, and tapes to help the serious student of God's Word in diligent, personal study. Never underestimate what God can do with so-called ordinary people who are motivated by the Spirit to study His Word!

*Training in the work.* Shepherding God's people demands a great deal of knowledge, wisdom, and practical skill—much of which is learned by doing. Training elders must include exposure to the shepherding task and experience in the work of building up the church. This places a heavy responsibility on the discipler. He must spend time with the disciple, pray with him, provide opportunities (and the necessary training and equipment) for service,and evaluate the disciple's performance.

### Involve the Whole Congregation

Since the eldership exists for the entire flock's well-being, the way it is implemented is vitally important. Although the existing leader(s) will lead in establishing and perpetuating the eldership, the whole congregation ought to be involved in the process. Everyone in the body is obligated to know those who labor among them, see that they are properly qualified, and make sure that no one is hastily appointed to church oversight. The entire congregation should be involved in praying, studying, and sharing suggestions and ideas. This can be an exciting time for the whole body. It is also an excellent time for the congregation to pray and fast (Acts 13:2,3; 14:23).

During the implementation process, there should be open communication and freedom to discuss and disagree in a loving, Christian way. Special meetings and surveys may be needed to explore the issues. One can expect many mistakes and complaints, but the Spirit equips Christians to forgive one another. Be especially careful to guard against jealousy, envy, or resentment over the appointment of new elders.

### Conclusion

I must say that many factors work against the successful establishment of a truly biblical church eldership:

- Men are spiritually lazy and prefer that someone else bear the heavy responsibility of caring for the Lord's people.
- Pastors, for the most part, are not going to give up their position or share it with other men, particularly if those men are not professionally trained.
- We have been programmed to think that only the ordained minister can perform the major religious duties of the church.
- We do not like change or breaking with cherished traditions.
- Many of us have never seen a church operate under biblical eldership and are fearful of the strife such change may cause.

Unless a congregation is fully convinced from Scripture that traditional clerical church structures are in error and that biblical eldership is God's design for church leadership, it will never develop a fully functioning eldership. All reform and restoration must be rooted in God's Word and the work of the Holy Spirit. So, the first priority is to reverently study God's Holy Word. That is why I have done so much exposition of Scripture in this book.

Despite the outward difficulties, the elder system of church oversight is profoundly better for the local church than anything devised by man. Unlike any other form of rule, eldership has full biblical support. Eldership best harmonizes with and promotes the true nature of the Christian church and places its oversight directly where it belongs—on the qualified men of the church family. So don't be disheartened. One who seeks to establish a fully biblical eldership is pursuing God's perfect will for His people. The strength, patience, and wisdom needed to implement such leadership—even in the midst of problems and hardships—can come through persevering prayer and dependence on our heavenly Father. Division can be avoided. God can be glorified. And the world can receive a witness to God's power through the lives of ordinary men and women in whom He has worked. So above all, pray!

---

**NOTES**

1. Jon Zens, "The Major Concepts of Eldership in the New Testament," *Baptist Reformation Review* 7 (Summer, 1978): 26.
2. *Ibid.* ·
3. Bruce Stabbert, *The Team Concept* (Tacoma: Hegg Bros. Printing, 1982), page 120.

# INDEX